JUDGING REFUGEES

To access state-based refugee protection regimes, refugee applicants must speak. They must narrate the basis of their claims in person, often before a single decision-maker, repeatedly and at length. In *Judging Refugees*, Anthea Vogl investigates the black box of the refugee oral hearing and the politics of narrative within individualised processes for refugee status determination (RSD). Drawing on a rich archive of administrative oral hearings in Australia and Canada, Vogl sets global trends of diminished and fast-tracked RSD against the critical role played by the discretionary spaces of refugee decision-making, and the gate-keeping functions of credibility assessment. *Judging Refugees* explores the disciplining role of 'good refugee' stories within RSD and demonstrates that refugee applicants must be able to present their evidence in model Anglo-European narrative forms to be judged as authentic and credible and ultimately, to be granted access to protection.

ANTHEA VOGL is a senior lecturer in Law at the University of Technology Sydney. She is an expert in the legal regulation of asylum, borders, refugees and non-citizens.

Cambridge Asylum and Migration Studies

At no time in modern history have so many people been on the move as at present. Migration facilitates critical social, economic, and humanitarian linkages. But it may also challenge prevailing notions of bounded political communities, of security, and of international law.

The political and legal systems that regulate the transborder movement of persons were largely devised in the mid-twentieth century, and are showing their strains. New challenges have arisen for policymakers, advocates, and decision-makers that require the adaptation and evolution of traditional models to meet emerging imperatives.

Edited by a world leader in refugee law, this new series aims to be a forum for innovative writing on all aspects of the transnational movement of people. It publishes single or coauthored works that may be legal, political, or cross-disciplinary in nature, and will be essential reading for anyone looking to understand one of the most important issues of the twenty-first century.

Books in the Series

The Child in International Refugee Law
Jason M. Pobjoy

Refuge Lost: Asylum Law in an Interdependent World
Daniel Ghezelbash

Demanding Rights: Europe's Supranational Courts and the Dilemma of Migrant Vulnerability
Moritz Baumgärtel

Climate Change, Disasters, and the Refugee Convention
Matthew Scott

The Global Governed?: Refugees as Providers of Protection and Assistance
Kate Pincock, Alexander Betts and Evan Easton-Calabria

The Evolution of Humanitarian Protection in European Law and Practice
Liv Feijen

Protection from Refuge: From Refugee Rights to Migration Management
Kate Ogg

Grasping Legal Time: Temporality and European Migration Law
Martijn Stronks

Conflict Refugees: European Union Law and Practice
Christel Querton

JUDGING REFUGEES

Narrative and Oral Testimony in Refugee Status Determination

ANTHEA VOGL
University of Technology Sydney

CAMBRIDGE
UNIVERSITY PRESS

CAMBRIDGE UNIVERSITY PRESS

Shaftesbury Road, Cambridge CB2 8EA, United Kingdom

One Liberty Plaza, 20th Floor, New York, NY 10006, USA

477 Williamstown Road, Port Melbourne, VIC 3207, Australia

314–321, 3rd Floor, Plot 3, Splendor Forum, Jasola District Centre, New Delhi – 110025, India

103 Penang Road, #05-06/07, Visioncrest Commercial, Singapore 238467

Cambridge University Press is part of Cambridge University Press & Assessment, a department of the University of Cambridge.

We share the University's mission to contribute to society through the pursuit of education, learning and research at the highest international levels of excellence.

www.cambridge.org
Information on this title: www.cambridge.org/9781108831857

DOI: 10.1017/9781108912402

First published 2024

A catalogue record for this publication is available from the British Library

Library of Congress Cataloging-in-Publication Data
Names: Vogl, Anthea, author.
Title: Judging refugees : narrative and oral testimony in refugee status determination / Anthea Vogl, University of Technology, Sydney.
Description: Cambridge, United Kingdom ; New York, NY : Cambridge University Press, 2024. | Series: Cambridge asylum and migration studies | Includes index.
Identifiers: LCCN 2023040251 (print) | LCCN 2023040252 (ebook) | ISBN 9781108831857 (hardback) | ISBN 9781108927437 (paperback) | ISBN 9781108912402 (epub)
Subjects: LCSH: Refugees–Legal status, laws, etc.–Australia. | Refugees–Legal status, laws, etc.–Canada. | Asylum, Right of–Australia. | Asylum, Right of–Canada. | Legal assistance to refugees–Australia. | Legal assistance to refugees–Canada., | Emigration and immigration law–Australia. | Emigration and immigration law–Canada.
Classification: LCC K3230.R45 V64 2024 (print) | LCC K3230.R45 (ebook) | DDC 342.7108/3–dc23/eng/20231003
LC record available at https://lccn.loc.gov/2023040251
LC ebook record available at https://lccn.loc.gov/2023040252

ISBN 978-1-108-83185-7 Hardback

CONTENTS

FOREWORD

Anthea Vogl argues that assessing a refugee claim involves much more than just applying the refugee definition to the facts of a particular case. It's rather a deeply culturally specific exercise in which those claiming protection are expected to narrate a story in a manner that is heard as credible by decision-makers in the receiving state. Whatever he or she has actually experienced or fears, the refugee claimant will fail unless able to tell a "good story."

To explain what is really happening in the refugee hearing, Vogl marries theoretical insights from narrative studies and related fields with original empirical work. The result is the most sophisticated analysis ever produced of the central dilemma of refugee status determination: how exactly do we come to understand the refugee's narrative, and what does that tell us about who we believe to be worthy of protection?

Beyond shining a light on the real dynamic at play in a refugee hearing, *Judging Refugees* connects the expectations of refugee applicants as narrators to the bigger picture of refugee law's gatekeeping function. Vogl cogently shows us that the duty of narration is a pernicious impediment to ensuring the fairness of the assessment process, with at least as much exclusionary power as the formal legal requirements for recognition of refugee status.

James C. Hathaway
Editor, Cambridge Asylum and Migration Studies

ACKNOWLEDGEMENTS

This book was possible because of the refugees who so generously participated in my research. I am deeply grateful for their openness to my project and their participation, even as they negotiated some of the most difficult moments in their applications for the right to remain safely in Australia or Canada. I also thank the lawyers, advocates and organisations who facilitated my fieldwork and supported this project, especially United Nations High Commissioner for Refugees (UNHCR) Canada, my Australian research partner organisation, and individual lawyers and advocates in Australia and Canada. The exigencies and often cruel timelines of seeking refugee protection and of refugee advocacy rarely make incorporating academic research projects easy or convenient. I truly appreciate both the fortitude and the patience involved.

I am indebted and grateful to Jenni Millbank, Catherine Dauvergne and Honni van Rijswijk for their boundless intellectual generosity, care and wisdom, and for their supervision of my doctoral research, which formed the basis of this book. I am immensely thankful to the Faculty of Law at University of Technology Sydney (UTS) and my colleagues there, for providing such a supportive environment from which to research, teach, think and learn. I work with the best people and my thanks in particular to Laurie Berg, David Carter, Penny Crofts, Sara Dehm, Lucy Fiske, Kathryn Greenman, Renata Grossi, Trish Luker, Elyse Methven, Alecia Simmonds, Michael Thomson and Ana Filipa Vrdoljak for your friendship, smarts and unshakable good humour, and to Katherine Biber especially, for mentorship, guidance and the wisest counsel on all things. I also thank Lesley Hitchens and Anita Stuhmcke for their mentorship and support, as well as my wonderful current collaborators, Susan Kneebone and Kate Ogg. My gratitude to the University of British Columbia (UBC) Faculty of Law, and to the many people who welcomed me there during the year I made UBC and Vancouver my home, and to Border Criminologies at the University of Oxford, for my time there and for creating and sustaining such an inspiring scholarly community.

David Carter, Penny Crofts, Sara Dehm, Catherine Dauvergne, Elyse Methven, Jenni Millbank, Alecia Simmonds, Honni Van Rijswijk and Eve Vincent each read and significantly improved versions of these chapters and so generously engaged with the book as it came together. I also thank Margy Thomas Horton and Fiona Yeh, for their exceptional editorial and research assistance and tireless attention to detail. My immense gratitude to Cambridge University Press and my publication team, most especially to the series editor, James Hathaway, for his support for the book, and to Marianne Nield, Tobias Ginsberg and Gemma Smith. Navigating daily life alongside a global pandemic while also finishing the manuscript was made possible by CUP's patience, assistance and collaboration. My thanks too for the insightful comments and feedback provided by the anonymous reviewers of my manuscript and to Robert Barsky and Michelle Foster for invaluable feedback as my dissertation examiners.

Writing a book is a labour of love (plus some other emotions besides) and none of it would be possible without the friendships that sustain me: to Alecia, Amy, Camilla, Catri, Dave, David and AJ, Elana, Elyse, Eve, Hannah and Alicia, Jenni, Katherine, Katie, Mark, Louis and Muriel, Marni, Maryam, Michael, Miriam, Patrick and Jonothan, Amanda and Olivia, Penny, Peach, Salote and Sara, thank you. I was also surrounded and happily distracted by my beloved family throughout: immeasurable thanks to all of my family, most especially to my parents Shahla and Edward, and to Martin, for their love, care and support; and to the smallest, most important family members, Marcel, Félix, Madeline and Poppy. And to Claire Van Vuuren, for everything.

Early versions of some of the book's arguments and themes appeared in the following publications: 'The Genres and Politics of Refugee Testimony' (2018) 30(1) *Law and Literature* 81 and 'Telling Stories from Start to Finish: Exploring the Demand for Narrative in Refugee Testimony' (2015) 22(1) *Griffith Law Review* 63.

ABBREVIATIONS

AAT	Administrative Appeals Tribunal
ADJR Act	Administrative Decisions Judicial Review Act
CCR	Canadian Council for Refugees
CIC	Citizenship and Immigration Canada
CRDD	Convention Refugee Determination Division
Cth	Commonwealth
DCO	designated country of origin
DIBP	Department of Immigration and Border Protection
DIEA	Department of Immigration and Ethnic Affairs
DORS	Determination of Refugee Status
EU	European Union
IAA	Immigration Assessment Authority
IARLJ	International Association of Refugee Law Judges
IRB	Immigration and Refugee Board of Canada
IRCC	Immigration, Refugees and Citizenship Canada
IRO	International Refugee Organisation
IRPA	Immigration and Refugee Protection Act
MRD	Migration and Refugee Division
MRT	Migration Review Tribunal
NGO	non-governmental organisation
PIF	personal information form
POE	port of entry
PSG	particular social group
RAD	Refugee Appeal Division
RALU	Refugee Analysis Liaison Unit
Refugee Convention	Convention Relating to the Status of Refugees, 28 July 1951, 189 UNTS 137, in force 22 April 1954 – as amended by the Protocol Relating to the Status of Refugees, 31 January 1967, 606 UNTS 267, in force 4 October 1967
RPD	Refugee Protection Division
RRT	Refugee Review Tribunal
RSAC	Refugee Status Advisory Committee

RSD	refugee status determination
RSRC	Refugee Status Review Committees
UMA	unauthorised maritime arrival
UNHCR	United Nations High Commissioner for Refugees
UNTS	United Nations Treaty Series

1

Introduction

To access state-based regimes for refugee protection, refugee applicants must speak. Within individualised processes for the determination of refugee status, refugees are required to present themselves before a decision-maker and convey, as best they can, the basis of their claim to protection. Generally, refugees must present their oral testimony in person, repeatedly and at length, unmediated by a legal representative or advocate, and in many cases without the benefit of documents, witnesses or other forms of evidence to support their claims. This book is about the oral testimony of refugee applicants. It is about the oral evidence that refugees are compelled to give, the stories they are required to narrate and the genres of storytelling they are required to master during administrative oral hearings for the assessment of refugee status in Australia and Canada. Specifically, the book examines how the testimonial evidence of refugee applicants is presented, interrogated and assessed within the refugee status determination (RSD) process and under domestic enactments of the Refugee Convention in both jurisdictions.[1] Its central question is what the presentation, interrogation and assessment of testimony during the oral hearing tells us about what is demanded of refugee applicants as testimony-givers and narrators within individualised RSD processes. It then asks what those demands, made of refugees and their testimony, reveal about the refugee subject whom Refugee Convention-signatory states judge as authentic, credible and ultimately, acceptable. I address these questions through the qualitative analysis of an original dataset of refugee oral hearings that took place before the Immigration and Refugee Board (IRB) in Canada and the former Refugee Review Tribunal (RRT) in Australia. Central to the book's project is the claim that we cannot understand how RSD operates, nor the black box of what is referred to as credibility assessment within RSD, without closely studying the oral hearing and its conduct in full. Such a study involves fixing our attention on the frequently surprising, unpredictable and largely unexamined and undocumented exchanges between decision-makers and refugee applicants within specific refugee oral hearings.

In examining the conduct and content of oral hearings in Australia and Canada, this book also aims to bring critical insights from within 'law and literature' scholarship, and its engagement with the relationship between law and narrative, to bear on how refugee

[1] *Convention Relating to the Status of Refugees*, opened for signature 28 July 1951, 189 UNTS 150 (entered into force 22 April 1954) – as amended by the *Protocol Relating to the Status of Refugees 1967*, opened for signature 31 January 1967, 606 UNTS 267 (entered into force 4 October 1967) ('Refugee Convention'). For the definition as adopted in Canada and Australia respectively: *Immigration and Refugee Protection Act*, SC 2001, c 27, s 96; *Migration Act 1958* (Cth) ss 5H, 36.

testimony is both presented by asylum seekers, and tested and judged by administrative decision-makers. How does placing narrative at the centre of an investigation into RSD reveal dynamics of interaction and processes of judgment that are central to the inclusion or exclusion of refugee applicants and to the intractable problem of credibility assessment? Certain strands of law and literature scholarship and popular discourse alike have cast narrative as emancipatory, and celebrated personal narratives and storytelling for both their political power and ability to contest legal norms and authority. What, then, does a focus on the role of narrative within RSD do to disrupt conceptions of narrative as necessarily empowering or as enabling resistance? Against accounts of narrative and storytelling as disrupting law's authority, this book proposes a different account of the role and political place of narrative and narrative forms within (refugee) law and legal authority.

In my analysis of refugee oral testimony during the hearing, I argue that refugee applicants are required to meet a demand for narrativity and specific narrative forms in the presentation of their evidence, as well as to demonstrate a capacity to account for themselves in line with 'stock' narratives of refugeehood and asylum seeking. In the Australian and Canadian refugee hearings that form the book's qualitative dataset, genre and storytelling operated as disciplining forms and the demand for narrative was critical to and implicated in the refugee-receiving state's power to exclude. Further, these demands for narrative were made in the context of administrative oral hearings that, in their form and conduct, directly impeded a refugee applicant's capacity to meet these narrative mandates. As such, refugee applicants were expected to provide evidence in conventional narrative forms. And yet, by virtue of the form and conduct of the hearing, they were prevented from doing so. To put this another way, in the chapters that follow, I argue that a refugee applicant's presentation and explanation of evidence in a distinctly narrative form is a core aspect of the assessment of refugee credibility and acceptability; and that the RSD oral hearing, as the primary site where applicants must demonstrate this capacity, actively impedes a refugee's ability to meet this demand. Finally, this frequently unmeetable demand for narrative, alongside its disruption and fragmentation during the oral hearing, is directly implicated in state practices of exclusion and deterrence of refugees seeking asylum within their territory.

The specific sites of the reception and testing of refugee testimony at the centre of the book are the closed oral hearing rooms of the Canadian IRB and the former Australian RRT. As such, the book is about individualised, onshore or inland administrative processes of refugee decision-making within the Refugee Convention-signatory states of Australia and Canada. This means it is about the testimony and judgment of the minority of asylum seekers who are able to access RSD processes at a time when the possibility of entering the walled and securitised territories of Refugee Convention-signatory states has become more and more remote, and for certain people, effectively impossible. The hearing rooms tucked away in inner-city buildings in Australia and Canada and one-on-one oral exchanges between decision-makers and refugee applicants may seem both inconsequential to and disconnected from a global context in which the militarisation and externalisation of borders, forcible 'turn-backs' of people seeking asylum on land and sea, and criminalisation and incarceration of those who do reach state territory, determine the reality of what we call 'refugee protection'. However, as the book demonstrates, RSD and the crude processes for judging a refugee's credibility that it encompasses, persist as a critical site of refugee inclusion and exclusion. Indeed, in addressing the oral hearing as a central and underexamined event within refugee law, the book sets global trends of diminished and fast-tracked processes of RSD against the critical role played by each refugee's ability to narrate and account for themselves in an attempt to access protection. Moreover, it presents the primarily closed and deeply individual spaces of refugee assessment, and their role in constituting the acceptable (and unacceptable) refugee, as connected to refugee law's gate-keeping and exclusionary functions.

My argument builds on the small but rich body of scholarship that has engaged with narrative and language within the law and politics of asylum-seeking and refugee status, often from within the fields of sociolinguistics, critical discourse analysis or literary studies rather than law.[2] Robert Barsky's foundational work on refugee testimony, which applied both literary and discourse theory to transcripts of Canadian refugee hearings, demonstrated that refugee applicants must not only *be* refugees, but they must be able to *present* and *construct* themselves as refugees.[3] For Barsky, the refugee hearing is primarily a test of the claimant's ability to construct an appropriate image of a 'Convention refugee' and to become a 'productive other' – in line with conceptions of a refugee set out within particular political and cultural discourses of the receiving state and of government decision-makers.[4] It is not the veracity of the claim that is tested within RSD procedures, but rather the claimant's competency in meeting the requirements of the process and in performing the style of speech and argumentation that the process requires. Jan Blommaert identified the problem of 'narrative inequality' or alternatively what Katrijn Maryns and Blommaert call an applicant's 'narrative resources' as shaping Belgian asylum determinations.[5] Blommaert argues that a complex set of discursive practices and language ideologies place unmeetable linguistic demands on asylum seekers, who are discredited for the use of disqualified or insufficiently narrative modes.[6] Blommaert suggests in turn, that narrative inequalities condition the distribution of social rights.[7] In line with this claim, I argue that such narrative inequalities (and narrative demands) within the RSD oral hearing find direct expression within existing credibility criteria, which absolutely 'condition the distribution' of access to asylum. Matthew Zagor's engagement with narrative and identity in refugee law also highlights the imperative of refugee speech and stylised forms of testimony, observing that

[2] See especially Robert F Barsky, *Constructing a Productive Other: Discourse Theory and the Convention Refugee Hearing* (John Benjamins, 1994); Jan Blommaert, 'Investigating Narrative Inequality: African Asylum Seekers' Stories in Belgium' (2001) 12(4) *Discourse & Society* 413; Marita Eastmond, 'Stories as Lived Experience: Narratives in Forced Migration Research' (2007) 20(2) *Journal of Refugee Studies* 248; Laurie Berg and Jenni Millbank, 'Constructing the Personal Narratives of Lesbian, Gay and Bisexual Asylum Claimants' (2009) 22(2) *Journal of Refugee Studies* 195; Katrijn Maryns, *The Asylum Speaker: Language in the Belgian Asylum Procedure* (Routledge, 2014); David A B Murray, 'The (Not so) Straight Story: Queering Migration Narratives of Sexual Orientation and Gendered Identity Refugee Claimants' (2014) 17(4) *Sexualities* 451; Agnes Woolley, 'Narrating the "Asylum Story": Between Literary and Legal Storytelling' (2017) 19(3) *Interventions* 376; Carol Bohmer and Amy Shuman, *Political Asylum Deceptions: The Culture of Suspicion* (Palgrave Macmillan, 2018); Laura Smith-Khan, 'Why Refugee Visa Credibility Assessments Lack Credibility: A Critical Discourse Analysis' (2019) 28(4) *Griffith Law Review* 406; Marie Jacobs and Katrijn Maryns, 'Managing Narratives, Managing Identities: Language and Credibility in Legal Consultations with Asylum Seekers' (2022) 51(3) *Language in Society* 372.

[3] Barsky, above n 2.

[4] Ibid 5–6.

[5] Blommaert, above n 2; Katrijn Maryns and Jan Blommaert, 'Stylistic and Thematic Shifting as a Narrative Resource: Assessing Asylum Seekers' Repertoires' (2001) 20(1) *Multilingua* 61; Maryns, above n 2.

[6] Blommaert, above n 2, 414.

[7] Ibid 428.

'the refugee has long been in a situation where protection depends upon the telling of one's story. Whether she wants to or not, a refugee must speak; and she must speak in a legal context and, preferably, a legal idiom'.[8]

This book insists that the RSD process requires far more of applicants than merely meeting the legal definition of a refugee. In so doing, it also aims to highlight the fact that we still have little sense of how refugees contend with these narrative demands during the oral hearing, or resist or challenge them. Indeed, as becomes apparent in the hearing excerpts, applicants with 'narrative resources' to deploy were at times steadfast and explicit in refusing decision-makers' questions or re-narrations of their evidence. In these exchanges between applicants and decision-makers, the requirement for a kind of narrative competency was evident in the stock stories of 'genuine' asylum seeking against which applicant testimony was interrogated, but also moved beyond this. Applicants had to account for the *form* of their evidence. They were expected to be able to justify its narrative arc, the actions of various characters, the relationship between events and outcomes, and the details that they (as narrator) had included or excluded; and they were required to do so in the face of decision-makers' subjective, unpredictable and at times idiosyncratic questioning. Indeed, refugee applicants must relate complex evidence of a life left behind, of persecution, departure and arrival, in the form of a story that presents events plotted in time, with explicable and linear causative links, and, *most of all*, that resolves in a decision to become a refugee – even where no such resolution exists.

The remainder of this introduction is divided into four sections. First, I introduce the book's qualitative dataset and the sites of oral testimony it examines. Next, I provide my account of what we know about the immense failures and injustices of credibility assessment within RSD; I explain why compelling research on the dysfunction of credibility determination has resulted in so little change and how these insights shape the questions and findings in the rest of the book. I then establish the profoundly mediated, co-produced and constrained nature of what I imperfectly term 'refugee testimony' and present the book's structure and chapter overview. Finally, I outline how the testimony of the refugee applicants who participated in this research will be presented throughout the book.

1.1 The Oral Hearing in Context

The book presents a detailed, qualitative analysis of fifteen refugee applicants' oral hearings, which took place before the IRB in Canada and the RRT in Australia between 2012 and 2015.[9] Since the period in which the hearings and the qualitative aspects of this research took place, refugee law and policy in both jurisdictions have been anything but

[8] Matthew Zagor, 'Recognition and Narrative Identities: Is Refugee Law Redeemable?' in Fiona Jenkins, Mark Nolan and Kim Rubenstein (eds), *Allegiance and Identity in a Globalised World* (Cambridge University Press, 2014) 311, 323.

[9] University of British Columbia Behavioural Research Ethics Board, *Approval Certificate No H12-01565*; University of Technology Sydney Human Research Ethics Committee, *Ethics Reference No 2011-486A*. The Appendix sets out the elements of each hearing, including the jurisdiction; gender of the applicant; basis of claim; country of origin; credibility determination; and outcome. Although I do not read the hearings quantitatively, for the sake of both interest and description, I note the data sample included: ten men and five women; and six negative outcomes and nine positive outcomes. All hearings and excerpts have been anonymised and de-identified to preserve confidentiality.

static. Notably in Australia this period has included reform to the administrative bodies charged with the assessment of protection claims. Indeed, in 2015, the RRT was amalgamated with the Administrative Appeals Tribunal (AAT), into a 'super tribunal' to deal with all Commonwealth matters of administrative review.[10] As a result, the RRT was replaced by the Migration and Refugee Division (MRD) of the AAT, albeit with minimal substantive change to the nature of administrative review provided within the new tribunal division or its fundamental operation. Then, as the manuscript of this book was being finalised, a new Labor Government in Australia announced the abolition of the AAT in its entirety, and plans for its replacement with a new administrative review body.[11] As I outline in Chapter 2, these changes were motivated by long-standing criticisms of the level of executive control over the Tribunal's process for the selection of members and, in particular, direct appointments of members with connections to sitting governments in the absence of a transparent, merits-based process.

Alongside reforms to the administration of and institutions responsible for RSD in Australia, Global North Refugee Convention-signatory states continue to be 'unwavering in their commitment' to avoiding responsibility under international refugee law and to implementing novel and extreme modes of refugee deterrence and *non-entrée* policies.[12] In both Australia and Canada, deterrence policies have moved both outwards from territorial and maritime borders to extraterritorial sites of migration control, and inwards to encompass reforms to RSD processes, including, but not limited to: early and opaque 'screening out' of certain applicants before claims are made in full; the rapid acceleration of RSD application timelines for select applicants; limiting access to and/or narrowing the scope of administrative and judicial review of primary decisions; and the withdrawal of government-funded legal assistance.[13] Indeed, tracing amendments to RSD in both states reveals that the quality of refugee decision-making has been progressively diminished for specific groups of asylum seekers, singled out for unique forms of deterrence or exclusion.[14]

Crucially for this project, though, in both Australia and Canada, the function, nature and conduct of the oral hearing – despite the reforms that have taken place around it –

[10] *Tribunals Amalgamation Act 2015* (Cth).

[11] Mark Dreyfus, Attorney General, 'Albanese Government to Abolish Administrative Appeals Tribunal' (Media Release, 22 December 2022).

[12] Thomas Gammeltoft-Hansen and James C Hathaway, 'Non-refoulement in a World of Cooperative Deterrence' (2015) 53(2) *Columbia Journal of Transnational Law* 235, 235.

[13] For examples of the acceleration of decision-making across time and jurisdiction, see Thomas Spijkerboer, 'Stereotyping and Acceleration – Gender, Procedural Acceleration and Marginalised Judicial Review in the Dutch Asylum System (2005)' in Gregor Noll (ed), *Proof, Evidentiary Assessment and Credibility in Asylum Procedures* (Martinus Nijhoff Publishers, 2005) 67; Angus Grant and Sean Rehaag, 'Unappealing: An Assessment of the Limits on Appeal Rights in Canada's New Refugee Determination System' (2016) 49 *UBC Law Review* 203; Linda Kirk, 'Accelerated Asylum Procedures in the United Kingdom and Australia: "Fast Track" to Refoulement?' in Maria O'Sullivan and Dallal Stevens (eds), *States, the Law and Access to Refugee Protection: Fortresses and Fairness* (Hart, 2017) 243; Emily McDonald and Maria O'Sullivan, 'Protecting Vulnerable Refugees: Procedural Fairness in the Australian Fast Track Regime' (2018) 41 *University of New South Wales Law Journal* 1003; Jessica Hambly and Nick Gill, 'Law and Speed: Asylum Appeals and the Techniques and Consequences of Legal Quickening' (2020) 47(1) *Journal of Law and Society* 3.

[14] Kirk, ibid.

has remained remarkably fixed.[15] Moreover, the effect of these diverse reforms is that they have put even greater pressure on refugee testimony and its presentation during the first- or second-instance oral hearing, as vital to the success of a claim. In this way, where refugee applicants are granted access to an oral hearing – and this is not always the case[16] – reforms diminishing the quality of RSD have been implemented 'on both sides' of oral hearings, in terms of shortened timelines in the lead up to the assessment of testimony, and the limiting of the avenues, scope and quality of review following its presentation. As such, the legal and procedural stakes of an applicant's expression of their testimony have rarely been higher, at the same time as the injustices of giving and assessing refugee testimony, as charted in the following chapters, remain as intractable as ever.

The hearings in the book took place across four cities in Australia and Canada.[17] I accessed them through my in-person attendance at the hearing itself, or through the full audio recordings of a hearing, or both.[18] For each hearing included in the study, I also had access to the written decision and reasons. In Canada, the IRB is responsible for the first-instance determination of the claim. In Australia, the former RRT conducted *de novo* administrative review of an initial negative decision made by a delegate of the Australian Immigration Minister.[19] An oral hearing, with limited exceptions, is required before both the IRB and RRT.[20] Both bodies are required to determine refugee claims on the merits and in full, and in both cases a refugee applicant presents such testimony directly to a single administrative decision-maker.[21] The decision-maker directly questions and tests the applicant's oral evidence and holds substantial discretion over precisely how the hearing is run and what aspects of the claim are discussed and for how long. Interpreters frequently mediate these exchanges.

An applicant's lawyer or advocate may be present in both jurisdictions, but it is the decision-maker who questions the applicant in the first instance in Canada, and legal advocates in Australia have no right to question their clients during the hearing.[22]

15 Ibid.

16 As detailed in Chapter 3, in some instances governments have excluded select groups of asylum seekers from accessing RSD altogether or implemented procedurally unfair screening processes that effectively remove access to the RSD procedure: see Regina Jefferies, Daniel Ghezelbash and Asher Hirsch, 'Assessing Refugee Protection Claims at Australian Airports: The Gap between Law, Policy, and Practice' (2020) 44(1) *Melbourne University Law Review* 162.

17 Sydney and Melbourne (Australia); and Montréal and Vancouver (Canada).

18 The multiple forms of data were both a strength and a limitation of the project: a strength insofar as each form of data provides different kinds of information and representations of the hearing, and a limitation in that the 'comparability' of some data is undermined by the diversity of forms.

19 Refugee applicants arriving by boat and without authorisation in Australia have variously been prohibited from accessing administrative review before the RRT and the AAT (discussed below) and subject to non-statutory processing regimes. Current RSD procedures for 'unauthorised maritime arrivals' are also addressed in Chapter 3, but for an account of RSD historically available to 'maritime arrivals' see Michelle Foster and Jason Pobjoy, 'A Failed Case of Legal Exceptionalism? Refugee Status Determination in Australia's "Excised" Territory' (2011) 23(4) *International Journal of Refugee Law* 583.

20 *Migration Act 1958* (Cth) s 425; *Immigration and Refugee Protection Act*, SC 2001, c 27, s 170(b).

21 Though, a decision in the applicant's favour can be made on the papers in both jurisdictions: *Migration Act 1958* (Cth) s 425(2)(a) and *Immigration and Refugee Protection Act*, SC 2001, c 27, s 170(f).

22 While advocates may be present in both jurisdictions, the applicant must present their evidence directly in response to the decision-maker's questioning. In Canada, an applicant 'may, at their own expense, be represented by legal or other counsel', though some legal aid is available in Ontario, Québec and British

Lawyers are both physically and figuratively 'to the side' of the presentation of oral evidence in each jurisdiction. Although the Canadian and Australian hearings took place at different stages of RSD, both the former RRT and IRB constituted the last stage of decision-making where an applicant presents their claim in an oral hearing before a decision-maker empowered to make findings of both law and fact.[23] Both Australia and Canada have ratified and domestically enacted the key obligations under the Refugee Convention, and each has a semi-independent, administrative decision-making body for the purposes of determining refugee claims.

The book's argument and findings are applicable to the assessment of refugee testimony in Global North refugee-receiving states where deterrence is a central aspect of the asylum regime and oral testimony is central to the RSD process. My analysis of the oral hearing in Australia and Canada raises questions that can be productively asked in other jurisdictions, particularly where the assessment of in-person oral testimony is governed by a version of the credibility criteria I describe below.[24] The book's findings contribute to a growing but still limited empirical literature on conduct of refugee decision-making, in relation to which Nick Gill and Anthony Good observe that 'it is remarkable that so little empirical research has been carried out into how RSD structures actually operate in practice'.[25] I agree. Despite the significant variance in the formal design and conduct of administrative RSD processes,[26] my arguments in relation to the dysfunction of credibility determinations within RSD and the assessment of oral testimony provide insight and lines of inquiry for all states with individualised, testimony-driven processes for RSD. Such research provides a much-needed 'antidote to the emphasis on either [only] legal doctrine or outcome' in studies of refugee decision-making.[27] While my data spans two jurisdic-

Columbia and advocates are permitted to question their clients and make submissions: *Immigration and Refugee Protection Act*, SC 2001, c 27, s 167(1). In Australia, 'a person appearing before the Tribunal to give evidence is not entitled to be represented before the Tribunal by any other person' and advocates are generally not permitted to question the applicant at all, though in practice they are permitted to make submissions at the close of the hearing: *Migration Act 1958* (Cth) s 427(6)(a).

23 Unsuccessful applicants before the RRT were permitted to seek judicial review only. Applicants who do not succeed before the Refugee Protection Division (RPD) of the IRB may seek merits review before the Refugee Appeal Division (RAD), but an appeal to the RAD must generally proceed without a hearing. Certain exceptions exist, including if the Minister participates in the hearing and wishes to present evidence; if evidence is presented that arises after the original hearing or that was not reasonably available; and if in the Board's opinion the documentary evidence raises a 'serious' and 'central' question with respect to credibility, which would justify the Board allowing or rejecting the claim: *Immigration and Refugee Protection Act*, SC 2001, c 27, s 110(3), (4) and (6).

24 As the following section explains, since credibility standards are drawn from the UNHCR *Handbook on Procedures and Criteria for Determining Refugee Status under the 1951 Convention and the 1967 Protocol Relating to the Status of Refugees*, this includes most Convention-signatory states with individualised RSD procedures: below nn 34, 37.

25 Nick Gill and Anthony Good (eds), 'Introduction' in *Asylum Determination in Europe: Ethnographic Perspectives* (Palgrave Macmillan, 2019) 6. Indeed, this collection makes a major contribution to empirical understandings of the operation of European RSD procedures.

26 See for example Gill and Good's short, insightful summary of some key differences in fundamental aspects of procedure in European states: ibid 13 (figure 1.2).

27 Gill and Good, above n 25, 19.

tions, I do not adopt a formally comparative methodology. Instead, the book demonstrates the demand for narrative across comparable refugee-receiving jurisdictions, where the presentation of oral testimony and credibility assessment remain core elements of the determination process, with attention to relevant differences in law, practice and procedure in both jurisdictions.

The dataset of countless pages of transcripts, observational notes, reasons and audio files provides a detailed picture of the presentation and reception of oral evidence in the fifteen RSD hearings that I observed. I address the multiple barriers to accessing RSD and oral hearings or interviews in Chapter 1, which also explains the basis upon which particular hearings were included in the research, and how refugee participants were recruited. The scope and limits of the dataset are, in part, a consequence of the enduring difficulty of accessing executive and administrative refugee status decision-making in jurisdictions where RSD is not undertaken in open courts or tribunals, and only a minority of decisions are published. I treat the hearings, both individually and collectively, as a rich source of qualitative data and use close reading and grounded theory as the basis for each chapter's arguments and thematic analysis.[28] Indeed, my focus on RRT and IRB oral hearings locates the project within a body of important work exploring the day-to-day operation and outcomes of administrative refugee decision-making *despite* barriers to access. The challenges of accessing lower-level decisions, let alone the hearings in full, unites much of the work in this field, with valuable recent exceptions, some of which highlight the comparatively open nature of hearings within European Union jurisdictions.[29] Given the limited amount of work that has accessed or assessed the oral hearing and its conduct, the dataset and hearings provide a valuable source of data and insight.

Existing research on credibility assessment, alongside establishing the unique factors that render RSD as the 'most intensely narrative mode of legal adjudication',[30] are logical points of departure for the remainder of the book. As such, in the next section, I explain the bases, profound failings and gate-keeping functions of credibility assessment and set these against one of the book's unifying concerns: that credibility assessment and the appraisal of refugee testimony is 'often the single most important step' in the determination of refugee status.[31]

1.2 Refugee Testimony and the Intractable Problem(s) of Credibility Assessment

Scholarship addressing credibility assessment is best described as a sustained, multi-jurisdictional and at times exasperated critique of existing standards and practice.[32] Here,

[28] Further details about research design, including methods of recruitment of research participants, criteria for research participants' inclusion in the dataset and my approach to qualitative analysis are addressed in Chapter 2.

[29] Most notably here, the ethnographic studies included in Nick Gill and Anthony Good, *Asylum Determination in Europe: Ethnographic Perspectives* (Palgrave Macmillan, 2019).

[30] Jenni Millbank, '"The Ring of Truth": A Case Study of Credibility Assessment in Particular Social Group Refugee Determinations' (2009) 21(1) *International Journal of Refugee Law* 1, 2.

[31] Michael Kagan, 'Is Truth in the Eye of the Beholder? Objective Credibility Assessment in Refugee Status Determination' (2002) 17 *Georgetown Immigration Law Journal* 367, 367. See also Gregor Noll (ed), *Proof, Evidentiary Assessment and Credibility in Asylum Procedures* (Martin Nijhoff, 2005); UNHCR, 'Beyond Proof: Credibility Assessment in EU Asylum Systems: Full Report' (May 2013).

[32] Audrey Macklin, 'Truth and Consequences: Credibility Determination in the Refugee Context' in International Association of Refugee Law Judges (ed), *The Realities of Refugee Determination on the Eve of a New Millennium: The Role of the Judiciary* (International Association of Refugee Law Judges,

I take stock of what scholars across disciplines have established about credibility assessment and the implications of this research for the immense burden placed on refugee testimony within RSD. I structure existing critiques of credibility assessment into three overlapping strands, each of which is implicated in the demand for narrative required of refugee applicants.

1.2.1 The Credibility Criteria as False Proxies for Truth

The Refugee Convention defines a refugee as a person who holds a 'well-founded fear of being persecuted for reasons of race, religion, nationality, membership of a particular social group or political opinion' in their country of origin and who is 'unable, or owing to such fear ... unwilling to avail himself [*sic*] of the protection of that country'.[33] An applicant's claim may fail because their evidence fails to meet one or more aspects of this definition. However, the determination of a claim to protection may also be based, in part or in full, on a decision-maker's finding that the person seeking protection cannot be believed. To put this another way, a finding that the evidence presented – or the person presenting it – is not credible (or, as is often the case, some slippage between the two). In determining this critical question of a refugee applicant's credibility, decision-makers must generally decide whether the applicant's account of their evidence meets the criteria of coherence, plausibility and consistency.[34] The controversial criterion of an applicant's demeanour also endures as a credibility standard in Australia and Canada, albeit one subject to repeated judicial caution as to its use and reliability.[35] These criteria are drawn from the UNHCR Handbook on

1998) 134; Kagan, above n 31; Cécile Rousseau et al, 'The Complexity of Determining Refugeehood: A Multidisciplinary Analysis of the Decision-Making Process of the Canadian Immigration and Refugee Board' (2002) 15(1) *Journal of Refugee Studies* 43; Guy Coffey, 'The Credibility of Credibility Evidence at the Refugee Review Tribunal' (2003) 15(3) *International Journal of Refugee Law* 377; Noll, above n 31; Millbank, above n 30; Hilary Evans Cameron, 'Refugee Status Determinations and the Limits of Memory' (2010) 22(4) *International Journal of Refugee Law* 469; Jane Herlihy, Kate Gleeson and Stuart Turner, 'What Assumptions about Human Behaviour Underlie Asylum Judgments?' (2010) 22(3) *International Journal of Refugee Law* 351; Robert Thomas, *Administrative Justice and Asylum Appeals: A Study of Tribunal Adjudication* (Hart, 2011) (especially chapter 5); Benjamin N Lawrance and Galya Ruffer, *Adjudicating Refugee and Asylum Status* (Cambridge University Press, 2015); Sean Rehaag, 'I Simply Do Not Believe: A Case Study of Credibility Determinations in Canadian Refugee Adjudication' (2017) 38 *Windsor Review of Legal and Social Issues* 38; Laura Smith-Khan, 'Different in the Same Way? Language, Diversity, and Refugee Credibility' (2017) 29(3) *International Journal of Refugee Law* 389.

33 Refugee Convention, above n 1, Article 1A.

34 UNHCR, *Handbook on Procedures and Criteria for Determining Refugee Status under the 1951 Convention and the 1967 Protocol Relating to the Status of Refugees* (HCR/IP/4/Eng/REV1, 4th ed, 2019) 44 ('the Handbook').

35 While it is increasingly regarded as an unreliable and inaccurate indicator of credibility, demeanour remains a factor that decision-makers may rely on with caution. As the UNHCR *Beyond Proof* report sets out: '[a] determination of credibility by reference to demeanour has a subjective basis that will inevitably reflect the views, prejudices, personal life experiences, and cultural norms of the decision-maker': UNHCR, above n 31, 186. The Australian RRT Guidelines on credibility set out that '[t]he Tribunal should also be aware of the effect of cultural differences on demeanour and oral communication' and that the RRT should exercise particular care if it relies on demeanour in 'circumstances where a person provides oral evidence through an interpreter or where a person is not before the Tribunal and can only be observed via a video-link': Administrative Appeals Tribunal Migration and Refugee Division, 'Guidelines on the Assessment of Credibility' (2006, updated 2015) [6.1]. The Canadian IRB's guidance on credibility directs decision-makers not to rely solely on demeanour because it 'is not an infallible guide

Procedures and Criteria for Determining Refugee Status, which sets out that an applicant's statements 'must be coherent and plausible, and must not run counter to generally known facts'.[36] The Handbook is a UNHCR document, first produced in 1979 in response to requests from Convention-signatory countries for guidance on RSD procedures, and many Convention signatories have adopted some version of the criteria of consistency, coherence and plausibility as determinants of credibility.[37] This is true in Australia and Canada, where the criteria of consistency, plausibility and coherence are used to determine credibility, as set out within credibility guidelines and case law.[38]

In the face of the widespread adoption of these standards, the most fundamental and uncontroversial knowledge about how autobiographical memory functions calls into question consistency, coherence and plausibility as a basis for assessing the credibility of testimony.[39] That is to say, the criteria used to test refugee applicants' credibility are at complete odds with existing understandings of the relationship between first person testimony, autobiographical memory and how memory operates.[40] As a result, refugee law's indicia of credibility place unreasonable expectations on refugees' accounts of their past and, to put it simply, are absurd proxies for truth. Research bringing knowledge from the disciplines of psychology and psychiatry to bear on RSD processes has repeatedly critiqued and discredited the foundational, structuring assumptions and

as to whether the truth is being told, nor is it determinative of credibility'. However, the document nonetheless goes on to state that:

> [i]n assessing demeanour, the decision-maker ought not to form impressions based on the physical appearance or political profile of a witness, *but on objective considerations that flow from the witness's testimony,* such as the witness's frankness and spontaneity, whether the witness is hesitant or reticent in providing information, and the witness's attitude and comportment (behaviour).

Immigration and Refugee Board, 'Assessment of Credibility in Claims for Refugee Protection' (Legal Services, updated 2020) [2.3.7] (emphasis added); see also Jill Hunter et al, 'Asylum Adjudication, Mental Health and Credibility Evaluation' (2013) 41 *Federal Law Review* 471, 483.

36 UNHCR, above n 34, 44. In its Note on Burden and Standard of Proof, UNHCR adds that '[c]redibility is established where the applicant has presented a claim which is coherent and plausible, not contradicting generally known facts, and therefore is, on balance, capable of being believed': UNHCR, 'Note on Burden and Standard of Proof in Refugee Claims' (1998) [11].

37 The Handbook was released by the UNHCR as part of its supervisory responsibility under the Refugee Convention (Articles 35 and 36) and the 1950 Statute of the UNHCR (paragraph 8). It represents the 'accumulated views of the UNHCR, State practice, Executive Committee Conclusions, academic literature and judicial decisions' at national and international levels. It was rereleased in 1992, 2011 and 2019. In all subsequent editions, substantive content remains unchanged from the original version. The later editions, however, contain an updated list of the UNHCR's *Guidelines on International Protection*: UNHCR, above n 34, 1–2.

38 Chapter 5 sets out in detail domestic credibility guidelines and jurisprudence.

39 See especially Hunter et al, above n 35; Laurence J Kirmayer, 'Failures of Imagination: The Refugee's Narrative in Psychiatry' (2003) 10(2) *Anthropology & Medicine* 167; Jane Herlihy and Stuart W Turner, 'Asylum Claims and Memory of Trauma: Sharing Our Knowledge' (2007) 191(1) *The British Journal of Psychiatry* 3.

40 Jane Herlihy and Stuart W Turner, 'The Psychology of Seeking Protection' (2009) 21 *International Journal of Refugee Law* 171; Evans Cameron, above n 32.

standards of credibility assessment.[41] Such research 'has provided compelling evidence to suggest that autobiographical remembering is not an exact replaying of an event'.[42] Moreover, this work examines and categorically rejects 'the assumption that people can reliably, consistently and accurately recall autobiographical memories' and that applicants who give discrepant or inconsistent accounts of their experiences are necessarily fabricating evidence.[43]

Notably, the requirement for consistency refers not just to internal consistency across countless retellings, translations and explanations, as well as with the events as they took place. It also assesses the 'external' consistency of an applicant's account, against facts about life in the applicant's home country and available 'country of origin information' (COI) about the conditions or circumstances that the applicant has fled. This brings not only the incomplete and uneven sources of 'accepted' COI into the frame, but also decision-makers' subsequent interpretation of them and their own pre-existing assumptions about life and culture in the applicant's country. Gibb and Good drily note that the frequent characterisation of COI as 'objective evidence' of external consistency is 'a formulation that seems to ignore the contextualization and interpretation to which all such knowledge is subject'.[44]

The dysfunction of the credibility criteria is exacerbated further still by the fact that refugee testimony is often, and often primarily, about traumatic events, violence or atrocity.[45] As Shuman and Bohmer write, trauma leaves gaps.[46] It disrupts the relationship between fact, memory and knowledge.[47] It distorts time and experience, in both the past and the present, and as some have argued, may exceed language itself and what is sayable.[48] Theories of traumatic memory suggest that the recall of traumatic events may have 'little verbal narrative to tie them together'; that they are 'not marked as being in the past'; and/or that they 'cannot be brought to mind by conscious attempts to recall'.[49]

41 Herlihy and Turner, above n 40, 175.

42 Jane Herlihy, Laura Jobson and Stuart Turner, 'Just Tell Us What Happened to You: Autobiographical Memory and Seeking Asylum' (2012) 26(5) *Applied Cognitive Psychology* 661, 662. See especially Hunter et al, above n 35; Kirmayer, above n 39; Herlihy and Turner, above n 39.

43 Herlihy, Jobson and Turner, above n 42, 662; Jane Herlihy and Stuart Turner, 'Should Discrepant Accounts Given by Asylum Seekers Be Taken as Proof of Deceit?' (2006) 16(2) *Torture: Quarterly Journal on Rehabilitation of Torture Victims and Prevention of Torture* 81.

44 Robert Gibb and Anthony Good, 'Do the Facts Speak for Themselves? Country of Origin Information in French and British Refugee Status Determination Procedures' (2013) 25(2) *International Journal of Refugee Law* 291, 321; see too Jasper van der Kist, Huub Dijstelbloem and Marieke de Goede, 'In the Shadow of Asylum Decision-Making: The Knowledge Politics of Country-of-Origin Information' (2019) 13(1) *International Political Sociology* 68.

45 Herlihy and Turner, above n 40, 173. One key assumption that the authors challenge is that 'an experience of severe violence or torture will be so important that it will be remembered very clearly over the long term': at 73. See also David B Pillemer, *Momentous Events, Vivid Memories* (Harvard University Press, 1998).

46 Amy Shuman and Carol Bohmer, 'Narrative Breakdown in the Political Asylum Process' (2021) 134(532) *The Journal of American Folklore* 180, 191.

47 Dominick LaCapra, *Writing History, Writing Trauma* (John Hopkins University Press, 2nd ed, 2014) 41–42.

48 Shoshana Felman, *The Juridical Unconscious: Trials and Traumas in the Twentieth Century* (Harvard University Press, 2002).

49 Herlihy and Turner, above n 43; Herlihy and Turner, above n 39.

Studies of refugee claims made on the basis of gendered harms and sexuality, in particular, have demonstrated the exceptional injustice of the credibility criteria of coherence and consistency in the context of shame, trauma and the prevalence of delayed or difficult disclosure associated with such harms.[50]

These expectations of refugee testimony persist despite the fact that official RSD guidelines frequently and openly acknowledge that refugee testimony and in particular traumatic testimony cannot be assessed against the usual indicia of credibility,[51] precisely because it is marked by the absence of 'coherence, structure, meaning, comprehensibility'.[52] Indeed the *Beyond Proof: Credibility Assessment in EU Asylum Systems* report – an immense, multi-agency report aimed at improving credibility assessment within the European Union – attested to ongoing and urgent concerns about the quality and basis of credibility assessment.[53] Domestic, regional and international guidelines on credibility, gender and sexuality, as well as the UNHCR Handbook itself, highlight – at times with nuance and sensitivity – the difficulties faced by applicants in formulating and then presenting autobiographical testimony. However, credibility assessment must be understood as a political rather than procedural problem. I build this argument below, but the need to analyse RSD as steadfastly part of regimes of refugee deterrence is evident in the fact that existing credibility standards persist and that they do so in the face of extensive, intelligent and practical suggestions for reform.[54] Even where existing

[50] Helen Baillot, Sharon Cowan and Vanessa E Munro, 'Reason to Disbelieve: Evaluating the Rape Claims of Women Seeking Asylum in the UK' (2014) 10(1) *International Journal of Law in Context* 105; Debora Singer, 'Falling at Each Hurdle: Assessing the Credibility of Women's Asylum Claims' in Efrat Arbel, Catherine Dauvergne and Jenni Millbank (eds), *Gender in Refugee Law: From the Margins to the Centre* (Routledge, 2014) 98; Thomas Spijkerboer (ed), *Fleeing Homophobia: Sexual Orientation, Gender and Asylum* (Routledge, 2013); Nicole LaViolette, '"UNHCR Guidance Note on Refugee Claims Relating to Sexual Orientation and Gender Identity": A Critical Commentary' (2010) 22(2) *International Journal of Refugee Law* 173; Berg and Millbank, above n 2; Jenni Millbank, 'From Discretion to Disbelief: Recent Trends in Refugee Determinations on the Basis of Sexual Orientation in Australia and the United Kingdom' (2009) 13(2–3) *The International Journal of Human Rights* 391.

[51] Domestic guidelines in Canada and Australia are addressed in detail in Chapter 5.

[52] Molly Andrews, 'Beyond Narrative: The Shape of Traumatic Testimony' in Matti Hyvärinen (ed), *Beyond Narrative Coherence* (John Benjamins, 2010) 148; Shuman and Bohmer, above n 46, 191.

[53] UNHCR, above n 31. As the Beyond Proof summary report notes, '[a] distinctive feature of this research was its focus on the implementation of the credibility assessment in practice by first-instance decision-makers': at 9. Although the report only relates to EU Member States, it notes 'there is a pressing need for comprehensive and up-to-date guidance on credibility assessment'; that UNHCR has 'embarked on the review of its own guidance with a view to producing updated guidelines on credibility assessment that reflect recent developments in international refugee law'; and that the report's findings will be taken into account in the preparation process for new UNHCR standards: UNHCR, 'Beyond Proof: Credibility Assessment in EU Asylum Systems: Summary Report' (May 2013) 8–9. While there was a second credibility report addressing credibility in the context of child refugee applicants and a UNHCR-convened Expert Roundtable on Credibility in 2015, there were no new UNHCR credibility standards at the time of writing. See UNHCR, 'Summary of Deliberations on Credibility Assessment in Asylum Procedures', Expert Roundtable in Hungary (2015); UNHCR, 'The Heart of the Matter – Assessing Credibility when Children Apply for Asylum in the European Union' (December 2014).

[54] See for example International Association of Refugee Law Judges, 'International Judicial Guidance for the Assessment of Credibility' in Allan Mackey et al, *A Structured Approach to the Decision Making Process in Refugee and Other International Protection Claims* (IARLJ, 2016); Gábor Gyulai et al, *Credibility Assessment in Asylum Procedures: A Multidisciplinary Training Manual*, Volume 1 & 2 (Hungarian Helsinki Committee 2013, 2015).

policy and guidelines clearly state that expectations of coherence, consistency and plausibility should be modified, reformulated or abandoned altogether for particular types of claims or claimants, the normative framework remains central to the demands placed on oral testimony.

1.2.2 RSD Cultures of Suspicion and the Politics of Refugee Deterrence

Domestic refugee laws, policies and politics in Global North states are designed to achieve the deterrence of 'onshore' refugees, and failing that, their punishment. The endurance of discredited credibility criteria must be understood in this context. Researchers across jurisdictions have described RSD, and the determination of an applicant's credibility within it, as characterised by a 'culture of disbelief',[55] 'a culture of suspicion',[56] 'adversarial posturing'[57] and a 'presumptive scepticism'.[58] These descriptions are so common they have attained a sound bite quality within the field.[59] Their persistence across time and jurisdiction reflect the connection between refugee decision-making and the politics and practical consequences of state policies orientated towards refugee exclusion. Which is to say, states' systematic 'illegalization' of onshore refugees is directly implicated in the suspicion and doubt that structures credibility assessment and the judgment of refugee testimony.[60] Refugees who dare to cross a border without authorisation to seek protection are not only cast as 'illegal' and as 'security threats' through the racialised securitisation of migration, but totalised as 'illegals'.[61] What is at times lost in the legal literature on credibility is that it is *only* those who surmount state-imposed barriers and 'unlawfully' cross militarised borders – that is, those already cast as bogus – who ultimately appear before RSD bodies in order to be judged. Making this critical connection between ever-expanding global deterrence policies and the judgment of individual applicants within RSD, Michael Kagan writes that '[o]ne by one and case by case, asylum seekers must navigate the tension between refugee protection and migration control as they struggle to be deemed "credible"'.[62]

[55] James Souter, 'A Culture of Disbelief or Denial? Critiquing Refugee Status Determination in the United Kingdom' (2011) 1(1) *Oxford Monitor of Forced Migration* 48, 48. See also James A Sweeney, 'Credibility, Proof and Refugee Law' (2009) 21(4) *International Journal of Refugee Law* 700, 703; Millbank, above n 30, 16.

[56] See Bohmer and Shuman, above n 2.

[57] Susan Kneebone, 'The Refugee Review Tribunal and the Assessment of Credibility: An Inquisitorial Role' (1998) 5 *Australian Journal of Administrative Law* 78, 94.

[58] Rosemary Byrne, 'Assessing Testimonial Evidence in Asylum Proceedings: Guiding Standards from the International Criminal Tribunals' (2007) 19(4) *International Journal of Refugee Law* 609, 607.

[59] Souter, above n 55, 48. In suggesting that the idea of 'cultures of disbelief' has become a sound bite, Souter argues that the term 'denial' and a culture of denial more accurately describe the refusal of decision-makers to recognise refugee status within the UK: at 49.

[60] Catherine Dauvergne, *Making People Illegal: What Globalization Means for Migration and Law* (Cambridge University Press, 2008); Audrey Macklin, 'Disappearing Refugees: Reflections on the Canada-US Safe Third Country Agreement' (2005) 36 *Columbia Human Rights Law Review* 365.

[61] Dauvergne, above n 60.

[62] Michael Kagan, 'Believable Victims: Asylum Credibility and the Struggle for Objectivity Culture & Society' (2015) 16(1) *Georgetown Journal of International Affairs* 123, 124; see also Bridget M Haas and Amy Shuman (eds), *Technologies of Suspicion and the Ethics of Obligation in Political Asylum* (Ohio University Press, 2019).

The framing and explanation of a politics of doubt and distrust within RSD can be widened further still and connected to a broader, post-colonial literature explaining the figure of the 'illegitimate', racialised and fake refugee. Sherene Razack argues that settler colonial states' narration of the nation as 'besieged' by bogus asylum seekers conceals a racist logic. This 'simple' logic casts refugees arriving without permission (i.e., those who rely on onshore RSD) as unidentifiable, racialised masses betraying the state's trust, and seeking access to entitlements which belong to white, settler citizens.[63] The state, in such circumstances, is permitted to defend itself from exploitation by illegitimate, 'undocumented' masses, which in turn relies on a 'national story of white innocence and the duplicity and cunning of people of colour'.[64] As against the produced, Eurocentric image of a 'normal' asylum seeker – 'white, male and anti-communist' – post–Cold War asylum seekers are characterised as 'new', mass arrivals, abusing Western hospitality and without genuine claims to protection.[65]

These narratives of race and nationhood enter the hearing room and highly individualised processes of credibility assessment because, as I am attempting to underline, the refugee applicant giving testimony who is judged as dubious or deceitful is simultaneously the queue jumper, the bogus refugee and the economic migrant who dared to move across national borders and exploit the sovereign exception embedded within the Refugee Convention.[66] Bridging cultures of disbelief within RSD and states' physical and political acts of refugee exclusion (or expulsion) is critical to the assessment of the politics of refugee testimony during the oral hearing. To ignore such theorisation involves imagining the doubt that has defined credibility assessment as materialising out of thin air, or assuming that well-designed procedural reform could solve 'the credibility problem', which it certainly has not to date – despite the best efforts of exceptional thinkers and experts on the topic.[67]

Decision-making 'cultures of disbelief' or 'refusal mindsets' would present a problem in any adjudicative context. For refugee applicants, though, it is critical to note from the outset that these predispositions fly in the face of a core, structuring principle of RSD: namely that refugee applicants should be given the benefit of the doubt.[68] The imperative of affording refugee applicants this benefit is precisely because of the singular context of refugee decision-making, whereby a life or death decision must frequently be made on the strength of an applicant's testimony alone.[69] Instead of the benefit of the doubt, doubt itself shapes the reception of refugee narrative. Refugee applicants in turn must actively manage and

63 Sherene H Razack, 'Simple Logic: Race, the Identity Documents Rule and the Story of a Nation Besieged and Betrayed' (2000) 15 *Journal of Law and Social Policy* 181. For an application of this argument to refugee law in Britain, and the category of refugee as a means for a 'generous' Britain to 'shed the association between its colonial history and the migration of its former subjects' see Nadine El-Enany, *Bordering Britain: Law, Race and Empire* (Manchester University Press, 2021) 133.

64 Razack, above n 63, 187.

65 BS Chimni, 'The Geopolitics of Refugee Studies: A View from the South' (1998) 11(4) *Journal of Refugee Studies* 350, 357.

66 See especially Patricia Tuitt, *False Images: Law's Construction of the Refugee* (Pluto Press, 1996).

67 For examples of critical engagement with practical and procedural reforms, see above nn 53–54.

68 UNHCR, above n 34, 43–44. For a clarifying account of this standard, and its practical operation in Canadian and UK refugee law, respectively, see Hilary Evans Cameron, *Refugee Law's Fact-Finding Crisis: Truth, Risk, and the Wrong Mistake* (Cambridge University Press, 2018) chapter 4; Anthony Good, '"The Benefit of the Doubt" in British Asylum Claims and International Cricket' in Daniela Berti and Anthony Good (eds), *Of Doubt and Proof: Ritual and Legal Practices of Judgment* (Routledge, 2015) 119, 121–26.

69 UNHCR, above n 34, 43–44.

negotiate the burden of suspicion during the hearing, a challenge that is exacerbated by the conduct of the hearing that I describe in the book and the elusive, unreachable 'standards' of credibility assessment that they are required to fulfil.[70]

1.2.3 *Gender, Race, Culture and Decision-Makers' Narrative Worlds*

The credibility literature has plainly and repeatedly demonstrated that decision-makers bring their culturally specific, raced and gendered understandings of the world around them to the question of who refugees are, how they should behave and what amounts to credible testimony. While questions of decision-maker subjectivity and standpoint are nothing new to studies of fact-finding and judgment, the vast discretion afforded to administrative refugee decision-makers renders the regulation of their discretion and subjectivity a central theme in evaluating both RSD and credibility determinations. There are of course limits on how decision-makers apply their worldviews when determining the credibility of a refugee's evidence.[71] However, as Hilary Evans Cameron has shown, the challenges posed by decision-maker subjectivity and predisposition – and the challenges of fact-finding across culture, language and time – are exacerbated by the lack of a clear legal or normative framework for *basic* fact-finding within Canadian RSD and beyond.[72]

Studying RSD generally and determinations of credibility specifically, then, involves a study of refugee decision-makers just as much as an inquiry into burdens and standards of proof or the jurisprudence of credibility assessment. Large, data-driven, quantitative studies of refugee status assessments have demonstrated the central role played by individual decision-makers in determining RSD outcomes in multiple jurisdictions.[73] These studies have reinforced the role of the decision-maker through their analysis of vast disparities in decision-maker recognition rates, including evidence of decision-makers with comparable caseloads having overall rejection rates ranging from 95 per cent (for one decision-maker) down to 5 per cent (for another).[74] Statistical variance across comparable caseloads has led

[70] In one of the few studies addressing the conduct of first instance asylum interviews, Nienke Doornbos found that officers frequently tested applicants in regards to peripheral or minor details, which led to communication 'breakdowns' and the applicants being unable to articulate their claims: Nienke Doornbos, 'On Being Heard in Asylum Cases: Evidentiary Assessment Through Asylum Interviews' in Gregor Noll (ed), *Proof, Evidentiary Assessment and Credibility in Asylum Procedures* (Martin Nijhoff, 2005) 103.

[71] I address these in detail in Chapter 5.

[72] Evans Cameron, above n 68, 7–24 especially.

[73] For analysis in different jurisdictions and across various stages of decision-making, see Jaya Ramji-Nogales, Andrew I Schoenholtz and Philip G Schrag (eds), *Refugee Roulette: Disparities in Asylum Adjudication and Proposals for Reform* (New York University Press, 2009); Philip G Schrag, Andrew I Schoenholtz and Jaya Ramji-Nogales, *Lives in the Balance: Asylum Adjudication by the Department of Homeland Security* (New York University Press, 1st ed, 2014); Sean Rehaag, 'Troubling Patterns in Canadian Refugee Adjudication' (2008) 39 *Ottawa Law Review* 335; Daniel Ghezelbash, Keyvan Dorostkar and Shannon Walsh, 'A Data Driven Approach to Evaluating and Improving Judicial Decision-Making: Statistical Analysis of the Judicial Review of Refugee Cases in Australia' (2022) 45(3) *University of New South Wales Law Journal* 1085.

[74] IRB decision-makers with major caseloads ranged in their positive grant rates from 7 per cent to over 95 per cent: Rehaag, above n 73. In the USA the recognition rate among immigration court judges deciding matters from the same country of origin in the same New York registry ranged from 5 per cent to 96 per cent: Ramji-Nogales, Schoenholtz and Schrag, above n 73. And in Australia the success rate of applications for judicial review before individual judges (rather than primary determinations) ranged from over 20 per cent to less than 1 per cent: Ghezelbash, Dorostkar and Walsh, above n 73.

to analogies of RSD with games of pure chance – a spin of the roulette wheel – based on the assigned decision-maker. This is the case even though, as others have argued, such quantitative findings regarding the impact of individual decision-makers must be read alongside other factors, including the presence and quality of legal counsel and advice.[75]

One of the insights of work addressing the highly subjective and even hunch-driven nature of credibility assessment[76] is that refugee decision-makers do not merely decide if an applicant's *evidence* is credible or meets the requirements of the Refugee Convention's definition of a refugee. Applicants must also convince decision-makers that they authentically fit the social and political category of 'refugee'. Razack, Makua Matua and Susan Masarrat Akram are among a number of scholars who have compellingly argued that presumptions about who or what is 'credible' and plausible within RSD frequently turn on orientalist and racialised characterisations of asylum seekers – of their countries of origin as barbaric; the liberal nation-state as saviour; and refugees as 'victims' in need not only of protection but of saving.[77] Omid Tofighian and Behrouz Boochani draw a direct connection between the exclusionary ideologies that hold up colonial border regimes and assertions of sovereignty, and the epistemic basis for contradictory and dehumanising tropes associated with refugees and displaced peoples. These include the 'desperate supplicant'; the 'trickster'; the 'tragic and miserable victim'; and the 'struggling [and battling] overcomer'.[78] These characterisations and expectations have been cast as a measure of one's 'refugeeness', an awkward term which in its capaciousness captures the demanding, contradictory and regularly dehumanising ways in which Global North states judge those seeking access to the category of 'refugee', and determine how 'acceptable' refugees ought to behave.[79] This has significant implications for exploring the place of narrative forms and 'stock' refugee stories in RSD. Refugees must adopt a form of passive victimhood and a desire to be saved from the indignity of illiberal and non-white cultures and beliefs;[80] however, as I seek to show, they must equally display agency, self-possession and a clear will towards liberal

75 Jamie Chai Yun Liew et al, 'Not Just the Luck of the Draw? Exploring Competency of Counsel and Other Qualitative Factors in Federal Court Refugee Leave Determinations (2005–2010)' (2021) 37(1) *Refuge: Canada's Journal on Refugees* 61; Ghezelbash, Dorostkar and Walsh, above n 73.

76 Macklin, above n 32, 134.

77 Sherene Razack, 'Domestic Violence as Gender Persecution: Policing the Borders of Nation, Race, and Gender' (1995) 8 *Canadian Journal of Women and the Law* 45; Makau Mutua, 'Savages, Victims, and Saviors: The Metaphor of Human Rights' (2001) 42 *Harvard International Law Journal* 201; Susan Musarrat Akram, 'Orientalism Revisited in Asylum and Refugee Claims' (2000) 12 *International Journal of Refugee Law* 7. Razack argues that '[t]he simplest and most effective means' for women to gain protection on the basis of gender 'is to activate in the panel members an old imperial formula of the barbaric and chaotic Third World and by implication, a more civilized First World': at 69. See also Liisa H Malkki, 'Refugees and Exile: From "Refugee Studies" to the National Order of Things' (1995) 24 *Annual Review of Anthropology* 495; Liisa H Malkki, 'Speechless Emissaries: Refugees, Humanitarianism, and Dehistoricization' (1996) 11(3) *Cultural Anthropology* 377.

78 Omid Tofighian, 'Behrouz Boochani and the Manus Prison Narratives: Merging Translation with Philosophical Reading' (2018) 32(4) *Continuum* 532, 535; Behrouz Boochani, *No Friend But the Mountains: Writing from Manus Prison* (Picador, 2018) 365–66.

79 Marie Lacroix, 'Canadian Refugee Policy and the Social Construction of the Refugee Claimant Subjectivity: Understanding Refugeeness' (2004) 17(2) *Journal of Refugee Studies* 147; Trish Luker, 'Performance Anxieties: Interpellation of the Refugee Subject in Law' (2015) 30(1) *Canadian Journal of Law and Society* 91.

80 Mutua, above n 77; see too Jenni Millbank and Anthea Vogl, 'Adjudicating Fear of Witchcraft Claims in Refugee Law' (2018) 45(3) *Journal of Law and Society* 370.

freedom, a theme which shapes Chapters 3 and 6.[81] The refugee story must conform with cognisable and plausible narratives of refugeehood, *but* at the same time it must not be too 'scripted, rehearsed or borrowed' such that is deemed too generic and therefore also fabricated.[82] So while the refugee applicant's testimony must be plausible, coherent and consistent as a refugee story, there is no one model refugee story, or one fixed stereotype, with which a refugee must conform.[83]

As has been so frequently observed, there is no absolute requirement that a refugee be credible to be granted asylum.[84] And yet, incredible refugees are rarely granted refugee status. Further, despite clear guidance that coherence and consistency are incompatible with autobiographical memory as such, and absurd standards by which to judge attempts to disclose and account for traumatic events, the standards persist. Each strand of the problem of credibility charted here is entwined with the burden of speech and demand for narrativity faced by refugees during the oral hearing, and these critiques, which fundamentally reject the credibility of credibility assessment, move in and out of the foreground in each of the book's chapters.[85]

1.3 The Impossibility of Refugee Testimony in RSD: Law, Lawyers, Interpreters

Like so much scholarship addressing refugee decision-making and credibility assessment, in the book I refer to 'refugee testimony' to describe the evidence presented by refugees as the basis for a protection claim. However, the testimony that I describe and analyse is not purely the 'refugee's testimony'. Instead, it is speech co-produced, shaped and constrained by the socio-legal requirements of the RSD process and the multiple actors involved in its production in Australia and Canada. The evidence referred to as 'refugee testimony' is what Marie Jacobs and Katrijn Maryns carefully describe as 'co-constructed' and continuously mediated by multiple actors within the RSD process.[86] The cast of people co-producing refugee testimony within RSD include, at least, interpreters, decision-makers and lawyers involved in preparing a claim and advising an applicant. As Laurie Berg and Jenni Millbank put it, '[h]ow the asylum claim is articulated depends on the relational interaction between advocate or decision-maker and asylum seeker at every stage of the process'.[87] Barsky even notes the

[81] Simon Behrman also argues that refugee law requires asylum seekers to adopt an 'extremely limited and distorted form of agency', which as narrow as it is, includes an essential expression of agency in one's engagement with 'the process of refugee status determination as a precondition to receiving the benefits of asylum': Simon Behrman, 'Accidents, Agency and Asylum: Constructing the Refugee Subject' (2014) 25(3) *Law and Critique* 249, 249, 257.

[82] Bohmer and Shuman, above n 2, 29.

[83] Julia Dahlvik describes bureaucrats in the Austrian asylum administration system as 'reproducing and reinventing' the system, and the determination regime as 'volatile' and contingent on these processes of street-level beliefs and construction: Julia Dahlvik, 'Asylum as Construction Work: Theorizing Administrative Practices' (2017) 5(3) *Migration Studies* 369.

[84] Bohmer and Shuman, above n 2; Lawrance and Ruffer, above n 32, 10.

[85] Smith-Khan, above n 2.

[86] Jacobs and Maryns, above n 2; see also Maryns, above n 2; Smith-Khan, above n 2; Jessica Hambly, 'Interactions and Identities in UK Asylum Appeals: Lawyers and Law in a Quasi Legal Setting' in Nick Gill and Anthony Good (eds), *Asylum Determination in Europe: Ethnographic Perspectives* (Palgrave Macmillan, 2019) 195.

[87] Berg and Millbank, above n 2, 196–97.

(former) role of hearing stenographers and the conditions of their work in the production of testimony in Canada, which was performed under subcontract, paid as 'piece work' and transcribed under difficult conditions, with varying degrees of accuracy.[88] The usually imperceptible and unacknowledged role that RSD decision-makers, in particular, play in shaping the oral testimony attributed to applicants is evident throughout the book. Laura Smith-Khan explains the problem with assigning sole authorship of texts produced in the application process 'discursively . . . to asylum seekers'; namely that they are held responsible for and judged as credible against communication that is produced by multiple actors, the content of which is simply not within their control.[89] This is a theme, finding and problem that comes to the fore in the analysis that follows.

This, in turn, highlights a limitation of this research: the hearing-based data cannot account for or evaluate the influence of other actors – and significantly of lawyers or interpreters – in shaping the testimony available for assessment. In my dataset, it is only when lawyers actively intervene in applicants' oral testimony or when there is an acknowledged issue with linguistic interpretation that these actors come into the frame of analysis. Here, research that has examined the fallibility of processes of linguistic and cultural translation (among lawyers, expert witnesses and interpreters alike) provides crucial context for the testimony represented here.[90] As Jacobs and Maryns have shown, lawyers, advocates and other actors may shape evidence through sincere misunderstanding or misinterpretation of testimony, but they may equally actively impose their own ideologies to reorient refugee narrative, imposing perceived markers of credibility or 'institutionally accepted forms of narration'.[91] My research, however, only assesses testimony in the form presented during the oral hearing, where it is reshaped by decision-makers and interpreters once again – but attributed, completely and finally, to the refugee applicant.

Finally, while a core aim of the book is to investigate how the event of the refugee oral hearing is conducted in Australia and Canada, it is not an institutional or ethnographic study of the decision-making bodies responsible for RSD in either jurisdiction. Ethnographic or bureaucratic studies of the 'asylum field'[92] stretch far beyond the study of a sample of refugee hearings or even of one decision-making body such as the RRT, AAT or IRB. Rather, such work reads asylum decision-making in the context of multiple, overlapping institutions and the tensions between them.[93] This scholarship has consistently found

[88] Robert F Barsky, *Arguing and Justifying: Assessing the Convention Refugees' Choice of Moment, Motive and Host Country* (Ashgate, 2000) (especially Chapter Three: 'Interpreting and Transcribing the Other').

[89] Smith-Khan, above n 2, 406, 426.

[90] See especially Hambly, above n 86; Smith-Khan, above n 32; Maryns, above n 2; Robert Gibb and Anthony Good, 'Interpretation, Translation and Intercultural Communication in Refugee Status Determination Procedures in the UK and France' (2014) 14(3) *Language and Intercultural Communication* 385; Jan Blommaert, 'Language, Asylum, and the National Order' (2009) 50(4) *Current Anthropology* 415.

[91] Jacobs and Maryns, above n 2, 3; but see also Stephen Meili, 'U.K. Refugee Lawyers: Pushing the Boundaries of Domestic Court Acceptance of International Human Rights Law' (2013) 36 *Boston College International and Comparative Law Review* 1123; Siobhán McGuirk, '(In)Credible Subjects: NGOs, Attorneys, and Permissible LGBT Asylum Seeker Identities' (2018) 41(1) *PoLAR: Political and Legal Anthropology Review* 4.

[92] John R Campbell, *Bureaucracy, Law and Dystopia in the United Kingdom's Asylum System* (Routledge, 2016).

[93] Ibid; see especially Gill and Good, above n 29; Robert Thomas, *Administrative Justice and Asylum Appeals: A Study of Tribunal Adjudication* (Bloomsbury Academic, 2011). For a formally comparative account of regimes and administrative systems of RSD in Australia and Canada, see Rebecca Hamlin, *Let*

that refugee decision-makers operate in extremely high-pressure environments and that they regularly face immense time constraints, resource challenges and backlogs. This is certainly the case in Australia, where as noted, the AAT itself is being disbanded and redesigned as this book goes to print, in part because of the intractable backlog of matters before it. Angus Grant and Sean Rehaag note that RSD in Canada involves a high-volume, high-stakes caseload and constant pressure to decide matters quickly.[94] Such pressures are connected to insufficient state funding alongside state imperatives to speed up asylum determinations – but equally, as I have argued, connected to rhetoric about dealing 'efficiently' with 'bogus' or 'opportunistic' claimants besieging (to use Razack's language) RSD mechanisms.[95]

In reading the rest of this book, though, constant calls from Global North states for more efficient and accelerated RSD will strike readers as at odds with the at times lengthy and painstakingly detailed exchanges led by decision-makers during hearings and circuitous discussions of aspects of evidence that seem ancillary to the refugee definition. The set of hearings that I present take place within, but cannot be fully accounted for by, high-level analysis of the broader 'asylum field' or governance of RSD as such. As I hope becomes apparent, reading the hearings in full, as complete qualitative texts, is the only way to think through and analyse the often-singular course of each hearing; the intimate and particular back-and-forth exchanges between refugees and decision-makers; and the demands made in real-time of refugee applicants and their testimony.

1.4 Judging Refugees: Chapter Overview

The chapters that follow integrate a theoretical and conceptual argument about the function of narrative within refugee decision-making and Global North states' demands of 'acceptable' refugees, with a detailed and intensely specific empirical analysis of how such demands manifested within fifteen refugee hearings. Following this introduction (Chapter 1), Chapter 2 presents the book's argument in favour of a critical politics of narrative. Specifically, it engages with the theoretical insights of law and literature, and law and 'outsider storytelling' scholarship as articulated by critical race, Indigenous and feminist law scholars, to explain how narrative and narrative genres are implicated in RSD and the politics of whom states cast as the 'credible' refugee. It also presents a working definition of narrative and of the 'model' Anglo-European narrative form, which I argue shapes the reception and assessment of testimony. In making a case for the use of narrative methods in evaluating refugee decision-making, the chapter critiques aspects of the 'law and literature' project that present storytelling and narratives either as distinct from legal discourse or as necessarily disruptive of law's authority.

Chapter 3 addresses the history of the refugee oral hearing in Australia and Canada. It explains how and why the oral hearing became a central event within RSD processes in each jurisdiction and traces the role of refugee testimony up until the introduction of a

Me Be a Refugee: Administrative Justice and the Politics of Asylum in the United States, Canada, and Australia (Oxford University Press, 2014).

94 Grant and Rehaag, above n 13.

95 For examples of such rhetoric in Canada and Australia, see Anthea Vogl, 'A Matter of Time: Enacting the Exclusion of Onshore Refugee Applicants through the Reform and Acceleration of Refugee Determination Processes' (2016) 6(1) *Oñati Socio-Legal Series* 137.

semi-independent administrative process for RSD and into the present day. In setting the scene for my analysis of hearings before the IRB and former RRT, the chapter demonstrates that the introduction of an oral hearing before a semi-independent executive decision-maker in both jurisdictions represented a shift towards enhanced administrative rights and justice for onshore refugee arrivals. However, the chapter also establishes that formal RSD procedures were introduced as both states became increasingly focused on the deterrence of refugee arrivals and limiting onshore claimants. In both jurisdictions the same legislation that introduced statutory RSD procedures also implemented harsh new modes of refugee deterrence. Particularly in Australia, the hearing itself was implemented alongside mandatory detention and presented quite explicitly as a means to both insulate executive decision-making from judicial interference and identify and exclude 'bogus' claimants.

Chapters 4–7 form the heart of the book. Each chapter is dedicated to putting narrative to work in analysing the assessment of refugee testimony in the oral hearings and dataset. Chapter 4 argues that a distinct 'stock story' of who refugees are and how they behave featured throughout the observed hearings. This story, which I name the 'stock narrative of becoming a refugee', is one of refugee departure, flight and arrival and exemplifies the elements of model Anglo-European narrative forms presented in Chapter 2. Implicitly or explicitly, in form and content, the refugee stock story formed an all-too-neat normative standard against which refugee applicants' evidence – and credibility – was tested and judged.

Chapter 5 shifts from examining the demand for a particular refugee story during the hearings, to considering how narratives were used to test oral evidence. It presents a key finding from the hearings: that decision-makers often engaged in 'narrative contests' with the applicant, presenting their own counter-narratives of how events *should* have taken place if the story presented were to meet the credibility standard of plausibility. The chapter details how the criterion of 'plausibility' forges a direct link between credibility assessment and the narrative form, as well as the minimal law or policy that governs the testing of oral evidence during the hearing in Australia and Canada. In the chapter, a laptop, an injured shoulder and an escape from state custody all become subjects of and opportunities for narrative contestation. When engaging in these narrative contests, the narrative expectations of decision-makers were often deeply subjective, idiosyncratic and unpredictable. Decision-maker 'questioning' went beyond asking refugee applicants for further information or explanation. Instead, the hearings involved decision-makers presenting alternative, hypothetical accounts of events that would have taken place, if the story (and by implication the applicant) were credible. This chapter also demonstrates that in navigating these exchanges, certain applicants displayed high levels of agency and resistance vis-à-vis decision-makers' own narrative assumptions and their vast power to direct the applicant's evidence and the hearing.

These connected themes – of decision-makers' discretionary control over the hearing and applicants' attempts to control their evidence – are addressed in detail in Chapter 6, which takes up narrative theory's attention to the conditions for narration, audience and context. In this chapter, I argue that applicants' testimony was frequently and severely fragmented due to the structure and conduct of the hearing, the control exercised by decision-makers, and the manner and style of their questioning. The process of narrative fragmentation leads to the finding that, in the majority of hearings observed, the applicant was both expected to present testimony in a narrative form and then actively impeded from doing so. Further, where applicants displayed confidence and an ability to present evidence in a narrative form – to 'argue and justify'[96] their own story – this was done in spite of, rather than because of, the structure and setting of the observed hearings.

Chapter 7 returns to an argument articulated in Chapter 1, namely that interrogating narratives within the hearing in terms of their (overlapping) genres, and with attention to implicit and explicit generic aspects of decision-makers' appraisal of testimony, provides further insight into the 'authentic' refugee whom state authorities are willing to accept. The chapter takes up Joseph Slaughter's engagement with the genre of human rights discourse, and his argument that we can understand the conception of human personhood evident within human rights discourse through the genre and plot of the *Bildungsroman* (the realist novel).[97] The chapter shows that Slaughter's account of the realist novel's plot trajectory, involving 'the movement of the subject from pure subjection to self-regulation' is evident in the testimonial forms required of refugee applicants.[98] Like the protagonist of the classic *Bildungsroman* and human rights narratives, refugee applicants were expected to narrate a linear progression from 'outsider' status towards full civic incorporation through the seeking of protection and the resolution of refugee status.[99] In this generic mode, the 'good' refugee's story moves steadily towards a resolution that *is* the seeking of refugee status and thereby, the realisation of a liberal personhood, marked by self-possession and autonomy, and readiness to become a refugee-citizen.[100] Finally, following what Agnes Woolley has described as 'the entanglement of literary and legal technologies in the asylum decision-making process', the conclusion (Chapter 8) returns to the book's central questions and arguments.[101] It considers the implications of the book's findings for the conduct and place of oral hearings within RSD, and the impossibility of a just assessment of refugee applicants' oral testimony against the current credibility criteria and the direct link between such criteria and a global politics of refugee deterrence, punishment and exclusion.

Presenting Refugee Testimony and the Oral Hearings

Every hearing included in my dataset involved an interpreter, even though at times the applicant spoke in the language of the Board or Tribunal (English or French). In the hearing excerpts reproduced here, I have edited out all speech not conducted in English but attempted to preserve the presence of the interpreter by indicating where the applicant is speaking directly and where the interpreter is speaking on behalf of the applicant. In each excerpt, I use the term 'Applicant' to denote where the interpreter is speaking for the applicant; 'Applicant in person' to denote where the applicant is speaking directly; and 'Interpreter' where the interpreter is speaking directly. The terms 'member' and 'advocate' are used in their ordinary sense.

[96] Barsky, above n 88.

[97] Joseph R Slaughter, 'Enabling Fictions and Novel Subjects: The Bildungsroman and International Human Rights Law' (2006) 121(5) *Publications of the Modern Language Association* 1405; Joseph R Slaughter, *Human Rights, Inc.: The World Novel, Narrative Form, and International Law* (Fordham University Press, 2007).

[98] Slaughter, *Human Rights, Inc.*, above n 97, 7–9.

[99] Ibid 249.

[100] Mutua, above n 77, 201; and see Makau Mutua, *Human Rights: A Political and Cultural Critique* (University of Pennsylvania Press, 2013).

[101] Woolley, above n 2, 378.

In this research, I present segments from individual hearings after contextualising them in relation to the applicant's claim, and where relevant, in relation to the conduct and sequence of the hearing. I note that the excerpts, in some instances, are quite long. They are often more than mere snippets and extend beyond a couple of lines of transcript. I have included these longer excerpts to convey a sense of the hearings and the dialogue within them – as messy or confusing as these exchanges at times were – and to preserve as much as possible of the affect and tone of the exchanges.[102] Of course, 'preserving' the hearing is not possible especially given the use of excerpts, the move from speech to text, and in absence of the interpreter's non-English translations. Hopefully, though, in the longer exchanges something more than the mere text is apparent, and the data adds value to the existing archive of published decisions, hearing summaries and brief excerpts from hearing transcripts. While some written decisions in Canada and Australia include short, verbatim excerpts from the hearings, they predominantly include the decision-maker's highly condensed summary of evidence, which in turn becomes the official and only record of the applicant's testimony and is yet another example of the decision-maker's role in co-producing testimony that is finally attributed to the applicant.

Finally, in writing on the law of RSD, and state-based procedures for judging refugee lives and entitlements, it is difficult to escape state-centric language and terminology. I primarily refer to the people included in this study as 'refugee applicants' because of my narrow focus on their interface with institutional processes for RSD and the domestic and international law that governs these procedures. At times I refer to 'irregular' or 'undocumented' migrants, but do so when explicitly referring to or analysing state-centric categorisations of people who seek to cross borders. I use the modifier 'onshore' to refer to all refugee applicant participants in my research. In Canada, those who seek status within Canadian territory are often called 'inland' (or sometimes 'point of entry') claimants. In Australia, they are called onshore applicants. I use the Australian terminology for the sake of consistency and clarity throughout the book. An appendix outlining the fundamental elements of each claim, including the applicant's country of origin, gender, alleged grounds of persecution and the hearing outcome is included at the end of the book.

[102] I note that I have included non-verbal aspects of the hearing, including pauses and some interpretations of tone and emphasis, in square brackets within the dialogue. While transcription conventions advise one not to 'interpret' tone, at times I have included my own interpretations – both because these struck me as valuable details as I observed the hearings, and because a 'pure' representation of dialogue and tone is beyond my reach in any event.

2

Law, Literature and Narrative in the RSD Oral Hearing

This book's argument – that refugee status determination (RSD) processes require refugee applicants to account for evidence in a prototypical narrative form at the same time as impeding an applicant's capacity to do so – calls for attention to theoretical conceptions of narrative and genre, as well as to narrative as constitutive of legal forms of judgment, reasoning and authority. Equally, my argument calls for a critical politics of narrative within RSD, and attention to how narrative is implicated in refugee-receiving states' *generic* demands of refugee applicants and their testimony. The purpose of bringing narrative into the frame of refugee law and status determination is captured by Mark Antaki's account of the 'critical work' of law and literature, which 'consists not in romantically completing law with literature, ethics with aesthetics, but in confronting how we have been disciplined to separate them, to separate sense from sensibility'.[1] In this chapter, then, I explain how and why the theoretical and methodological approaches associated with law and literature, and more specifically law and narrative scholarship, are uniquely suited to responding to the questions at the heart of this book.

The present chapter draws upon law, narrative and storytelling scholarship as articulated by critical race, Indigenous and feminist law scholars to frame my exploration of refugee testimony. Such scholarship has been sharply attuned to the politics of narrative. It has insisted on the relationship between narrative, and the capacity to formulate 'acceptable' stories, with the distribution of rights, justice and power. It has demanded an interrogation of the function of narrative within law that has structured the questions I ask in relation to the politics of refugee protection and the conduct of RSD: of whom are narratives demanded? Who is required to conform to or convey specific narratives for recognition? Who, in turn, gets to judge, sanction or reject stories and determine 'truth' and credibility – and to what ends? And, what do refugee stories deemed as credible tell us about paradigms of refugee denial (and acceptance) that structure refugee decision-making?

As such, the first section of this chapter constructs a framework for engagement with narrative and narrative forms within refugee assessment. This framework engages with modes of legal analysis and law and literature scholarship that have reinscribed the disciplinary boundaries between law and narrative – boundaries that this research in turn seeks to open up and interrogate in relation to RSD. I then move from a general engagement with law and narrative into an explanation of the specific methodology applied here, which makes use of narrative forms and theory to interrogate the conduct of the oral hearing and the assessment of refugee testimony. Here, I establish a working definition of narrative and introduce the elements of narrative that I employ throughout the book. Lastly, the chapter

[1] Mark Antaki, 'Genre, Critique, and Human Rights' (2013) 82(4) *University of Toronto Quarterly* 974, 978.

addresses aspects of the dataset and research design not covered in Chapter 1, to explain how and on what terms I accessed the oral testimony presented in the chapters that follow. This section details the significant barriers to accessing refugee oral testimony within RSD processes in Australia and Canada and contends that the closed nature of hearings and preservation of confidentiality must be considered alongside what this entails for oversight of the hearing as a site of narrative, judgment and the co-construction of refugee testimony.

2.1 Law and Narrative

Narrative-based approaches in legal scholarship have treated legal texts as legitimate subjects of literary criticism and narrative forms as intrinsic to legal rhetoric.[2] Narratives are an element of law's normative world and claim to authority. Robert Cover's resonant contention that no legal institution or prescription 'exists apart from the narratives that locate it and give it meaning' and that 'for every constitution there is an epic, for every decalogue a scripture' has shaped law's engagement with literature and narrative, and the treatment of legal judgments and interpretative acts as legitimate subjects of literary criticism and rhetorical inquiry.[3] Such analysis, though, has mainly proceeded with an acute awareness that legal judgment and acts of interpretation, as distinct from other social texts and hermeneutics, 'signal and occasion the imposition of violence on others'. As Cover argued, using a turn of phrase that has echoed through law and literature scholarship, classrooms and my own engagement with refugee law decision-making, '[l]egal interpretation takes place in a field of pain and death'.[4] And, while 'the practical activity' and studies of legal decision-making alike 'blithely ignore it', even the most routine acts of legal interpretation 'depend upon the social practice of violence for [their] efficacy'.[5]

Conceiving of law *as* literature, as certain strands of law and literature scholarship do, is not a claim that law (and its moral prescriptions) are *the same as* literary texts, but rather that legal authority and rhetoric rely on or deploy methods to convince, reason and persuade that are traditionally associated with literary texts and studies. Law, however, generally uses language, style and rhetoric less openly and less transparently than texts designated as literature. As Peter Goodrich articulates it:

> [l]aw is a literature which denies its literary qualities. It is a play of words which asserts its absolute seriousness . . . it is a language which hides its indeterminacy in the justificatory

[2] Peter Brooks, 'Narrative in and of the Law' in James Phelan and Peter J Rabinowitz (eds), *A Companion to Narrative Theory* (Blackwell, 2005) 415; see generally Peter Brooks and Paul D Gerwirtz (eds), *Law's Stories: Narrative and Rhetoric in the Law* (Yale University Press, 1996).

[3] Robert M Cover, 'Foreword: Nomos and Narrative' (1983) 97 *Harvard Law Review* 4, 4.

[4] Robert M Cover, 'Violence and the Word' (1986) 95(8) *The Yale Law Journal* 1601, 1601.

[5] Ibid 1601, 1613. Judges, for Cover, hold a violent, jurispathic office in selecting and enforcing legal meaning and outcome over all others: 'confronting the luxuriant growth of a hundred legal traditions, [judicial decision-makers] assert that this one is law and destroy or try to destroy the rest': Cover, above n 3, 53. Linking this idea with that of narrative genre, Honni van Rijswijk writes 'Law's archive as "commandment" suggests that the genre of law is a certain kind of aggressive realism. The legal archive is a domain in which social relations and inequalities are structured and adjudicated, and in which law asserts access to a reality that law alone can adjudicate and resolve': Honni van Rijswijk, 'Archiving the Northern Territory Intervention in Law and in the Literary Counter-Imaginary' (2014) 40(1) *Australian Feminist Law Journal* 117, 122.

> discourse of judgment; it is procedure based on analogy, metaphor and repetition and yet it lays claim to be a cold or disembodied prose.[6]

Along similar lines, Peter Brooks gets to the heart of the central but frequently unacknowledged place of narrative in law:

> The place and status of narrative in the law and in legal studies strike me as uncertain and ambiguous. On the one hand, trial advocates know – have known, presumably, since antiquity – that success in the court of law depends upon telling an effective and persuasive story ... On the other hand, one looks in vain in legal doctrine, and in judicial opinions, for any explicit recognition that 'narrative' is a category for adjudication: that rules of evidence, for instance, implicate questions of how stories can and should be told.[7]

The absence of any mention of narrative within the formal standards governing credibility in Australia and Canada, at the same time as a 'good story' is vital to decision-making, accords with Brooks' observation that 'one looks in vain' but rarely finds any acknowledgement of the role of narrative in legal authority.

Following work that has analysed the place of the narrative form in law, legal reasoning and argument in general,[8] in this chapter and those that follow, I explore *how* we should consider and deal with narrative within refugee status decision-making specifically. There is the tendency among certain forms of legal scholarship to sentimentalise storytelling, especially fictional literature, as a source of superior and 'nuanced' truth and as necessarily providing a better and more accurate account of social phenomena than the law. And related to these sentimental and universalising claims about literature is law and legal scholarship's readiness to 'colonise' and instrumentalise other forms of knowledge (including literature),[9] without attention to the politics, interpretative debates and methods of other disciplines or epistemologies. One aspect of sentimental approaches to the power of literature is the claim that law 'needs' literature or narrativity to 'save', improve or complete it.[10] The argument that law needs literature implies that the law itself is not literary, that it must seek out

6 Peter Goodrich, *Law in the Courts of Love: Literature and Other Minor Jurisprudences* (Taylor & Francis, 2002) 112.

7 Peter Brooks, 'Inevitable Discovery: Law, Narrative, Retrospectivity' (2003) 15 *Yale Journal of Law & the Humanities* 71, 71.

8 See especially Guyora Binder and Robert Weisberg, *Literary Criticisms of Law* (Princeton University Press, 2000); Wai Chee Dimock, *Residues of Justice: Literature, Law, Philosophy* (University of California Press, 1997); Desmond Manderson, *Kangaroo Courts and the Rule of Law: The Legacy of Modernism* (Routledge, 2012); Karin Van Marle and Stewart Motha (eds), *Genres of Critique: Law, Aesthetics and Liminality* (Sun Press, 2014). Binder and Weisberg analyse law as interpretation, narration, rhetoric, language and culture, and trace the history of each of these approaches in both legal and literary theory. In their focus on law as an arena for composing and contesting identity, status and character, both authors express a loud aversion to sentimentalised accounts of law and literature scholarship: Binder and Weisberg, 9–17.

9 See, in particular, the special edition: Juan Marcellus Tauri, Maria Giannacopoulos and Bronwyn Carlson, 'Introduction: "Fuck the Law": Decolonizing Nomophilitis with the Discourse of Love' (2019) 4(1) *Journal of Global Indigeneity*.

10 Manderson, above n 8, 20; Jane B Baron, 'The Rhetoric of Law and Literature: A Skeptical View' (2004) 26 *Cardozo Law Review* 2273; Antaki, above n 1.

'literature' and literary methods from an external source, reinscribing the social boundaries of each discipline.[11]

Desmond Manderson identifies a similar approach within law and literature studies, which he argues treats 'stories' in novels as an 'unproblematic vehicle for information about people's lives, and for the truth of their particular perspective'.[12] He identifies certain approaches to the novel as a source of truth, proof or as 'the realisation of particular perspectives' and argues that a more 'evidential approach to literature could hardly be imagined'.[13] Indeed, the law's use of literature as a source of 'truthful', objective and authentic experience is an extreme example of law instrumentalising literary forms and knowledge. Moreover, seeking out literary modes to 'enrich' or broaden law's accounts of reality assumes that law, as such, is governed by the technical application of legal rules; that it is 'instrumental, rational, non-emotional, mechanical, and seriously doctrinal'[14] and 'needs to be supplemented and corrected by the humane values of literature'.[15] This view of literature, as monolithic and monolithically moral or edifying, gives literature a claim to 'good authority'[16] similar to claims that law, as a scientific and rational form of knowledge, is also a source of good (albeit different) authority.[17] The universalised claim, explicit or implicit, that literature can give us a better 'sense of the complex nature of the human condition'[18] is one that I am directly writing against in critiquing the use of narrative as a means of exclusion within RSD. Assuming literature's inherently 'humanising potential' ignores the interpretative and disciplinary processes at play in the creation, use and abuse of literary narratives in the generation of knowledge, power and *de*humanisation – both within and beyond legal forms of authority.

2.2 Race, Narrative and Outsider Storytelling

Of course it is not new to observe that law is a discourse that relies on language, rhetoric and narrative,[19] even if doctrinal legal scholarship has often failed to adopt a critical or at all

[11] Austin Sarat et al, 'The Concept of Boundaries in the Practices and Products of Sociolegal Scholarship: An Introduction' in Austin Sarat et al (eds), *Crossing Boundaries: Traditions and Transformations in Law and Society Research* (Northwestern University Press, 1998).

[12] Desmond Manderson, 'Mikhail Bakhtin and the Field of Law and Literature' (2012) 8 *Law, Culture and the Humanities* 1, 7.

[13] Ibid. Manderson identifies and critiques one example of such an approach in Martha C Nussbaum, *Poetic Justice: The Literary Imagination and Public Life* (Beacon Press, 1995).

[14] Robert Weisberg, 'The Law-Literature Enterprise' (1989) 1(1) *Yale Journal of Law & the Humanities* 1, 16; see also Baron, above n 10, 2775.

[15] Kevin Crotty, *Law's Interior: Legal and Literary Constructions of the Self* (Cornell University Press, 2001) 14.

[16] On this point, see Goodrich, above n 6; and for an application of Goodrich and a critique of the novel as a form, see Patricia Tuitt, 'Literature, Invention and Law in South Africa's Constitutional Transformation' in Karin Van Marle and Stewart Motha (eds), *Genres of Critique: Law, Aesthetics and Liminality* (Sun Press, 2014) 75.

[17] Manderson, above n 8, 20–22; see also Manderson, above n 12. Manderson calls this law and literature's 'romantic fantasy', namely that literature is salvific and can 'complete' law: Manderson, above n 8, 20.

[18] For Manderson, such work reflects a tendency among law and literature scholars to cling to a 'time before the crisis of modernity shook literature's claims to a determined and complete textuality': Manderson, above n 8, 20.

[19] For a clear discussion of law and literature's common interest in and reliance upon rhetoric, see James Boyd White, 'Law as Rhetoric, Rhetoric as Law: The Arts of Cultural and Communal Life' (1985) 52

welcoming approach to interdisciplinary knowledge produced under the broad banner of law and the humanities. By contrast, law and storytelling scholarship – in particular work located within and written by Indigenous, critical race and feminist legal theory and theorists – has been exceptionally attentive to the politics of narrative and narrative forms within even the most ostensibly technical realms of legal reasoning and language. From the late 1980s onwards, critical race scholars in particular produced powerful and enduring works calling attention to narrative and 'stock stories' within the law, and used narrative theory and criticism to disrupt law's claims to liberal equality, race neutrality and objectivity. Outsider storytelling scholarship, or what Mari Matsuda labelled 'outsider jurisprudence' used counter-storytelling to disrupt law's claims to facially neutral, 'common sense' narratives about how the world works and its endorsement of certain stories as fact and/or reliable evidence. What is designated as fact or believable, as Patricia Williams so arrestingly demonstrates in her own account of racial discrimination, is a matter of perspective, personal history and experience.[20] In turn, such work has presented the counter-stories told by so-called marginalised or 'outsider' groups as powerful tools for challenging the law's implicit and explicit racism, and the racialised narratives that underpin ostensibly abstract or gender- or race-neutral legal principles and judgments.[21]

Attention to storytelling methodologies, narrative and experience is also central to Indigenous scholarship, decolonising methodologies and storytelling practice. As Alison Whittaker and Nicole Watson write 'the violent matrix between stories, how we evaluate them as First Nations feminist scholars, and how we are undermined in our speaking of law and all that it entails' are enduring themes among First Nations scholars writing on law and power.[22] First Nations scholars' attention to the role of story and knowledge production asks who gets to tell stories and of whom storytelling is demanded, but also demands engagement with the ethical, pedagogical and political uses of Indigenous stories and narratives, within and beyond law.[23] Larissa Behrendt details how the colonial legal system 'works tenaciously'

University of Chicago Law Review 684; see also Jack Balkin and Sanford Levinson, 'Law and the Humanities: An Uneasy Relationship' (2006) 18 *Yale Journal of Law & the Humanities* 155.

20 Patricia J Williams, *The Alchemy of Race and Rights* (Harvard University Press, 1991).

21 See Symposium, 'Legal Storytelling' (1989) 87 *Michigan Law Review* 2073; and in particular, see Richard Delgado, 'Storytelling for Oppositionists and Others: A Plea for Narrative' (1989) 89 *Michigan Law Review* 2411; Kim Lane Scheppele, 'Foreword: Telling Stories' (1989) 87 *Michigan Law Review* 2073; Mari J Matsuda, 'Public Response to Racist Speech: Considering the Victim's Story' (1989) 87 *Michigan Law Review* 2320. And for legal texts that use storytelling as a technique, see, e.g., Williams, above n 20; Derrick A Bell, *And We Are Not Saved: The Elusive Quest for Racial Justice* (Basic Books, 1987).

22 Alison Whittaker and Nicole Watson, 'First Nations Women: Law, Power, Story' (2019) 45(2) *Australian Feminist Law Journal* 179, 181.

23 Jo-ann Archibald Q'um Q'um Xiiem, Jenny Bol Jun Lee-Morgan and Jason De Santolo, 'Introduction' in Jo-ann Archibald Q'um Q'um Xiiem, Jenny Bol Jun Lee-Morgan and Jason De Santolo (eds), *Decolonizing Research: Indigenous Storywork as Methodology* (Bloomsbury, 2019) 1, 5–9; Margaret Kovach, *Indigenous Methodologies: Characteristics, Conversations, and Contexts* (University of Toronto Press, 2nd ed, 2021). This collection reaches well beyond a critique of colonial exploitation of Indigenous stories that I address here and presents the centrality of storytelling traditions and 'Indigenous storywork' as a means of knowing, teaching, learning, survival and liberation for Indigenous peoples. I note in particular *Stó:lō* scholar Jo-ann Archibald Q'um Q'um Xiiem's conception of 'storywork' in this volume encompasses a distinct methodology and pedagogy drawn from her work and storytelling with *Salish* and *Stó:lō* Elders: Jo-ann Archibald Q'um Q'um Xiiem, *Indigenous Storywork: Educating the Heart, Mind, Body, and Spirit* (UBC Press, 2008).

to counter and dismiss Indigenous stories.[24] This work, as Behrendt demonstrates, operates alongside the narrative tricks used by authorities, legal and otherwise, to create and reinforce white myths and stories about First Nations people, and the material benefits and profit reaped from such stereotypes.[25] Here, in contrast to RSD credibility assessment's naïve application of concepts such as plausibility, consistency and coherence as proxies for truth, we find an insistence that the terms on which stories and discourse are transformed into 'facts' as fundamentally connected to colonial logics, and acts of dispossession and control.[26] Jo-ann Archibald Q'um Q'um Xiiem et al illuminate the role of Indigenous storywork in moving beyond the colonising constraints of Western theories and paradigms, whereby 'Indigenous stories, experiences and understandings are the core of the meaning-making process' rather than unstable or unreliable sources of knowledge, in need of colonial judgment or verification.[27]

Critical race, outsider and Indigenous storytelling has not simply highlighted the narrative voices and narrative styles that are marginalised or actively discredited by the law and legal epistemologies. In articulating a critical approach to law and narrative, critical storytelling scholarship has demanded a better understanding of the law's reliance on narrative, and the linguistic strategies that the law adopts to render the stories and experiences of those who hold power as truth. This has come with an acute awareness of whom the law casts as 'storytellers'.[28] Indeed, the claim that stories are a powerful or even natural method of engagement for groups labelled as 'outsiders' or forced to be 'marginal' is implicated in the uncritical representation of stories (and storytellers) 'as sentimental, personal and individual' – as opposed to law, which is objective, universal and limitless.[29] As Razack observes, a troubling aspect of such approaches is that they attribute the qualities and 'unsound' epistemology of storytelling to women or to people of colour and Indigenous people, the 'others' of the West and whiteness.[30] Here, the question of which stories are sanctioned and to what use they will be put are not determined by the storytellers. As Jo-ann

[24] Larissa Behrendt, 'Indigenous Storytelling: Decolonising Institutions and Assertive Self-Determination: Implications for Legal Practice' in Jo-ann Archibald Q'um Q'um Xiiem, Jenny Bol Jun Lee-Morgan and Jason De Santolo (eds), *Decolonizing Research: Indigenous Storywork as Methodology* (Bloomsbury, 2019) 175, 178.

[25] Larissa Behrendt, *Finding Eliza: Power and Colonial Storytelling* (University of Queensland Press, 2016).

[26] Archibald Q'um Q'um Xiiem, above n 23.

[27] Archibald Q'um Q'um Xiiem, Lee-Morgan and De Santolo, above n 23, 11.

[28] Sherene Razack, *Looking White People in the Eye: Gender, Race, and Culture in Courtrooms and Classrooms* (University of Toronto Press, 1998) 37.

[29] Delgado, for example, writes that '[s]tories humanize us. They emphasize our differences in ways that can ultimately bring us closer together': 'Storytelling for Oppositionists and Others: A Plea for Narrative' in David Ray Papke (ed), *Narrative and the Legal Discourse – A Reader in Storytelling and the Law* (Deborah Charles Publications, 1991) 289, 312. For a perspective on and critiques of the 'truth' or particular 'voice' of outsider narratives see, e.g., Daniel Farber and Suzanna Sherry, 'Telling Stories out of School: An Essay on Legal Narratives' (1992) 45 *Stanford Law Review* 807; Robert F Barsky, *Arguing and Justifying: Assessing the Convention Refugees' Choice of Moment, Motive and Host Country* (Ashgate, 2000) chapter 6; Kathryn Abrams, 'Hearing the Call of Stories' (1991) 79(4) *California Law Review* 971.

[30] Razack, above n 28, 37. Razack draws on the work of Trinh T Minh-Ha, 'Not You/Like You: Post-Colonial Women and the Interlocking Questions of Identity and Difference' in Gloria Anzaldúa (ed), *Making Face, Making Soul/*Haciendo Caras: *Creative and Critical Perspectives by Feminists of Color* (Aunt Lute Foundation Books, 1990) 373.

Archibald Q'um Q'um Xiiem et al emphasise, 'Indigenous story-making' and 'story-taking' was vital to both Western processes of colonisation and to Western research, whereby colonial researchers and 'story-makers' misrepresented, misappropriated and stole Indigenous stories to their own ends.[31] Indeed, appealing solely to the transformative power, potential and virtue of narratives and 'telling stories', even when stories are told in opposition to dominant narratives and norms, can obscure the conditions in which such texts are produced; the power relations involved in who must 'tell' these stories; and when, and on whose terms, stories will be listened to, (mis)appropriated or judged as good or true.[32] Certain stories, counter-narratives and narrative forms can, however, reveal the nuance, unfamiliarity and power of stories that have been dismissed, discredited or explicitly silenced by legal standards, principles or decision-makers. As well, certain works of literature can be productively read as directly challenging law's demand for particular types of narrative. Such counter-narratives do not necessarily attempt to lay claim to truth or to universality,[33] but under certain conditions for their telling, they can challenge and call into question law's own 'stock stories'.[34] This is the case even accepting that storytelling is not necessarily a political 'good' in and of itself.

Sujatha Fernandes' work relentlessly interrogates the politics of storytelling and asks what is at stake and for whom in the mobilisation of storytelling, and under what conditions stories reproduce dominant relations of power.[35] In so doing, Fernandes encapsulates a point central to storytelling within RSD: that those who are able 'to make their personal experiences legible to the mainstream through drawing on dominant narratives and devices are given a platform' and are recognised; but this occurs at the same time as others, whose narratives are neither legible nor conforming, are sidelined or excluded.[36] In the case of RSD, those who are unable to trade in narratives and story-forms that are cognisable (or who fail to account for their deviations from dominant stories) may be discredited and quite explicitly not recognised *as* refugees.

All of the above relates to the project at hand. In my turn to narrative and narrative forms in this book, I eschew claims that narrative will empower or bring justice to so-called outsider groups merely by virtue of its form or its expression. My methodology characterises the narrative form required of refugee applicants as a culturally specific version of storytelling and testimony which operates both as a tool of exclusion and means of designating 'acceptable' and worthy refugee applicants from unacceptable potential future citizen subjects. And, following Barsky's contention that a refugee's capacity to *construct*

31 Archibald Q'um Q'um Xiiem, Lee-Morgan and De Santolo, above n 23, 5.

32 Patricia Ewick and Susan S Silbey explain this approach succinctly: '[s]ome scholars contend that narratives have significant subversive or transformative potential. . . . By allowing the silenced to speak, by refusing the flattening and distorting effects of traditional logico-scientific methods and dissertative modes of representation, narrative scholarship participates in rewriting social life in ways that are, or can be, liberatory': Patricia Ewick and Susan S Silbey, 'Subversive Stories and Hegemonic Tales: Toward a Sociology of Narrative' (1995) 29 (2) *Law & Society Review* 197, 199.

33 Martha-Marie Kleinhans, 'Rewriting Outsider Narratives: A Renaissance of Revolutionary Subjectivities' (2007) 2 *Charleston Law Review* 185, 201.

34 For Barsky's argument along these lines, see Robert Barsky, *Clamouring for Legal Protection: What the Great Books Teach Us About People Fleeing from Persecution* (Bloomsbury Academic, 2023).

35 Sujatha Fernandes, *Curated Stories: The Uses and Misuses of Storytelling* (Oxford University Press, 2017).

36 Ibid 3, 6.

herself as a refugee is at the heart of RSD[37] – an assessment often utterly indifferent to the underlying need for refugee protection – my analysis certainly does not characterise the story-form demanded of refugee applicants as an inherently positive, authentic or enabling form of evidence.[38] As I express throughout the book, it is not difficult, in the context of the RSD oral hearing, to remain highly sceptical of the view that narrative forms are redemptive or alternatively, that counter-narratives will inevitably destabilise the power of law's rule and norms. For refugee applicants, the experience of the hearing, the demand for narrative and the plenary power of decision-maker to control the story reinforce that the opportunity to construct a narrative neither necessarily empowers the speaker nor contests law's authority.

2.3 Conventional Narrative Form(s) and RSD

What narrative is, it may come as no surprise, has in large part been taken for granted by legal academics seeking to put narrative to work.[39] Narrative is at times defined in a purely oppositional mode, as 'not legal argument' or 'not abstract reasoning'; and as associated with the individual, the personal and the contextual.[40] This approach is unworkable when attending to the narrative forms that are *part of* legal reasoning, even if the question of what constitutes a narrative is a vexed one.[41] Dominick LaCapra observes, and I agree, that '[i]t is curious that theorists who know much better nonetheless seem to assume the most conventional form of narrative (particularly nineteenth-century realism read in a rather limited manner), when they generalize about the nature of narrative, often to criticize its conventionalizing or ideological nature'.[42] LaCapra gives a helpful account of the main aspects of this conventional, novelistic narrative, describing it as involving 'a beginning, a middle and an end, whereby the end recapitulates the beginning after the trials of the middle, and gives you (at least on the level of insight), some realization of what it was all about – there's a sense in which the conventional narrative is redemptive'.[43] This description of narrative aligns with the many accounts of narrative that feature in law and narrative scholarship, wherein scholars adopt 'conventional' narrative forms as proxies for all modes of narrative and narrativity within legal texts. Not an issue confined to legal scholarship, the construction of the 'prototypical story formula' based in conflict and

37 Robert F Barsky, *Constructing a Productive Other: Discourse Theory and the Convention Refugee Hearing* (John Benjamins, 1994); Barsky, above n 29 especially chapter 6.

38 See too Manderson, above n 8; Binder and Weisberg, above n 8.

39 For example, the relationship between 'story' and 'narrative', used interchangeably in legal scholarship, is a vexed issue within narrative theory; see Martin McQuillan (ed), *The Narrative Reader* (Psychology Press, 2000) 3–6.

40 See, for example, Paul Gerwirtz, 'Narrative and Rhetoric in the Law' in Peter Brooks and Paul Gerwirtz (eds), *Law's Stories: Narrative and Rhetoric in the Law* (Yale University Press, 1998) 135.

41 McQuillan, above n 39, 4. I note here that my engagement with narrative does not include or rehearse the history, central debates and differing approaches to narrative study within narrative theory. While these subjects are beyond the scope of my project, for a solid treatment of the history of narrative from Russian formalism to structuralist and scientific theories of narratology, and through to poststructuralism (and for a critique of this linear history), see David Herman, *Basic Elements of Narrative* (John Wiley & Sons, 2011) 23–33; McQuillan, above n 39, ix–xii; Hayden White, *The Content of the Form: Narrative Discourse and Historical Representation* (Johns Hopkins University Press, 1987).

42 Dominick LaCapra, *Writing History, Writing Trauma* (Johns Hopkins University Press, 2nd ed, 2014) 64.

43 Amos Goldberg, 'Interview with Professor Dominick LaCapra' (Eclipse of Humanity, Yad Vashem, 9 June 1998) <www.yadvashem.org/articles/interviews/dominick-lacapra.html>.

resolution[44] is, as Sujatha Fernandes writes, 'highly reductive of the vast oral and narrative practices that it purports to represent'.[45]

A precise definition of the narrative form, though, is particularly difficult to determine when attempting to answer the threshold question of 'when is a text narrative?' or conversely, when is it not one? In contrast to orthodox definitions drawn from culturally located, 'model' narrative forms, Martin McQuillan argues that narrative is any minimal linguistic act that depends for its meaning on an intersubjective use of language. In this way, he proposes that 'pass the salt' could be a narrative because it depends on context for its meaning, involves an intersubjective experience and potentially describes 'events existent in a chain of temporal causality or at least contingency'.[46] In interrogating far more restrictive and 'standard' definitions of narrative, McQuillan also identifies and critiques the novel form as 'paradigmatic of all narrative production', particularly within orthodox theories of narrative. McQuillan writes that 'reliance of narrative models upon the form of the novel is a consequence of the discipline of narrative theory's beginnings within departments of literature in the French, and later Anglo-American academy'.[47] Fernandes also observes that narrow Western accounts of narrativity erase story-forms that extend beyond the paradigm of the novel. As she notes '[s]torytelling in the contemporary era has involved constructing a genealogy of an essentialized, universal formula out of what are fairly diverse oral traditions and narrative practices'.[48] Popular and scholarly accounts of storytelling, she writes, 'often extrapolate from the Western experience to present the idea of storytelling as universal and timeless'.[49]

Rejecting universal or 'orthodox' explanations of the narrative form allows us to both identify which narratives cleave to 'model' Anglo-European forms and those that do not, but which may be classed as narratives nonetheless. Certainly, authors who deliberately disrupt orthodox narrative structures as a literary storytelling device are nonetheless producing narratives, even if the narratives are non-linear or disorienting. Non-linear and fractured testimonial narratives – which may be associated with traumatic rupture or events and that reflect 'the effects of trauma making rents in the tissues of memory' – can similarly be classed and defined as narratives.[50] Indeed, a wide range of linguistic acts may fall into the category of narrative, but as McQuillan argues, there are still certain narratives that are held up as model forms, and such narratives carry weight by virtue of their status as 'standard' narratives within the specific cultural, social and political contexts of their telling. Distilling the definition of narrative provides a way to consider 'unconventional' narratives as narratives nonetheless – but most helpfully for my purposes, it allows us to identify and ask questions about the precise genres of narrative that are demanded of particular legal subjects. I adopt a broad conception of narrative here, but as I explain, it is a model or standardised Anglo-European narrative form that is demanded of refugee applicants.

44 See, e.g., Jerome Bruner, 'The Narrative Construction of Reality' (1991) 18(1) *Critical Inquiry* 1.

45 Fernandes, above n 35, 4.

46 McQuillan, above n 39, 8; Seymour Benjamin Chatman, *Coming to Terms: The Rhetoric of Narrative in Fiction and Film* (Cornell University Press, 1990).

47 McQuillan, above n 39, 9.

48 Fernandes, above n 35, 4.

49 Ibid.

50 Tess Coslett, Celia Lury and Penny Summerfield (eds), *Feminism & Autobiography: Texts, Theories, Methods* (Routledge, 2000) 9.

The conventional Anglo-European narrative form is not and should not be a stand-in for a definition of narrative. Indeed, even the designation 'conventional' reinforces the centrality of the Anglo-European novel as the paradigmatic narrative form. However, for the purposes of this project and the chapters that interrogate the refugee oral hearing in this book, it is precisely the *conventional* or what I refer to as the *model Anglo-European narrative form* or *model narrative form* that is demanded of refugee applicants. This model narrative form, I argue, structures the reception, testing and judgment of refugee testimony. The elements of this particular mode of narration are central to my analysis of the hearing, its conduct and assessments of refugee credibility within RSD.

Patricia Ewick and Susan S Silbey provide an exceptionally clear definition of this model narrative form, and synthesise a number of theories of narrative to express its three core elements.[51] Concisely stated, these core elements of a model Anglo-European narrative are: the selective appropriation of past events and characters; a temporal ordering of the events within the narrative; and a relationship between characters and events and to some overarching structure, 'often in the context of opposition or struggle', a criterion that is otherwise called emplotment or 'relationality of parts'.[52] Further, and crucially, the requirement for temporal and structural ordering is implicated in a requirement for both '"narrative closure" and "narrative causality": in other words, a statement about how and why the recounted events occurred'.[53] In my argument about narrative in refugee testimony, I present the demand for testimony as aligning with this version of the narrative form. The refugee narrative, however, often calls for a chronological or sequential ordering (rather than merely locating events in time) and *direct* causative relationships between events and their outcomes. And, as I discuss in Chapter 7, for refugee applicants the demand for closure is not a demand for any manner of resolution – but a resolution that involves the seeking of refugee status, which LaCapra would contend, is therefore what the story was all about.

In a careful reflection on the 'proliferating interest' in narrative within academic research, Ewick and Silbey also provide a 'sociology' of how narrative has been used within sociolegal scholarship,[54] identifying three ways in which narrative-based methodologies have entered scholarship. The first involves narrative as the object of inquiry, encompassing research that focuses on how narratives function in mediating reality and constituting identities.[55] Second, narrative may be the method of inquiry, whereby scholars collect or examine existing narratives as a means of 'accessing or revealing some other aspect of the social world'.[56] Finally, narratives may also be the product of research.[57] Following Ewick and Silbey's taxonomy of narrative within sociolegal research, this book primarily focuses on

[51] See Herman, above n 41, 23–33; McQuillan, above n 39, ix–xii.

[52] Ewick and Silbey, above n 32, 200.

[53] Ibid.

[54] Ibid 201.

[55] Ibid 202. Ewick and Silbey include here research that addresses how actors rely on narrative to communicate and make sense of their worlds; some of this research also explores the 'conditions of narration' and how these conditions may give rise to reasonable, appropriate or persuasive narratives in a particular setting.

[56] Ibid. Such work need not focus on what constitutes a particular narrative or the ways in which narratives are produced; it involves a sociological study through narrative, rather than dealing with narrativity as the object of inquiry.

[57] Ibid 203–04. Indeed, even in fields where scholars are not self-consciously creating narrative, sociolegal and sociological scholarship nonetheless produces narratives about an area or topic of inquiry.

narrative as the *object of inquiry*, and asks how narrative and narrative forms mediate reality, constitute identities and shape meaning in the RSD hearing room.

Finally, it bears making explicit that personal testimony and stories produced in spaces of, or for the purposes of, legal adjudication are distinct from narratives cast outside of law's explicit mandates, and as such should be considered as unique modes of testimony. Certainly, narratives reproduced within legal texts or by certain actors *for* legal judgment – in particular narratives strategically articulated by 'outsiders' *in order to* access rights or justice – cannot be analysed as voluntary tellings of the self outside of an adjudicative context constrained by rules of content and narration. Here, Carolyn Steedman's articulation of the concept of an 'enforced narrative' is immensely helpful, particularly when thinking through the nature of narrative produced for and by the refugee oral hearing, and what it can (and cannot) tell us.[58] Examining the narrative accounts that the labouring poor in seventeenth- and eighteenth-century England were required to provide in order to receive poor relief, Steedman demonstrates that such testimonial narratives are anything but 'a straightforward telling of self'.[59] Instead, Steedman argues, enforced narratives such as the voices of the labouring poor revealed a kind of narrative that was demanded and enforced by the 'emerging administrative state', and which it could in turn fashion 'according to requirements', alienate and expropriate.[60] As well, enforced narratives demonstrate how those from whom narrative are exacted contend with, conform to or resist such demands. This conception of an 'enforced narrative' captures law and literature's attention to narrative forms sanctioned (or dismissed) within legal authority, and the implicit and explicit discursive and substantive rules that govern such stories. This point is also central to Maryns' scholarship, which excavates the often-unacknowledged discursive rules and frames that shape what is 'sayable' within RSD hearings and in the 'long and complicated textual trajectories' of refugee testimony throughout the assessment process.[61] I also note the relevance of what Steedman so neatly names the 'autobiographical injunction', which the state imposes on certain subjects as the basis for accessing anything from rights to resources. The genre of acceptable refugee testimony, which I address in Chapter 7, might also be characterised as a kind of autobiographical injunction. Following Steedman, that chapter considers the 'expectations, orders and instructions' that require refugee subjects to *produce* certain kinds of autobiographical narratives, which I argue conform with makings of a modern, self-narrating, white 'European' or Western self.[62]

As well, while refugee applicants' oral evidence is cast within refugee law and legal scholarship *as* testimony, this evidence is distinct from established conceptions and theorising of the testimonial form and genre/s of testimony. As Van Rijswijk has noted, in both therapeutic or quasi-legal settings (and frequently in response to extraordinary events) the testimonial genre is often accepted at face value.[63] Indeed, in contrast to adversarial or inquisitorial legal proceedings, sites of testimony such as truth commissions or public

58 Carolyn Steedman, 'Enforced Narratives: Stories of Another Self' in Tess Cosslett, Celia Lury and Penny Summerfield (eds), *Feminism and Autobiography: Texts, Theories, Methods* (Routledge, 2000) 25.

59 Ibid 36.

60 Ibid.

61 Katrijn Maryns, *The Asylum Speaker: Language in the Belgian Asylum Procedure* (Routledge, 2014) 6.

62 Steedman, above n 58, 28.

63 Honni van Rijswijk, 'Testimonial Justice in Transnational Contexts: The Limitations and Possibilities of the Testimonial Form' in Werner Gephart, Jenny Hellmann and Raja Sakrani (eds), *Legal Cultures in Transition* (Klostermann, 1st ed, 2015) 101.

archiving projects, adopt a posture of faith towards testimony-givers, and personal testimony may be considered as a basis for both historical truth and fact and the truth of individual experience.[64] The form and reception of refugee evidence during the RSD hearings could not be further from such testimonial forms or settings. While this is not to ignore the discursive limits of testimony and witnessing,[65] the distinct and adjudicative nature of RSD oral hearings and their attendant cultures of disbelief reinforce why I consider refugee speech presented in the oral hearing through the lens of narrative, rather than the lens and politics of testimonial forms. Following on from this framing, the next section explains the precise sites of refugee decision-making I accessed, and the nature and limits of the refugee testimony I observed.

2.4 The Dataset, Narrative Theory and Observation as Method

The aim of this project's empirical component was to access, in full, administrative oral IRB and RRT hearings for RSD in Australia and Canada. In this section, I address methodological aspects of the project not described in Chapter 1, specifically recruitment, criteria for inclusion in the case set, my approach to observation and analysis of the hearings and, finally, my reflections on the challenges of accessing the refugee oral hearing in both jurisdictions.

To access hearings in Canada, I recruited research participants through a partnership with UNHCR Canada, which has a statutory right to observe RSD hearings,[66] as well as through members of the Canadian immigration bar in Montréal and Vancouver. In Australia, participants were recruited through a partnership with a medium sized, community-based refugee legal service. I adopted broad and open criteria in determining which oral hearings to include in this research, namely that the applicant had applied for a protection visa and that the application involved a full hearing before either the RRT or the IRB.[67] I did not limit the hearings on the basis of a particular set of criteria, such as the Refugee Convention ground on which the claim was made or the applicant's region of origin, nationality or gender. Adopting restrictive criteria for the 'type' of hearing or claimant included in the project may have enhanced the comparability of the hearings. However, the factors which most affect testimony and the assessment of credibility, as canvassed in Chapter 1, are not necessarily determined by the legal basis of a claim; my aim was not to understand how the IRB and RRT treated

64 Anne Orford, 'Commissioning the Truth' (2006) 15(3) *Columbia Journal of Gender and Law* 858 cited in van Rijswijk, above n 63.

65 Rosanne Kennedy, Lynne Bell and Julia Emberley, 'Decolonising Testimony: On the Possibilities and Limits of Witnessing' (2009) 15(3) *Humanities Research* 1.

66 *Immigration and Refugee Protection Act*, SC 2001, c 27, s 166(e).

67 Cases were not selected on a random basis. My partner organisations and refugee lawyers who participated as research partners collaborated in selecting the hearings included in the research. My agreement with research partners was that I would attend and access RRT or IRB hearings where this was logistically possible and where advocates felt it was appropriate and practicable to approach clients to participate. In Australia, when choosing potential participants, the advocacy organisation considered the effect of my presence, and specifically the possible negative effect of my involvement in highly sensitive hearings. Partner organisations in Canada did not explicitly articulate this consideration. All research partners aimed for a mix of basis of claim and applicant country of origin. The Appendix sets out various elements of each hearing, including the jurisdiction; gender of the applicant; basis of claim; country of origin; credibility determination and outcome.

particular kinds of claims but to investigate the nature of the oral hearing, the presence of decision-makers' narrative-driven expectations and modes for testing oral testimony as such.[68]

A factor that did shape and limit the dataset was that in both Australia and Canada, the included hearings were those of applicants who were represented by an experienced refugee advocate. Particularly in Australia, the applicants' representation came via a community-based refugee advocacy organisation, where applicants in contact with the organisation were likely to have access to a range of services, support mechanisms and information. Access to high-quality legal assistance fundamentally affects the applicant's experience of the determination process and its outcome. And, in the case of the lawyers involved in this research, legal assistance was provided by lawyers with significant refugee law and RSD expertise. As a result, the applicants represented here are a narrow subset of asylum seekers with access to high-quality legal assistance both in the preparation and presentation of their claims.[69]

Participant observation is a rather counter-intuitive term that describes a means of gathering data where the researcher (participant) observes a particular social event or phenomenon *without* directly participating or actively intervening.[70] Participant observation was primarily developed in the context of long-term anthropological and sociological fieldwork with particular groups of people or societies. However, the method is increasingly used in studies where the researcher observes events or occasions as they occur (such as court hearings) rather than understanding them through other qualitative research methods such as interviews and discussions with participants.[71] Raymond Gold's typology of four observational research roles – of which 'participant-as-observer' is one – explains the participant observer as someone who is known to those being observed but does not play an active role in the setting.[72] By contrast, Loïc Wacquant suggests the fieldwork researcher's role should always be one of active 'observant participation' and suggests social inquiry must be 'embedded and embodied' and requires the researcher to enact a role in the phenomena being studied.[73]

[68] There are also a number of studies that examine RSD decision-making by comparing particular classes of claim, particularly claims that involve gender-based harms, as discussed in Chapter 1. These studies reveal the advantage of comparing like claims with like claims, and in particular the importance of revealing the narratives and assumptions at play for certain groups. See, e.g., Laurie Berg and Jenni Millbank, 'Constructing the Personal Narratives of Lesbian, Gay and Bisexual Asylum Claimants' (2009) 22(2) *Journal of Refugee Studies* 195; Helen Baillot, Sharon Cowan and Vanessa E Munro, '"Hearing the Right Gaps": Enabling and Responding to Disclosures of Sexual Violence within the UK Asylum Process' (2012) 21(3) *Social & Legal Studies* 269; David A B Murray, 'The (Not So) Straight Story: Queering Migration Narratives of Sexual Orientation and Gendered Identity Refugee Claimants' (2014) 17(4) *Sexualities* 451.

[69] As Chapter 1 notes, due to the limits of observing the oral hearings as my primary source of data, I could not assess or account for the influence of advocates in the preparation and structuring of claims.

[70] Patricia Adler and Peter Adler, 'Observational Techniques' in Norman Denzin and Yvonna Lincoln (eds), *Handbook of Qualitative Research* (Sage, 3rd ed, 2005) 377.

[71] See, e.g., the influential work of John M Conley and William O'Barr on conducting ethnographies of legal institutions (including the courtroom) and on spoken legal discourse: John M Conley and William M O'Barr, *Rules versus Relationships: The Ethnography of Legal Discourse* (University of Chicago Press, 1990).

[72] Raymond L Gold, 'Roles in Sociological Field Observations' (1958) 36(3) *Social Forces* 217.

[73] Loïc Wacquant, 'For a Sociology of Flesh and Blood' (2015) 38(1) *Qualitative Sociology* 1.

For the observational parts of the research, I was in the hearing room, visible to all participants. In each case, I was required to explain my presence once the hearing had started. I did not participate in formal proceedings beyond this introduction and did not speak again for the duration of each hearing. For hearings where my data comprised the full, recorded audio of the hearing and transcript rather than in-person attendance, my method is best described as complete observation.[74] In one sense, these case files are a less 'contaminated' source of data.[75] However, there is no clear answer to the question of what effect my predominantly passive presence in the room had on the conduct of the hearings observed. It would be too simplistic to say that my presence was an advantage or disadvantage to the applicant. One recurrent observation was that the atmosphere in the room shifted when one or more attendees in the room were there on behalf of the applicant. Since the hearing rooms are relatively small and there were only ever between five and nine people in the room, when three or more non-participating attendees were there this provided some sense of a 'public' that was absent when the only people in the room were the decision-maker, interpreter, applicant, the applicant's lawyer and myself.

The 'grounded' element of grounded theory refers to the idea that results or theories are located within the data itself; that is, theories 'start' with the data.[76] Kathy Charmaz provides one of the most useful explications of the approach, drawing on its foundational texts to provide a set of 'systematic, flexible guidelines' for the task of analysing data. She argues that grounded theory guidelines are ultimately an approach to dealing with and organising data, and that they do not dictate a methodological or theoretical approach.[77] I like Charmaz's explanation and her guidelines because they do not obscure how data is interpreted via obfuscating terminology or foster notions of 'objectivity' or a positivist empiricism. As such, I adopted a grounded theory approach to analyse the hearing data in light of my own theoretical framing of law, narrative and refugee testimony.

Before moving to consider the history of the oral hearing within RSD processes in the next chapter, I want to reflect on the difficulties I encountered in accessing asylum seeker testimony for the purposes of this project. Organising third-party researcher access to

[74] As noted, the data types include my own first-person observation of some hearings, the complete audio recordings of some hearings and the written transcriptions of some hearings or all of the above. In the Appendix, I outline the types of data that were available in relation to each hearing.

[75] An obvious disadvantage of audio files as a form of data was that I could neither experience the hearing nor see the participants. However, even for the hearings that I did attend, because I was required to sit at the back of the room, the only face I was able to fully see was that of the decision-maker. At times, I was able to glimpse the side of the applicant's face as they spoke, and in certain hearings, I was able to see the face of the interpreter if they sat to the side of the applicant's table.

[76] Kathy Charmaz, *Constructing Grounded Theory: A Practical Guide Through Qualitative Analysis* (Sage, 2006) 3. In explicating a grounded theory approach I note Richards and Richards point that often grounded theory is 'widely adopted as an approving bumper-sticker in qualitative studies' and that I do not engage with the epistemology of these methods: Lyn Richards and Tom Richards, 'The Transformation of Qualitative Method: Computational Paradigms and Research Processes' in Nigel G Lee and Raymond M Fielding (eds), *Using Computers in Qualitative Research* (Sage, 1991) 38, 43.

[77] Charmaz, above n 76, 9. Charmaz's approach is partly in response to original versions of grounded theory, which had a strong positivist bent; see, e.g., Barney Glaser, *Theoretical Sensitivity: Advances in the Methodology of Grounded Theory* (Sociology Press, 1978). The grounded theory method, particularly in Barney Glaser's approach, treating coding categories as strictly emergent from the data and based on them, is what Charmaz calls a rather 'direct, and, often, narrow empiricism'. See also Kathy Charmaz and Anthony Bryant (eds), *Handbook of Grounded Theory* (Sage, 2002).

refugee hearings in Australia and Canada is difficult. The RSD hearings are not publicly listed, and in both Australia and Canada, refugee hearings completely closed to the public.[78] In the period that the hearings took place, it was not only the applicant who was required to consent to third-party attendance, but also the IRB or RRT decision-maker.[79] The initial plan for fieldwork involved first-person observation and attendance at up to eight refugee hearings in both Australia and Canada. As noted, my access to the Australian hearings took place through a research partnership with a community-based refugee legal service. At the outset of this research, I attended two Australian hearings. The RRT consented to my attendance. However, following these hearings, the RRT contacted my partner organisation to inform them that I would not be permitted to attend further hearings in my capacity as a researcher, despite the client's informed, written consent to my attendance. The Tribunal communicated that my attendance was prohibited because hearings are required to be held in private and that my presence was not necessary for the conduct of the hearing.[80] Further, it was expressed that only those required for purposes of the performance of the Tribunal's functions were permitted to be present in the room.[81] Gaining access to refugee hearings in Canada was easier. Although the IRB's permission was required *alongside* the applicant's, as was a written application explaining my status as a researcher, unless the hearings I gained consent to attend were delayed or cancelled,[82] arranging my attendance was a comparatively straightforward process.[83] My verified status as a researcher, rather than a 'lay' observer, was key to the approval process.

While systems of law and justice are often described via visual and spatial metaphors of transparency and openness, conceptions of aurality and audibility are useful when reflecting on refugee testimony in the context of state-based RSD mechanisms. Since any kind of public 'hearing' of refugee applicants' speech is exceptionally difficult to access, the

78 *Migration Act 1958* (Cth) s 429; *Immigration and Refugee Protection Act*, SC 2001, c 27, s 166(c).

79 Hearing dates were often changed or rescheduled at the last minute. As well, in Australia, two applicants provided initial consent but then withdrew it directly prior to the hearing due to nervousness and concerns about the potential effect of my presence. These concerns and apprehensions were more prevalent among the Australian participants than the Canadian participants. At the time of the hearings, one of the central goals of Australian refugee policy was to deter refugee applicants travelling to Australia by boat, and both of the major political parties supported a policy of 'stopping the boats' and limiting Australia's onshore refugee program.

80 Telephone conversation between the author and head of the legal service on 25 November 2013.

81 Section 429 of the *Migration Act 1958* (Cth) sets out that the 'hearing of an application for review by the Tribunal must be in private'. In *SZAYW v MIMIA* (2006) 230 CLR 486, the High Court of Australia interpreted s 429 of the Act and held that 'it is consistent with the statutory purpose, and with common use of language, to treat the concept of privacy as embracing, not only agents of an applicant, but also persons whom an applicant desires to be present and thus to be made privy to what occurs at a hearing': *SZAYW v MIMIA* (2006) 230 CLR 486, [25]–[26].

82 Notably, on the day of one scheduled hearing in Canada – for which the applicant had waited over ten months – we all sat stiffly in a windowless, basement hearing room in the Montréal office of the IRB for 40 minutes, waiting for the Board Member to arrive. Only after some time did a staff member inform the advocate that the Member was sick and had forgotten to inform anyone of his absence. The hearing was rescheduled for the following week. The 30-odd minutes of waiting, mainly in silence, for the Member to arrive added to the months of waiting that had preceded the hearing.

83 This process was made easier by the existence of the Canadian Association of Refugee Lawyers, an association that, according to its website, 'serves as an informed national voice on refugee law and human rights, and promotes just and consistent practices in the treatment of refugees in Canada': *Canadian Association of Refugee Lawyers* <www.carl-acaadr.ca/about>.

institutional silencing of and barriers to accessing testimony was an overarching theme in relation to my fieldwork and in considering refugee speech for the purposes of applying for protection more generally. The difficulty of hearing refugee testimony is, in part, a consequence of the crucial protection of refugee confidentiality and the associated closed nature of RSD hearings. Another factor at play, less clearly explained by privacy concerns, is the very limited percentage of redacted decisions that are published in Australia and Canada[84] and – as I experienced in the Australian context – a lack of openness to oversight within the institutions responsible for RSD. If a public record of refugee testimony is available at all, as noted, it is a decision-maker's written account of the hearing, which may or may not contain decontextualised excerpts of refugee speech. Such accounts do however contain a lot of summarising, interpreting and discussion about what refugee applicants *have* said, and how it should be understood and judged. This research confirms the difficulty of accessing refugee testimony presented before administrative tribunals and this accounts for both numerically small datasets and the limited amount of research that has accessed the presentation of testimony in both jurisdictions.[85]

By highlighting the limited access to RSD for researchers and other observers, I do not mean to dismiss the need to maintain confidentiality or protection of an applicant's privacy as a central concern. This is even more critical at time when all manner of digital information is readily accessible by an applicant's home country government, when host states demand and collect biometric data and refugee data breaches have occurred in multiple jurisdictions. However, as the next chapter reveals, both the Australian and Canadian governments have long sought to maintain executive control and limited oversight over refugee decision-making. No doubt, mechanisms to protect refugees' privacy and confidentiality operate alongside governments' also controlling and withholding information about 'border management' and refugee arrivals in the name of national security. In both Australia and Canada, the scales are clearly tipped in favour of protection of confidentiality over values of transparency and accountability in relation to accessing the sites of RSD decision-

[84] In Australia, first-instance decisions are not made available at all. In 2021–22 and 2020–21, 17 per cent of the MRD's decisions were published (3,600 decisions published out of a total of 20,892 decisions in 2021–2022; 4,021 decisions published out of a total of 23,246 decisions in 2020–21): AAT, *Annual Report 2021–2022* (2022) 25, 30; AAT, *Annual Report 2020–2021* (2021) 28, 33. This recent publication rate is significantly lower than that in previous years. For example, the then MRT and RRT stated that they published 42 per cent of their decisions in 2011–12, and 43 per cent of their cases in 2010–11: MRT-RRT, *Annual Report 2011–2012* (2012); MRT-RRT, *Annual Report 2010–2011* (2011). Disaggregated data for publication of refugee protection decisions specifically in the MRD was not available; similarly, the MRT and RRT operated as a single agency and disaggregated data for each Tribunal's publication record was not available. In Canada, decisions that are deemed 'persuasive' are published on the IRB's website to promote consistent and efficient decision-making, as are certain decisions designated as 'jurisprudential guides': IRB, 'Policy Note on Persuasive Decisions' (19 May 2009); IRB, 'Policy on the Use of Chairperson's Guidelines and Jurisprudential Guides' (7 July 2022). The total percentage of RPD decisions published by the IRB is not available; however, an Access to Information request in 2008 revealed that 5 per cent of all sexual orientation cases over a four-year period had been published, which may give some indication of publication rates: Jenni Millbank, '"The Ring of Truth": A Case Study of Credibility Assessment in Particular Social Group Refugee Determinations' (2009) 21(1) *International Journal of Refugee Law* 1, 3.

[85] Though see valuable studies of the oral hearing conducted in both Australia and Canada despite these barriers and larger-scale projects possible in jurisdictions where asylum hearings are not closed to the public, detailed in Chapter 1.

making. This has in turn even further constrained oversight, analysis and critique of the terms on which refugee applicants are permitted to speak within RSD processes.

Following a history of the oral hearing in Australia and Canada in the next chapter, each of the book's analysis chapters presents one aspect of the findings that arose from combining the observational, qualitative methods I have described here and an interrogation of the form, presence and political implications of narrative within RSD processes.

2.5 Conclusion

Narratives and narrative forms constitute the law, its normative world and its claims to authority, as well as refugee law and RSD specifically. This chapter has set out how a methodology informed by a critical approach to law and narrative studies will be brought to bear on the presentation and assessment of onshore refugee applicants' testimony. For the purposes of this book, it matters *how* the fields of law, literature and narrative are understood when calling for refugee legal scholars to pay greater attention to literary modes of analysis. This becomes amply clear in the book's analysis chapters, which trace how narrative shapes and constrains the RSD oral hearing, as well as determines how the 'credible refugee' is permitted to narrate their testimony, and their lives to date. The argument that law *needs* narrative, or is apart from it, cannot be sustained in my reading of the oral hearing, which is replete with narrative, and as I argue, with a distinctly linear, teleological and Anglo-European form of narrative – all of which highlight the generic demands made of refugee applicants in real time during the oral hearing.

This book's use of narrative theory to evaluate the oral testimony accepted and rejected by refugee decision-makers requires a critical conception of narrative, which I have articulated here and develop throughout the book. Absolutely central to this project, and to the judgment of refugee testimony as such, is attention to the constraining functions of the narrative form. This involves persistently asking, which narratives are sanctioned, preferred and held up within RSD processes, and to what end? This is because, as Ewick and Silbey emphasise, only certain stories are 'culturally available' for telling and such stories repeatedly 'articulate and reproduce existing ideologies and hegemonic relations of power and equality'.[86] Before I examine the narratives that can be told within the RSD oral hearing – alongside those dismissed as implausible, incoherent and inconsistent – the next chapter locates the oral hearing within a longer history of RSD in Australia and Canada. It traces the history of RSD from the first oral interviews with onshore asylum seekers in both countries, through to the hearing in its current form. This history sheds light on the multiple purposes of the oral hearing, the nature of the hearing as a 'narrative occasion' and, particularly in Australia, on the hearing as a site that entrenched executive control over refugee decision-making and the terms on which refugee arrivals were able to access protection.

[86] Ewick and Silbey, above n 32, 212–13.

3

How Did We Get Here? A History of the Oral Hearing in Australia and Canada

This chapter addresses the history of the refugee oral hearing in Australia and Canada. It traces the genesis of both the IRB and the RRT and quasi-independent processes for the administrative review of refugee decision-making in both countries and explains when and why the oral hearing became a determinative event within RSD. Examining the history of the oral hearing in Australia reveals that the hearing was introduced in the context of major reforms that sought to limit and control onshore refugee arrivals – including the introduction of Australia's notorious policy of mandatory detention of unauthorised arrivals.[1] In Canada, the introduction of the oral hearing also coincided with new deterrence policies, although the hearing itself was introduced as the result of successful litigation under the *Canadian Charter of Rights and Freedoms* and was less explicitly presented as a means of limiting onshore arrivals through excluding 'bogus' claimants.[2]

In both jurisdictions the introduction of the oral hearing coincided with increasing state focus on and rhetoric about the 'genuineness' of refugee arrivals. This was precipitated in part by Australia and Canada's relatively new status as countries of first asylum and growing numbers of onshore asylum seekers. As this chapter demonstrates, the introduction of formal RSD processes, which significantly enhanced the procedural fairness and independence of RSD processes, came at a time when both states' rhetoric about 'fake asylum seekers' (and in Australia 'queue jumpers'), and their abuse of the right to asylum, was on the ascent.[3] Critically, the question of genuineness was to be tested *via* the oral hearing and oral testimony. In this context, a robust determination process was presented by both states as a way to ensure that only 'genuine' refugees were granted asylum. In Australia in particular, the introduction of the hearing was linked to a culture of gatekeeping and racist suspicion of onshore refugees, as well as a desire to insulate executive decision-making from judicial oversight, that continues to inflect contemporary RSD processes.

While the exact history of the oral hearing tracks a different course in each jurisdiction, the evolution of RSD processes in Australia and Canada is similar in key ways. Crucially, in neither jurisdiction were the oral hearing and statutory RSD procedures introduced by the

[1] *Migration Amendment Act 1992* (Cth).

[2] *Singh v Minister for Employment and Immigration* (1985) 1 SCR 177. *Canadian Charter of Rights and Freedoms*, Part 1 of the *Constitution Act, 1982*, being Schedule B to the *Canada Act 1982* (UK), c 11. Note too, the IRB was introduced as a 'quasi-judicial body with the status of a superior court of record', while in Australia, 'the constitutional separation-of-powers doctrine ensures that the Tribunal remains part of the executive branch of government': Catherine Dauvergne, *Humanitarianism, Identity, and Nation: Migration Laws of Australia and Canada* (UBC Press, 2005) 97.

[3] Klaus Neumann charts the language of 'queue jumping' as first appearing in Australia in 1976–77: Klaus Neumann, *Across the Seas: Australia's Response to Refugees: A History* (Black Inc, 2015) see Chapter 5.

government *only* to improve procedural fairness for refugee applicants or to provide them with the right to be heard, although these were important outcomes. Rather, concerns about government – and in particular executive – control of onshore migration; border regulation and efficiency each also played a part. Racialised anxieties about managing 'new', unauthorised, onshore refugee arrivals were front and centre, and mirrored racist exclusions in immigration policy. At the same time, though, as applicants made onshore claims, each government also came under pressure from the legal profession and from advocates to improve existing processes; and domestic enactments of the Refugee Convention and an increasing sense of international and 'humanitarian' commitments also played a role. As such, government concerns about growing numbers of onshore asylum seekers and only letting in 'genuine' refugees operated alongside the need for and introduction of more independent, accountable and transparent RSD procedures.

This chapter begins by charting this history of the emergence of the oral hearing in Australia and Canada from approximately the last quarter of the twentieth century onwards. It then addresses recent reforms, and the narrowing of access to and the quality of RSD processes in both jurisdictions. This later history reveals that the 'right' to fair and independent decision-making processes has become increasingly constrained in both jurisdictions, as limiting access to RSD has become a key means by which states enact policies of refugee deterrence and exclusion. Importantly, the emergence of the oral hearing occurred within the broader context of extensive offshore refugee and humanitarian resettlement programs in both states. These resettlement programs were part of both countries' post–World War II refugee and migrant intake,[4] and did not require formal status determination in Australia or Canada. Further, refugees and humanitarian migrants selected for entry under offshore programs were required to fit, to varying degrees, within criteria deemed to align with national interests and priorities. Indeed, until the 1980s there were no codified or even quasi-independent 'in country' status determination procedures, or oral hearings for individual onshore refugees.[5]

3.1 Refugee Determination and the Oral Hearing in Australia

Australia first began to develop a non-statutory process of onshore RSD in the late 1970s. From the post–World War II period to the 1970s, Australia had primarily received refugees 'whose status or needs for resettlement had been determined elsewhere according to various agreements between Australia and international organisations such as the International Refugee Organisation (IRO) and the UNHCR'.[6] In 1947, an assisted passage and resettlement agreement was put into place with the IRO. As part of this agreement, Australia accepted around 200,000 refugees (or persons displaced at the end of World War II), and by

[4] For detailed accounts of both immigration history and refugee policy in Canada and Australia, particularly in the post–World War II period, see Ninette Kelley and Michael J Trebilcock, *The Making of the Mosaic: A History of Canadian Immigration Policy* (University of Toronto Press, 2nd ed, 2010); John Lack and Jacqueline Templeton, *Bold Experiment: A Documentary History of Australian Immigration since 1945* (Oxford University Press, 1995); and in relation to the US and North America generally, see Gil Loescher, *Calculated Kindness* (Free Press, 1998).

[5] James C Hathaway, 'The Conundrum of Refugee Protection in Canada: From Control to Compliance to Collective Deterrence' (1991) 4(1) *Journal of Policy History* 71, 71; Peter Waxman, 'The Shaping of Australia's Immigration and Refugee Policy' (2000) 19(1) *Immigrants & Minorities* 53, 62–65.

[6] Roz Germov and Francesco Motta, *Refugee Law in Australia* (Oxford University Press, 2003) 33.

1976, Australia had admitted over 350,000 refugees.[7] Until well into the 1970s, the majority of these refugees or displaced persons were European.[8] Throughout this period, Australia's principal 'offshore' program was criticised 'for exploiting the refugee situation for population-building and work-force purposes [and] for taking very few of the "hard-core" cases'.[9] Michael Grewcock notes that 'no non-European refugees were granted entry between 1945 and 1965 and, even after the [White Australia] policy was relaxed in 1966 to allow visas for non-Europeans with special skills that local residents could not provide, European heritage and self-identification were decisive'.[10] Peter Waxman writes that the large majority of displaced persons selected for acceptance were young, of good health and character, and assimilable.[11]

The arrival of those who, in contemporary terms, might be called onshore refugees first occurred in Australia from the mid-1970s onwards. While Australia's early ascension to the Refugee Convention in 1954 brought the Refugee Convention into force, it was only at the end of the Vietnam War that Australia became a country of 'first asylum', as those fleeing post-war Vietnam arrived seeking protection.[12] Andrew Endrey writes that race was not all that distinguished this refugee movement from every other in Australian history; rather, it was also that the Indo-Chinese arriving by boat were the first 'self-selecting' humanitarian migrants of recent times.[13] Prior to these arrivals, there had been very few onshore refugee applicants. At the time, the Immigration Minister determined the outcome of onshore humanitarian applications as part of the discretionary power to grant entry permits under

[7] David Cox, 'Australian Refugee Policy and Developing Countries: Evolvement of Australian Refugee Policy, 1945–1985' in Reginald T Appleyard (ed), *The Impact of International Migration on Developing Countries: Conference on Migration and Development* (Organisation for Economic Co-operation and Development, 1989) 249, 249. Australia agreed to settle a minimum of 12,000 persons a year from camps in Europe: Germov and Motta, above n 6, 32. From 1947–52 alone, Australia had accepted 170,400 displaced persons: Waxman, above n 5, 68.

[8] Patricia Hyndman, 'Australian Immigration Law and Procedures Pertaining to the Admission of Refugees' (1987) 33 *McGill Law Journal* 716, 719. This was a consequence of the White Australia policy, which restricted non-British and non-European migration through a number of exclusionary measures. Hyndman also charts the history of Arthur Calwell's attempts to expel the people, who were allowed to come to Australia during the war, once the war had ended, attempts that were successfully challenged in *O'Keefe v Calwell* (1949) 77 CLR 261. An Act was then passed to permit these deportations, which did not take place because of a change of government, but restrictions preventing some family reunion and naturalisation remained: Ibid.

[9] Cox, above n 7, 249. 'Hard-core' is a term often used in reference to post-war immigration and refugee intakes, and it generally describes refugees or humanitarian entrants who were injured, sick, elderly or living with a permanent disability: Kelley and Trebilcock, above n 4, 344.

[10] Michael Grewcock, *Border Crimes: Australia's War on Illicit Migrants* (Institute of Criminology Press, 2009) 93.

[11] Waxman, above n 5, 68. According to the 1977 'Refugee Policy and Mechanisms Statement', refugee selection was influenced by capacity to integrate, the state of the economy, the refugees' background and locational choice within Australia, and the availability of services upon arrival: Commonwealth, *Parliamentary Debates*, House of Representatives, 24 May 1977, 1714 (Hon Michael Mackellar, Minister for Immigration and Ethnic Affairs).

[12] See Mary Crock, 'Judging Refugees: The Clash of Power and Institutions in the Development of Australian Refugee Law' (2004) 26 *Sydney Law Review* 51, 53.

[13] Waxman, above n 5, 70; Andrew Endrey, 'Outline of Australia's Response to Refugee Situations since 1975' (National Population Council, 1990).

the *Migration Act 1958* (Cth) (*Migration Act*).[14] When 'the first refugee boat' carrying Vietnamese asylum seekers arrived in April 1976,[15] there was limited media coverage of the event. The men on board were granted entry permits and sent to the St Vincent de Paul Charity for support.[16] Michael Grewcock details the reception of further boats in the same year:

> Two more boats, carrying 106 Vietnamese refugees, arrived in November and December 1976. All were permitted to enter and most were flown to the Wacol Migrant Hostel in Brisbane, where they resided while their status was considered.[17]

Between April 1976 and August 1981, 56 boats carrying a total of 2,100 people arrived in Australia.[18] The arrival of these boats of 'onshore' asylum seekers, as well as offshore Vietnamese refugees resettled in Australia post-1975, were the subject of the 1976 Senate Committee report 'Australia and the Refugee Problem: The Plight and Circumstances of Vietnamese and Other Refugees' ('Australia and the Refugee Problem' report).[19] Cox, writing in the early 1980s, betrays the prevalence of the anti-Asian racism at the time when he notes that after 1976, Australians found themselves 'confronted' by Asians on public transport, in shops and on the streets, and that 'reactions were *understandably mixed*'.[20] Grewcock notes that the Senate Standing Committee on Foreign Affairs and Defence was prompted to commission the Report not just by the influx of refugees in the late 1970s, but also by the ad hoc and inconsistent government responses to the initial phases of migration following the collapse of the Saigon regime in 1975.[21]

[14] Andreas Schloenhardt, 'Australia and the Boat-People: Twenty-five Years of Unauthorised Arrivals' (2000) 23 *University of New South Wales Law Journal* 33, 36. See also *Migration Act 1958* (Cth) s 6 (in time at 1958). Note, though, that Australia's political and social preoccupation with maritime arrivals often overlooks significant phases of arrival of other national groups fleeing political crisis and unrest after World War II. Amongst these groups were approximately 15,000 Hungarians in the mid-1950s (escaping the Russian crackdown in Hungary) and roughly 5,500 Czechs escaping the reinvasion of Prague after 1968. As well, about 18,000 Lebanese arrived during the civil war in Lebanon from 1975–78: see Waxman, above n 5, 69.

[15] Grewcock, above n 10, 97.

[16] Claire Higgins sets out the 'staged' Government media strategy at the time, which aimed (where possible) to keep the first arrivals out the media spotlight, and failing that, to 'humanise' those arriving with personal stories, and then as opposition to refugees built as an election approached in 1977, to focus on screening processes and Australia's commitment to international law and reputation: Claire Higgins, *Asylum by Boat: Origins of Australia's Refugee Policy* (New South Publishing, 2017) 43–46.

[17] Grewcock, above n 10, 97; and see also Nancy Viviani, *The Long Journey: Vietnamese Migration and Settlement in Australia* (Melbourne University Press, 1984).

[18] Department of Immigration and Ethnic Affairs, *Review of Activities to 30 June 1982* (Australian Government Publishing Service, 1982); Grewcock, above n 10, 97; and see further Nancy Viviani, *The Indochinese in Australia, 1975–1995: From Burnt Boats to Barbecues* (Oxford University Press, 1996); Schloenhardt, above n 14. Although the official date for the dismantling of the White Australia Policy was 1973, moves had been made to change the policy earlier: see Waxman, above n 5, 58.

[19] Senate Standing Committee on Foreign Affairs and Defence, *Australia and the Refugee Problem: The Plight and Circumstances of Vietnamese and Other Refugees* (Australian Government Publishing Service, 1976).

[20] David Cox, 'Refugee Settlement in Australia: Review of an Era' (1983) 21(3) *International Migration* 332, 332. My emphasis.

[21] Grewcock, above n 10, 96.

The 'Australia and the Refugee Problem' report clearly evinced the tension between the Government's reluctance to accept refugees whom the state had not directly chosen and the growing recognition and influence of international refugee law.[22] While Australia had ratified the Refugee Convention in 1954, long before some states, it was not until 1973 that Australia signed the 1967 Protocol, which finally broadened the application of the Convention to events occurring both outside of Europe and after 1951.[23] Also at play in the report was the liberal state's ideal of humanitarianism, which would support some form of international responsibility for the growing Indo-Chinese refugee populations.[24] Much of the 'Australia and the Refugee Problem' report was also devoted to outlining the policy and resettlement failures that had become apparent since the arrival of the first groups of Indo-Chinese refugees.[25] In particular, it argued that the absence of a clear set of policies in relation to asylum seekers 'reduces our practical ability to respond to crises, and in turn can become justification for not involving ourselves with particular situations'.[26] In response to the 'problem' of the refugee influx, the report recommended the creation of a 'comprehensive set of policy guidelines together with the necessary administrative machinery to be applied to refugee situations'.[27]

Following this report, the then-Immigration Minister presented the 'Refugee Policy and Mechanisms' to Parliament in May 1977, which set out four principles that were intended to guide Australia's nascent refugee policy and introduced new means 'to enable Australia to respond quickly to designated refugee situations', outlined below. The first two principles set out that 'Australia fully recognises its humanitarian commitment and responsibility to admit refugees for resettlement' and that 'the decision to accept refugees must always remain with the Government of Australia'.[28] These two key points in many ways represent the tension that has characterised onshore refugee policy up to the present moment.[29] Even

[22] Higgins records that boat turn-backs, interceptions and third country resettlement were already being debated within government: Higgins, above n 16, 117–18.

[23] Grewcock, above n 10, 92–93.

[24] For critique of this discourse in the Australian context see Jordana Silverstein, 'Refugee Children, Boats and Drownings: A History of an Australian "Humanitarian" Discourse' (2020) 17(4) *History Australia* 728.

[25] The 'Australia and the Refugee Problem' report also includes the original text of the leaflet given to the Vietnamese refugees whom the Government had flown in from Vietnam and Guam. The leaflet, which provides a profile of Australia 'as a nation' ('Australia, your new country is a mixture, with many varied points') and closes by stating that:

> Australia has had a lot of experience with migrants, especially in the last 25 years. The majority, about three in four, get along very well; the remainder because they failed, leave Australia. ... But, finally, whether you succeed or not is up to you. Now is the time to decide and see if you believe you will succeed like other migrants to Australia.

Senate Standing Committee on Foreign Affairs and Defence, above n 19, 118.

[26] Ibid 89; Germov and Motta, above n 6, 33–34; Francis Galbally, *Migrant Services and Programs: Report of the Review of Post-arrival Programs and Services for Migrants* (Australian Government Publishing Service, 1978).

[27] Senate Standing Committee on Foreign Affairs and Defence, above n 19, 89; Grewcock, above n 10, 96.

[28] Senate Standing Committee on Foreign Affairs and Defence, ibid.

[29] The two further points made in the statement set out that '[s]pecial assistance will often need to be provided for the movement of refugees in designated situations or for their resettlement in Australia' and that '[i]t may not be in the interest of some refugees to settle in Australia [and] their interests may be better served elsewhere', a situation that Australia's annual financial contribution to the UNHCR was intended to address: ibid.

though the statement itself was far from a detailed approach to onshore refugee determination or to Australia's international treaty obligations, the 'Refugee Policy and Mechanisms' constituted the beginnings of what has perhaps been overstated as 'a new Australian refugee policy'.[30]

While the reforms that followed the new policy did not introduce an oral hearing, even at this early stage the Government presented the codification of procedure as a means to determine which onshore applicants did not merit protection.[31] Grewcock argues that the policy and reforms did more than articulate the Government's preference for an organised approach to refugee entry and resettlement; it also intimated that a more restrictive response might yet develop towards unauthorised boat arrivals as a result of the policy's focus on the imperative of executive control.[32] During the period surrounding the release of the policy, the government increasingly articulated its 'concerns' about the genuineness of later phases of Indo-Chinese arrivals, with the Secretary of the Department of Immigration and Ethnic Affairs (DIEA) stating in 1982 that 'the arrangements for the individual determination of refugee status, and a general tightening of our refugee policies, are now ensuring that only genuine refugees are settled here under Australia's protection'.[33] However, these statements were often tempered by strong moral statements about Australia's obligation to those less fortunate and to share our wealth and prosperity with those who do not enjoy 'our political and social freedom'.[34]

As noted, a range of humanitarian programs for receiving offshore refugees had existed in Australia long prior to its acting as a country of first asylum for applicants arriving by boat. However, these programs afforded the Australian Government significant control over which refugees would finally be selected for admission. There were generally three primary criteria for selection: the reunification of immediate family; identification of those considered to have the highest capacity to assimilate; and the acceptance of a proportion of so-called 'hard-core' refugees.[35] Since criteria based on who would be a 'good' migrant played a critical role in hand-selecting offshore refugees for resettlement, Australia continued to be criticised for 'creaming' refugee situations.[36] The arrival of onshore refugee applicants interrupted Australia's ability to control its refugee program and policies. Concerns about the (still relatively minimal) numbers of arrivals and their genuineness, as well as international moves towards the standardisation of RSD protocols, both influenced Australia's early development of its own RSD process.

30 See, for example, Schloenhardt, above n 14, 38.

31 Michael Mackellar, 'Refugee Policy and Mechanisms Statement', Commonwealth, *Parliamentary Debates*, House of Representatives, 24 May 1977, 1714 (Minister for Immigration and Ethnic Affairs).

32 Grewcock, above n 10, 96. Grewcock also notes that it was as the number of onshore Indo-Chinese refugees increased – as opposed to post–World War II refugees arriving from Europe – that the beginnings of a formal RSD policy were articulated, which also marked the 'beginnings of a state infrastructure for monitoring and ultimately detaining and deterring unauthorised refugees': at 94.

33 Australian Council on Population and Ethnic Affairs, 'Regional Refugee Consultations' (Canberra, DIEA, 1982) cited in Cox, above n 7, 250.

34 Senate Standing Committee on Foreign Affairs and Defence, *Indo-Chinese Resettlement: Australia's Involvement* (Australian Government Publishing Service, 1982).

35 Cox, above n 20, 333. See Kelley and Trebilcock, above n 4 for a definition of 'hard-core' refugees.

36 Cox, above n 20, 333.

3.1.1 The Early Days of RSD

Following the publication of the 'Australia and the Refugee Problem' report in 1976 and as a result of the 1977 Refugee Policy and Mechanisms, the Australian Government established the Determination of Refugee Status (DORS) Committee and the Standing Inter-Departmental Committee on Refugees in 1977. The purpose of these committees was to consider refugee claims and make recommendations to the Immigration Minister.[37] Both bodies existed within the DIEA and their recommendations were without statutory foundation[38] and not binding on the Minister.[39] Indeed, from this point until 1989, the task of refugee determination remained wholly at the discretion of the executive, without any form of independent standards or enforceable oversight.[40]

The establishment of the DORS Committee was a key outcome of the 1977 Refugee Policy and Mechanisms.[41] Meeting regularly in Canberra, the DORS Committee functioned on a case-by-case basis and was required to apply the Refugee Convention's definition of a refugee. Where the applicant was 'screened in', whereby the initial claim to the DIEA was deemed to be suitable for assessment, the Department arranged for the applicant to be interviewed by a DORS case officer, and a transcript of this interview accompanied any application to the Committee.[42] The DORS Committee, constituted by four government officials from four different departments and a UNHCR representative in an advisory, non-voting capacity, made all claim assessments by majority vote, and assessments were passed on to the Minister as recommendations only.[43]

The year 1980 marked the first time that Australian domestic legislation made reference to the Refugee Convention. Prior to 1980, no legislative instrument referred to the question of refugee status or to the obligations that were owed to a person who was determined to be a refugee.[44] The new provision did not incorporate the Refugee Convention's terms, or set out how status was to be determined, or remove the complete discretion of the executive to determine who would be granted status. Rather, it set out that a non-citizen shall be granted an 'entry permit' if the 'Minister has determined, by instrument in writing, that he [*sic*] has

37 Schloenhardt, above n 14, 36.

38 Germov and Motta, above n 6, 65–67.

39 Schloenhardt, above n 14, 36.

40 Germov and Motta, above n 6, 65–67.

41 Committee members came from the DIEA, the Attorney General's Department, the Department of Prime Minister and Cabinet and the Department of Foreign Affairs and Trade. The role of the UNHCR representative was to offer a credibility assessment based on what was known about the applicant's country of origin; 'to provide information on the treatment of similar cases or similar legal points in other jurisdictions'; and 'to represent the international community's interests by providing its interpretation of fundamental concepts such as a "well-founded fear of persecution"': Dianne Ayling and Sam Blay, 'Australia and International Refugee Law: An Appraisal' (1987) 9 *University of Tasmania Law Review* 245, 259.

42 Hyndman, above n 8, 738. Unless the claim was considered 'manifestly unfounded' based on an initial meeting with an officer, in which case the DORS Committee could recommend it be rejected without a full interview: at 738.

43 Ibid 727. From 1980, the applicant was required to fill in an application form and submit any relevant documentary evidence to the Committee: Germov and Motta, above n 6, 66. From 1987, a more comprehensive 48-page application form was introduced. Hyndman notes that the whole process could take up to twelve months or longer: Hyndman, above n 8, 738, 742.

44 Germov and Motta, above n 6, 38.

the status of a refugee within the meaning of the [Refugee] Convention'.[45] Critically, in this same period, the Government was also introducing new legislation targeting 'people smugglers' and expanding the powers of the Coast Guard and executive powers to deport.[46] In 1980, the government passed the *Immigration (Unauthorised Arrivals) Act 1980* (Cth), which created a 'complex ensemble of immigration offences' and targeted the 'masters, owners, agents and charterers of vessels' who facilitated the arrival of 'boat-people' to Australia.[47] The Act also expanded executive powers to board, search and seize 'illegal' vessels and expanded executive powers to arrest and detain unlawful non-citizens.

For asylum seekers who were able to reach Australia, despite the introduction of the new DORS committee, obvious deficiencies in process persisted.[48] These included the DORS Committee's complete lack of independence from the Department; the lack of transparency or requirement for reasons;[49] the fact that the Committee was both the original decision-making body and the reviewing body; and the informal nature of the Committee, which effectively entailed that only applicants with knowledge and the correct contacts had access to the system.[50] The DORS Committee remained in place as the key body determining refugee status until 1990. Although there were changes to the way the Committee functioned, these changes – like the body itself – were policy based and not codified.

The difficulty of charting the basis upon which decisions to grant status or entry permits were made in this period reveals the persistence of executive discretion. The administrative arrangements, recommendations and decisions were scantly documented.[51] Patricia Hyndman writes that decisions were made on the basis of 'procedures and guidelines set out in departmental manuals and circulars', which were amended frequently.[52] Andreas Schloenhardt records that, in practice, political considerations strongly influenced the DORS determinations,[53] claiming 'the establishment of the DORS crystallised an increasingly severe approach of the Government to refugees; it was clear that refugees were just another, more difficult, class of immigrants and not a humanitarian exception'.[54] There was

[45] *Migration Act 1958* (Cth) s 6A(1)(c) (in time at 1980); Hyndman, above n 8, 734. The same section set out that if the Minister granted a person territorial asylum or determined there were 'strong compassionate grounds or humanitarian grounds' for entry, an entry permit could also be issued.

[46] Schloenhardt, above n 14, 39.

[47] *Immigration (Unauthorised Arrivals) Act 1980* (Cth) ss 6, 8; ibid 38.

[48] Relevantly, an applicant could request an informal review of the Committee's determination, in which case the DIEA or the Minister could, but was not required to, refer the matter back to the Committee: Hyndman, above n 8, 746. There was also the possibility of judicial review under the *Administrative Decisions (Judicial Review) Act 1977* (Cth). This avenue of appeal was rarely accessed, particularly up until the late 1980s: ibid 749.

[49] Note, though, that since *Minister for Immigration and Ethnic Affairs v Mayer* (1985) 57 CLR 290, the Minister must give reasons if requested to do so.

[50] Hyndman, above n 8, 746; citing the Australian Human Rights Commission, *Human Rights and the Migration Act*, Report No. 13, Australian Government Publishing Service (April 1985) [316]. Complaints could also be made to the Commonwealth Ombudsman.

[51] Germov and Motta, above n 6, 66.

[52] Hyndman, above n 8, 725. Some of these manuals produced by the DIEA included the *Determination of Refugee Status: Notes for the Guidance of Interviewing Officers* and *Examination of Passengers and Crew at Airports*. In a reminder of pre-Internet days, Hyndman also notes these manuals were apparently available for inspection at DIEA offices and government bookshops: at 725–26.

[53] Schloenhardt, above n 14, 37.

[54] Ibid.

neither any actual independence nor an attempt to create any semblance of it.[55] Certainly, the statutory right to an oral hearing before any kind of decision-maker was not included with the introduction of the DORS Committee.[56]

Part of the reason for the absence of a clearer legislative or codified framework into the early 1980s, to limit and control refugee entry, was the low number of onshore or boat arrivals. The government and media response reflected and generated deeply racialised anxieties about 'new' refugee arrivals. The early boat arrivals were described as a potential 'invasion' and the *Melbourne Sun* described the Vietnamese refugees as 'a trickle of unannounced visitors' that could become a 'tide of human flotsam'.[57] Indeed, Australia had only recently been identified as a 'first destination' for onshore Indo-Chinese refugee applicants.[58] Approximately 350 arrivals per year was a significant spike in onshore arrivals at the time, and Grewcock notes that in the early 1980s, the Government began with 'more systemic' attempts to question the legitimacy of Indo-Chinese refugee claims.[59] At this time, the concept of 'queue jumping' acquired a form of 'official sanction' and was used by Immigration Minister MacPhee in March 1982 in order to justify a review of refugee policy for the purpose of 'ensur[ing] that only genuine refugees are admitted under Australia's refugee programs'.[60]

3.1.2 *Orality and the Emergence of the RSD Oral Hearing*

Australia's relatively new executive process for onshore RSD was addressed in a number of reports in the 1980s.[61] In 1988, the then-Labor Government commissioned an independent committee to 'undertake a broad ranging look at its immigration policies'.[62] The committee's report, 'Immigration: A Commitment to Australia' (Fitzgerald Inquiry report), was expansive, and produced a model migration bill that led to a significant overhaul of the existing *Migration Act*.[63] The Fitzgerald Inquiry report declared that while the 'exodus' from

[55] Ibid.

[56] These changes took place in the broader context of the expansion of administrative justice and of mechanisms for the review of administrative decisions in Australia. See generally John Griffiths, 'Australian Administrative Law: Institutions, Reforms and Impact' (1985) 63(4) *Public Administration* 445.

[57] Viviani, above n 17, 69–70.

[58] Between April 1976 and August 1981, 56 boats arrived, carrying 2,100 people. The primary source of Indo-Chinese arrivals in this era was not a consequence of boat arrivals but rather offshore refugees accepted by the Australian Government. In roughly the same period (1974–81), 51,780 Indo-Chinese refugees were resettled in Australia: Department of Immigration and Ethnic Affairs, *Review of Activities to 30 June 1981* (Australian Government Publishing Service, 1981); see also Grewcock, above n 10, chapter 3.

[59] Grewcock, above n 10, 100.

[60] Department of Immigration and Ethnic Affairs, 'Annual Report 1983' (Australian Government Publishing Service, 1983) 27; and see Grewcock, above n 10, 100.

[61] For example, in 1986, the Administrative Review Council reported there was a need for an independent mechanism to review refugee determinations and noted that 'the [DORS] Committee cannot be said to provide an independent review of its own primary decisions': Administrative Review Council, 'Review of Migration Decisions' (Australian Government Publishing Service, 1986) 90.

[62] Fitzgerald Committee to Advise on Australia's Immigration Policies, 'Immigration: A Commitment to Australia' (Australian Government Publishing Service, 1988) ix.

[63] Minister for Immigration, Local Government and Ethnic Affairs and Senator the Hon Robert Ray, 'Minister Ray Hails Start of New Era in Immigration' (Media Release, 18 December 1989).

Indo-China had begun to dwindle, the 'seepage of people is nonetheless taxing the humane reception policies of neighbouring countries and exacerbating regional tensions'.[64] The report, which demonstrated the increasing hostility towards onshore arrivals, went on to note that the outflow was also 'of an increasingly migratory character'.[65] Obviously not predicting the influx of onshore applicants that would occur in the early 1990s, the report made its recommendation as follows:

> While recognising the importance of responding to refugee situations in our region, the Committee recommends that from 1988/89 Australia gradually disengage itself from Indochinese resettlement, in line with the decreasing outflow and diminishing numbers of refugees from Indochina and in the context of positive strategies for solutions to this problem.[66]

Soon after the publication of the report and this recommendation, in 1989 and the early 1990s numbers of onshore asylum seekers increased, and the government moved to codify and formalise RSD processes. Until 1989, there had been fewer than 500 refugee applications per year. Then, in 1989–90, there were 12,130 applications received, and in 1990–91, the number of onshore applications reached 16,428.[67] These figures are commonly explained as representing the large numbers of asylum seekers who fled China in the wake of the Tiananmen Square massacre and those who left former Soviet Bloc countries upon the lifting of exit restrictions at the end of the Cold War.[68] As part of the round of legislative amendments that followed the Fitzgerald Inquiry report, the Migration Regulations 1989 (Cth) were gazetted. These regulations, for the first time, provided transparent guidelines as to how refugee status was to be determined, reviewed and to whom it was to be granted.[69] The review procedure remained in place only briefly, as the immediate predecessor of the Refugee Review Tribunal, which began operating in 1993.[70]

A key part of the new procedure in this period involved further 'streamlining' of the primary decision-making stage: the distinction between the decision-maker and the case officer was removed. And, from 1992, all applicants were to be given an interview, along with 'an opportunity to comment during the interview and afterwards on any adverse material'.[71] The reforms also included the Minister's creation of the Refugee Status Review Committee (RSRC), the first separate body conducting a form of merits review of refugee determinations.[72] This new system for in-house review of primary refugee status decisions, like the DORS Committee with primary determinations, did not have the power to make final determinations; rather, it made non-binding recommendations to the

64 Fitzgerald Committee to Advise on Australia's Immigration Policies, above n 62, 83.

65 Fitzgerald Committee to Advise on Australia's Immigration Policies, above n 62.

66 Ibid 84.

67 Of which 77 per cent were from the People's Republic of China: Germov and Motta, above n 6, 34; Schloenhardt, above n 14, 42. Many of the applicants were Chinese citizens who initially entered the country as students and who, as a consequence of Tiananmen Square, made *sur place* refugee claims.

68 Schloenhardt, above n 14, 40–43.

69 Germov and Motta, above n 6, 39.

70 Ibid 68.

71 Ibid.

72 Jean-Pierre Fonteyne, 'Refugee Determination in Australia: An Overview' (1994) 6 *International Journal of Refugee Law* 253, 255.

Minister's delegate.[73] The RSRC, then, remained a body with no statutory basis[74] and Savitri Taylor notes that the RSRC 'certainly never gave the claimant an oral hearing'.[75] However, where required, the original decision-maker (the departmental delegate) could be invited by the RSRC to 'make a presentation' in regards to the assessment of the case.[76] If an RSRC panel did have questions for an applicant, it could request a departmental officer to conduct an interview with the applicant.[77]

As these new procedures were established in the early 1990s, and onshore refugee applicants were starting to number in the thousands rather than hundreds, the conditions and criteria for protection-related entry permits were constantly changing.[78] Then, with the passage of the *Migration Reform Act 1992* (Cth), the Government completely overhauled the system that had been built upon the 1989 Regulations.[79] These amendments gave rise to a process involving both an interview before a departmental delegate in the first instance as well as an oral hearing before the RRT, which was to conduct administrative review.[80] Critically, the same Act *also* introduced the policy that those arriving by boat and without documentation were to be subject to mandatory detention.[81] As such, one of Australia's harshest 'deterrence' policies, which persists under current law, was introduced alongside the introduction of the oral hearing and a semi-independent merits review mechanism.

In July 1992, the Minister announced that the RRT would function as a specialist, independent administrative tribunal and would take over the functions of the RSRC.[82] As such, beginning in July 1993, it would be the body responsible for reviewing all primary decisions made by the delegates of the Minister. The newly formed Tribunal was 'charged with conducting reviews *on the merits* of adverse departmental decisions in refugee determination cases'; this function continued as the Tribunal's primary function up to its incorporation into the AAT in 2015.[83] In the second reading speech for the *Migration Reform Act 1992* (Cth) Gerard Hand, then Immigration Minister, stated that 'credible independent merits review will ensure that the Government's clear intentions in relation to controlling entry to Australia, as set out in the *Migration Act*, are not eroded by narrow judicial interpretations'.[84] The comment reflected both the Government's border control

[73] Ibid. These RSRC operated from 1990 until 1 July 1993.

[74] Savitri Taylor, 'The Right to Review in the Australian On-Shore Refugee Status Determination Process: Is It an Adequate Procedural Safeguard against Refoulement?' (1993) 22 *Federal Law Review* 300, 315.

[75] Ibid 317.

[76] Ibid.

[77] Ibid 317, 323.

[78] Germov and Motta, above n 6, 41–43.

[79] Ibid 43. Note, though, that much of the Act did not come into force until 1994, at which time it had been amended by the *Migration Legislation Amendment Act 1994* (Cth).

[80] *Migration Reform Act 1992* (Cth). Additionally in 1991, the *Migration Act* finally incorporated, by direct reference, the full definition of a refugee as set out in the Refugee Convention and the 1967 Protocol: *Migration Amendment Act 1991* (Cth); *Migration Act 1958* (Cth) s 36(1), (2) (in time at 1991).

[81] *Migration Reform Act 1992* (Cth) s 13.

[82] Susan Kneebone, 'The Refugee Review Tribunal and the Assessment of Credibility: An Inquisitorial Role' (1998) 5 *Australian Journal of Administrative Law* 78, 79; Gerard Hand, Minister for Immigration, 'Migration Reform Bill 1992 Second Reading Speech' (4 November 1992).

[83] Fonteyne, above n 72, 255.

[84] Gerard Hand, Minister for Immigration, above n 82.

policy orientation and rhetoric as well as the growing tension between the executive and judiciary over the regulation of migration decision-making.

The Tribunal differed from the RSRC in significant ways. It was able to make final determinations about whether a decision would be remitted for redetermination, rather than simply make recommendations to the Minister; and it was a statutory body, which was to operate quasi-independently of the Department of Immigration. Unlike the RSRC, it was to make determinations with single-member benches, and it no longer had the power to make recommendations to the Minister for the exercise of discretion in humanitarian cases falling outside the Convention definition.[85] From the outset, the RRT was set up as an inquisitorial tribunal and was entitled to conduct its own inquiries. The applicant made all initial submissions in writing and was then given an opportunity to appear before the decision-maker at an oral hearing, unless a positive decision could be made on the papers.[86] The idea that the Tribunal was to be 'fair, just, economical, informal and quick' was stated in the original enabling legislation and this remained as the language and framing of the AAT, which succeeded the RRT.[87] Other features of the Tribunal that still govern its operation were that it was not bound by 'technicalities, legal forms, or rules of justice' and that it was to act according to principles of 'substantial justice and the individual merits of the case'.[88]

Jean-Pierre Fonteyne argues that the Tribunal was initially established partially in reaction to claims that the RSRC was 'stacked' with members of the Department of Immigration.[89] This basis for reform was echoed in the key justification for the much later abolition of the AAT, announced in 2022, being decision-makers' perceived lack of independence from and close connections to sitting governments. In the early 1990s, those critical of the former RSRC voiced concerns that if staff were simply transferred from the former RSRC to the Tribunal, then it too would be 'infected' in the way that the RSRC had been.[90] The Tribunal was indeed established in part because of the perceived lack of independence of the RSRC, as well as the fact that the Committee's decisions did not compel the Minister to grant status to those recognised as meeting the refugee definition.[91] During a hearing before the Joint Standing Committee on Migration Regulations, the Department explained this as follows:

> the Tribunal will do exactly the same job but will be seen to be more transparent and fairer than the RSRC, which in the minds of our critics is not transparent and not fair. The public perception of the unfairness of the RSRC is, presumably based on the ideas that this is a committee of bureaucrats.[92]

[85] Fonteyne, above n 72, 255.

[86] Ibid 256. Fonteyne notes that the legislation set out that there was no right to legal representation but that 'most applicants are in practice accompanied by a legal advisor at Tribunal hearings': at 256.

[87] In relation to the Migration and Refugee Division of the AAT, see *Administrative Appeals Tribunal Act* (Cth) s 2A (in time at 2022).

[88] *Migration Act 1958* (Cth) s 420 as at April 2015, amended by *Tribunals Amalgamation Act 2015* (Cth).

[89] Fonteyne, above n 72, 257.

[90] Ibid 257–58. See also Taylor, above n 74, 319.

[91] Germov and Motta, above n 6, 73.

[92] Joint Standing Committee on Migration Regulations, *Australia's Refugee and Humanitarian System: Achieving a Balance between Refuge and Control* (Australian Government Publishing Service, 1992) 127 (in camera evidence).

Alongside public opinion focused on the independence of RSRC, improving the fairness of the review process was, for the government, also about attempts to keep asylum appeals out of the court system and away from judicial interference. Fonteyne writes that a further key factor that led to the establishment of the RRT was ongoing government concern with 'what it viewed as the excessive use of the regular court system by unsuccessful refugee applicants – and the degree of success in persuading the courts to overturn [negative] departmental review determinations'.[93] Fonteyne also observes the connection between the two goals of improving perceived fairness and limiting the judicial review of decisions. The Department hoped that the new Tribunal and its de novo review role and oral hearing would assuage concerns about the 'bias' of departmental employees and that it would be 'perceived as sufficiently independent from the Department, so as to have a significant impact on the frequency with which rejected applicants would turn to the courts'.[94] The question of the independence of refugee decision-makers however persisted as a major issue, and, as noted, came to encompass debates about the AAT's appointment process for members, and was the subject of a major statutory review of the AAT in 2019[95] – but I return to later developments in Section 3.3.

The brief history above reveals that the creation of a fulsome oral hearing for protection visa applications, one that takes place before a decision-maker and includes rights to quasi-independent administrative review and a review hearing, was slow to come to Australia. It seems fair to observe that the Tribunal was created in a climate of animosity among legal professionals, advocates and the government, and in 'an atmosphere of concern about the cost of processing increased numbers of refugees in the period of the post-Tiananmen Square incident'.[96] The extent to which the RRT provided full merits review and an oral hearing was the result of pressure placed on the government for a fairer, transparent and more independent review process. The hearing also reflected government interest in maintaining executive control over the border, onshore determination processes and in quarantining decisions, as much as possible, from judicial review.[97] Resonating with a theme that reappears throughout the book, in Minister Hand's second reading speech for the *Migration Reform Act 1992* (Cth) he explicitly cast the new RSD process *as* a mechanism for border control,

93 Fonteyne, above n 72, 258.

94 Ibid. In fact, the opposite transpired, and given the right to appeal directly to the Court from the Tribunal, the number of appeals rose from 229 cases in 1991–92 to 2,339 in 1992–93: Schloenhardt, above n 14, 47.

95 Ian Callinan AC QC, 'Report on the Statutory Review of the Tribunals Amalgamation Act 2015' (Attorney-General's Department, 2019). One 2022 study suggested that 21 per cent of AAT members 'have a direct political affiliation, [with] almost all being to the [conservative] Coalition Government that has appointed them': Danielle Wood, Owain Emslie and Rebecca Joiner, 'Towards a Better AAT Appointments Process: Submission to the Senate Standing Committee Inquiry into the Performance and Integrity of Australia's Administrative Review System' (Grattan Institute, 24 November 2021) 3.

96 Kneebone, above n 82, 80. As noted above, the annual number of onshore arrivals had jumped from 500 in the mid-1980s to upwards of 10,000 arrivals per year in the early 1990s: Glenn Nicholls, 'Unsettling Admissions: Asylum Seekers in Australia' (1998) 11(1) *Journal of Refugee Studies* 61, 62; Joint Standing Committee on Migration Regulations, above n 92, [6.49].

97 On the battle between the executive and judiciary for power over final RSD decisions in Australia, see Crock, above n 12.

emphasising that the new Tribunal would 'lead to greater precision in our efforts to control the border'.[98]

The codification of RSD took place as Australia emerged as a country of first asylum. It reflected government concerns about the growing numbers of onshore refugees and its desire to settle only 'genuine' refugees from the region, alongside the need for a more independent, fair and transparent process. Indeed, there had been little need for a codified process, or an oral hearing, when the number of onshore arrivals was small and the government maintained full, executive discretion over which refugees Australia accepted and on what terms. Once introduced, the oral hearing and oral testimony provided by the applicant to an executive decision-maker became an essential aspect of RSD, and its improved procedural fairness and legitimacy. The hearings, at first instance and before the RRT, were presented by government as sites where claims could be decided fairly and efficiently within the executive arm, as well as where the government could both standardise and control the terms of decision-making and administrative review.

3.2 Refugee Determination and the Oral Hearing in Canada

3.2.1 The Beginnings of a Refugee Policy

The emergence of the RSD oral hearing charted a different course in Canada. Its introduction was shaped by both the protections provided under the *Canadian Charter of Rights and Freedoms* and judicial intervention into RSD processes. Similar geopolitical factors and government concerns, however, shape both histories. James Hathaway describes Canadian refugee policy up to the early 1990s as having evolved through 'three distinct traditions'.[99] Like in pre–World War II Australia, in the first identified stage, humanitarian entrants to Canada applied for admission under Canada's general immigration scheme. Hathaway describes this first tradition of refugee protection, which lasted until the mid-1960s, as 'a matter of immigration control'. The other two 'traditions' that Hathaway identifies are *compliance* with international obligations, which lasted from the 1960s through 1990s, and then, from the 1990s onwards, *collective deterrence*, characterised amongst other things by a constraining of domestic determination procedures. Hathaway, writing in 1992, described this final tradition as a prediction of what was to come and there is little to contradict his forecast that after the 1990s, Canada's 'asylum dilemma' would 'centre on the viability of a continued commitment to multilateral refugee protection as contemplated by the Refugees Convention in the context of an effective renunciation of the responsibility by many of [Canada's] traditional [European] allies'.[100]

As in Australia, the codification and regulation of RSD in Canada came late due to the persistence of the 'immigration control' period. Though, when codification finally was introduced, the oral hearing in Canada set a new high watermark of procedural fairness even as it attempted to preserve government control over refugee status determinations. Indeed, the introduction of the oral hearing took place as Canada moved into the period identified by Hathaway as marked by collective deterrence. As with the history of the Australian oral hearing, the Canadian hearing was accompanied by major improvements in

98 Gerard Hand, Minister for Immigration, above n 82.
99 Hathaway, above n 5, 71.
100 Ibid 72.

the overall fairness of RSD, but simultaneously the new procedure was presented as a means to ensure that only 'genuine' inland refugee applicants accessed Canadian protection.[101]

In the first tradition that Hathaway identifies, that of 'immigration control' in the period following World War II, Canadian refugee policy and practice were remarkably similar to policy and practice in Australia. Even though there were 'millions of Europeans to be protected, Canada responded cautiously by seeking out only the most "adaptable" European refugees from among those in need of resettlement'.[102] Refugee intake and selection as connected to nation-building projects and racist exclusions within migration policy was a defining aspect of settler-colonial practice, and of the nexus between migration policy and 'humanitarian' programs in both Australia and Canada. As in Australia, the refugees that Canada accepted were viewed as capable of assimilation and were not expected to place major demands on national resources.[103] And, like Australia, 'Canada refused to admit any of the "hardcore" European refugee population, including thousands of persons whose age, illness or handicap made them undesirable immigrants'.[104] So, while Canada established a number of situation-specific refugee programs throughout the early 1970s,[105] the refugees who were admitted were selected according to the criteria governing Canada's general immigration program. Indeed, Gerald Dirks traces Canada's particular reluctance to accept refugees who could not assist with working the land or growing the nation's commerce in the early twentieth century, through to the anti-Semitism of the 1930s, as well as Canada's reluctance to sign on to permanent international institutions established to care for refugees and migrants post World War II.[106]

In the late 1980s, Canada came to be a more prominent country of first asylum, even though throughout the early 1980s the number of onshore claims was still small in proportion to Canada's broader refugee program.[107] Before this period, although Canada was one of the key participating states in drafting the Refugee Convention, it did not sign the final version of the accord until 1969. At the heart of the decision not to sign the Refugee Convention were departmental and government concerns about the Refugee Convention's open-ended definition of 'refugee' and the implication that Canada would be bound to admit 'Asiatic' refugees under proper domestic implementation of the definition.[108] The scope of Canada's existing refugee programs allowed for a greater number of admissions

[101] Gerald E Dirks, *Controversy and Complexity: Canadian Immigration Policy during the 1980s* (McGill-Queen's University Press, 1995) 60–91.

[102] Hathaway, above n 5, 72. See generally David Brian Dewitt and John J Kirton, *Canada as a Principal Power: A Study in Foreign Policy and International Relations* (Wiley, 1983).

[103] Hathaway, above n 5, 72.

[104] Ibid.

[105] For refugees fleeing former Czechoslovakia and Hungary, and for Ugandan Asians, for example: Ibid. For details of each program, see Harold Troper, 'Canada's Immigration Policy since 1945' (1993) 48(2) *International Journal: Canada's Journal of Global Policy Analysis* 255.

[106] Gerald Dirks, *Canada's Refugee Policy: Indifference or Opportunism* (McGill-Queens University Press, 1977).

[107] Due to extensive offshore programs, during the 1980s (specifically 1988), Canada ranked fifth in the world for per-capita refugee intake, but in roughly the same period, onshore refugee intake still averaged well below 1,000 per annum from 1981 to 1984: James C Hathaway, 'Selective Concern: An Overview of Refugee Law in Canada' (1987) 33 *McGill Law Journal* 676, 686.

[108] Hathaway, above n 5, 74 citing Memorandum to the Minister of Citizenship and Immigration, File 566-10 (19 January 1953); Memorandum to the Minister of Citizenship and Immigration from Laval Fortier, Deputy Minister of Citizenship and Immigration, File 566-10 (29 May 1958).

than existed in many Convention-signatory states. Nonetheless, several successive immigration ministers argued against signing on the racist grounds that the refugee definition was in conflict with Canada's restrictive immigration legislation, and that the Refugee Convention's rule of *non-refoulment* had 'undesirable' implications for applicants within Canadian territory.[109] Indeed, in the period up to the early 1970s, decisions regarding status and protection remained at the discretion of the executive. The Refugee Convention was cast as undermining exclusionary raced-based – or rather, openly racist – policy objectives.[110]

A 1966 White Paper on Immigration led to a shift in policy and an expansion of the Canadian post-war definition of a refugee.[111] The White Paper found that Canada's refugee definition was 'orientated towards Europe at a time when we boast a global view' and that the existing statutory definition appeared to be 'exclusive and politically orientated' and 'very restricted in time'.[112] The White Paper led to Canada's ascension to both the Refugee Convention and its 1967 Protocol in 1969[113] and to the first incorporation of a Convention-based definition of a refugee into Canadian law in 1973.[114] Despite the above statutory reforms in 1973,[115] Canada's onshore refugee policy remained a matter of executive discretion. The then Immigration Appeal Board had the power to apply an enacted version of the Refugee Convention definition; however, it was not bound to do so, and the matter of refugee protection could only be raised on appeal rather than at the initial stage of an application.[116]

3.2.2 *The* Singh *Decision and the Establishment of the Oral Hearing*

The first formal process to adjudicate asylum claims in Canada came with the 1976 *Immigration Act*.[117] Under the *Immigration Act 1976*, the Refugee Status Advisory Committee (RSAC) was responsible for identifying refugees in the first instance. In coming to its recommendation, the Committee reviewed a transcript of an applicant's formal examination under oath and then provided an opinion to the Minister.[118] While the

109 Ibid 74–75. This was the case despite opposing views from Canada's Department of External Affairs, which argued ascension to the Refugee Convention was required to improve Canada's international standing and influence: 75.

110 Ibid 74–75; see also Marilyn Lake and Henry Reynolds, *Drawing the Global Colour Line: White Men's Countries and the Question of Racial Equality* (Melbourne University Publishing, 2008); Audrey Macklin, 'Asylum and the Rule of Law in Canada: Hearing the Other (Side)' in Susan Kneebone (ed), *Refugees, Asylum Seekers and the Rule of Law: Comparative Perspectives* (Cambridge University Press, 2009) 78.

111 Jean Marchand, 'White Paper on Immigration' (Department of Manpower and Immigration, 1966); cited in Christopher J Wydrzynski, 'Refugees and the Immigration Act' (1979) 25 *McGill Law Journal* 154, 159; see also Kelley and Trebilcock, above n 4, 352–58.

112 AJ Banerd, 'Memorandum to the Director, Planning Branch' (Department of Manpower and Immigration, 23 November 1967) 8; cited in Hathaway, above n 5, 75; see also Marchand, above n 111.

113 Gerald Dirks, 'The Green Paper and Canadian Refugee Policy' (1975) 7 *Canadian Ethnic Studies* 61.

114 *An Act to Amend the Immigration Appeal Board Act*, SC 1973–74, c 27.

115 Hathaway, above n 107, 683–84; see also Wydrzynski, above n 111.

116 *Immigration Appeal Board Act*, SC 1966–67, c 90, s 11.

117 *Immigration Act*, SC 1976–77, c 52.

118 Unsuccessful applicants could make an application on humanitarian and compassionate grounds to the Special Review Committee: Kelley and Trebilcock, above n 4, 404.

applicant was required to give evidence to a government officer, there was no formal oral hearing before a decision-maker.[119] Like Australia in this period, the Canadian Government sought to exert control over onshore refugee arrivals as the number of arrivals increased; and then, as now, the Canadian Government 'imposed selective visa controls which prevented many refugees from coming to Canada in order to present a claim for asylum'.[120] The 1976 *Immigration Act* also incorporated into Canadian law a detailed expression of the Convention refugee definition, rather than a mere reference to it. At this time, many bureaucrats and politicians nonetheless persisted in trying to preserve complete executive discretion over refugee decision-making, as well as to maintain a broadly protectionist stance vis-à-vis onshore claimants. As Hathaway explains:

> Persons in Canada who met the Convention definition as codified in the [1976 Immigration] Act were to be protected from removal to a country in which persecution was feared, but the decision to grant or withhold permanent resident status remained, at least in theory, an immigration prerogative.[121]

The RSAC remained in place until the Government's major reform of refugee determination in response to the 1985 Supreme Court of Canada decision, *Singh v Minister for Employment and Immigration*.[122] In the landmark *Singh* decision, the Supreme Court of Canada held that Canada's existing RSD procedures breached the principles of fundamental justice, set out in section 7 of the *Canadian Charter of Rights and Freedoms*, by failing to grant applicants an oral hearing before a decision-maker at any point in the decision-making process.[123] Notably, the Government had argued in *Singh* that the existing process did not breach principles of fundamental justice, or in the alternative that if they were breached, under section 1 of the *Charter*, oral hearings would be too resource-intensive to be practicable.[124]

In the *Singh* decision, Justice Wilson, writing on behalf of Chief Justice Dickson and Justice Lamer, set out that

> where a serious issue of credibility is involved, fundamental justice requires that credibility be determined on the basis of an oral hearing. Appellate courts are well aware of the inherent weakness of written transcripts where questions of credibility are at stake and thus are extremely loath to review the findings of tribunals, which have had the benefit of hearing the testimony of witnesses in person. I find it difficult to conceive of a situation in which compliance with fundamental justice could be achieved by a tribunal making significant findings of credibility solely on the basis of written submissions.[125]

The Canadian Government's response was 'a complete overhaul' of the refugee determination process in 1987, including passing provisions for the introduction of

119 Hathaway, above n 107, 684.
120 Ibid 704.
121 Hathaway, above n 5, 77.
122 *Singh v Minister for Employment and Immigration* (1985) 1 SCR 177.
123 Ibid.
124 The Supreme Court rejected these arguments: ibid 218–19.
125 Ibid 213–14; citing *Stein v The Ship 'Kathy K'* (1976) 2 SCR 802, 806–08.

a tribunal process for first-instance refugee determinations.[126] In response to *Singh*, in 1989, the Immigration and Refugee Board (IRB) began operating. The Convention Refugee Determination Division (CRDD) of the IRB was responsible for determining refugee applications.[127] Under the new procedure, applicants appeared before an immigration adjudicator, housed within the Canadian immigration department, Immigration Canada, in order to be screened into or out of the process. Applicants who were determined to be eligible for an oral hearing then appeared before a two-member panel of the CRDD. The hearing process was intended to be non-adversarial and a member of the Refugee Hearing Office acted as counsel to the CRDD panel. In order for a positive determination to be made, only one of the two panel members was required to find in the applicant's favour. Applicants were granted access to interpreters as a matter of right, and to legal aid in certain provinces.[128]

Hathaway identifies the 1987 reforms of the *Immigration Act* as part of a 'new wave of control mechanisms'.[129] He writes that the benefits of the new CRDD and introduction of the oral hearing 'were overshadowed' by the government's 'unfortunate' decision to advance a distinctly protectionist agenda as part of the same legislative reform that established the CRDD'.[130] The new legislation included granting the Immigration Minister the right to interdict ships carrying undocumented aliens and turn them back without determining any claims to protection; and also introduced 'safe third country' provisions and criminal sanctions for people smuggling.[131] The protectionist context of the CRDD's introduction conformed with Canadian Government policy at the time, which remained primarily geared towards expanding offshore rather than onshore programs.[132] Indeed, in the year of the *Singh* hearing and the year following the decision, the number of onshore claimants drastically increased, from 8,400 in 1985 to 18,000 in 1986, with projections at the time of

[126] Bill C-55, *An Act to Amend the Immigration Act, 1976 and to Amend other Acts in Consequence Thereof*, 2d Sess, 33d Parl, 1986–87 ('Bill C-55'); Catherine Dauvergne, 'How the Charter Has Failed Non-Citizens in Canada: Reviewing Thirty Years of Supreme Court of Canada Jurisprudence' (2013) 58(3) *McGill Law Journal* 663, 668; *Singh v Minister for Employment and Immigration* (1985) 1 SCR 177, 213–14.

[127] The CRDD became the Refugee Protection Division of the IRB in 2002 under the *Immigration and Refugee Protection Act* (IRPA).

[128] See *Immigration Act*, SC 1976–77, c 52, s 69.1(8), which set out that one member of the Refugee Division may hear and determine a claim where the claimant consents. See also Peter W Billings, 'A Comparative Analysis of Administrative and Adjudicative Systems for Determining Asylum Claims' (2000) 52 *Administrative Law Review* 253, 280–81.

[129] Hathaway, above n 107, 704.

[130] Hathaway, above n 5, 81.

[131] Bill C-84, *An Act to Amend the Immigration Act, 1976 and the Criminal Code in Consequence Thereof*, 2d Sess, 33d Parl, 1986–87 ('Bill C-84'). 'Safe third country' rules are discussed in detail in chapter 3, but generally require refugee applicants to lodge their claim in the first country of arrival where effective protection could be sought, and can operate to bar or limit an application if protection is not claimed at the earliest opportunity.

[132] In this period, the Government also implemented an Expedited Process within the CRDD, under which a Refugee Hearing Officer could recommend a claimant for CRDD recognition. Claimants from major source countries with high acceptance rates were eligible. The reform was positive for the affected groups. However, the primary motivation for the process was the imperative of managing the number of applications before the CRDD, which had finalised over 21,000 claims from over 100 states in its first two years: Hathaway, above n 5, 83.

up to 25,000 claims in 1987.[133] And finally, judicial appeal rights from both the first-stage eligibility interview and the CRDD determination were limited. Then, as now, applicants required special leave to appeal to the Federal Court of Canada, and while the eligibility determination could be appealed, such an appeal would not ordinarily stay a removal order.[134] Simultaneously, though, the form of the new hearing and process – particularly the two-member panel and a quasi-judicial process at first instance – was at the time a high watermark of quality in RSD processing.[135] The new process was, 'widely regarded as one of the fairest refugee determination processes in the world'.[136] Unlike in Australia, at the time of its introduction, the hearing was not explicitly framed as a means to preserve, as efficiently as possible, executive control of refugee determinations and refugee acceptance rates throughout the late 1980s remained high.

In Australia, the RRT was not introduced by means of a government-opposed judicial ruling.[137] Nonetheless, in both jurisdictions, an oral hearing came about in response to criticism of existing, executive forms of RSD. In Australia, the government sought to introduce reforms that preserved executive discretion as much as possible whilst remaining true to the policy goal of creating fair determination procedures and finding a means to manage its obligations under the Refugee Convention. In Canada, in spite of moves towards broader policies of deterrence, at the time of its implementation in 1987, Canada's system of RSD was indeed regarded as 'world-class' and the 'Rolls Royce' of RSD systems.[138] The two-member constitution of first-instance decision-making panels, and the requirement that only one decision-maker find in the applicant's favour, was akin to a direct implementation of the 'benefit of the doubt' standard that applies to refugee status decision-making.[139] Equally, providing the applicant with a full oral hearing at first instance, rather than upon review, has been recognised as a form of RSD best practice,[140] which not only saves resources lost through poor-quality first-instance determinations, but also entails that the applicant is able to present a claim before a quasi-independent body with greater procedural fairness protections from the outset. In reflecting on the *Singh* decision almost three decades later, Dauvergne writes that *Singh* has become part of the mythic foundation of Canadian

[133] Hathaway, above n 107, 705.

[134] Hathaway, above n 5, 83.

[135] See Jessica Hambly, Nick Gill and Lorenzo Vianelli, 'Using Multi-member Panels to Tackle RSD Complexities' (2020) 65 *Forced Migration Review* 4.

[136] Dauvergne, above n 126, 668.

[137] Billings, above n 128, 282. In Australia, shortly before the RRT was established, a case arguing that natural justice required that each refugee claimant be given an oral hearing failed before the Federal Court of Australia: *Zhang De Yong* (1993) 118 ALR 165 at 179; see also *Simsek v MacPhee* (1982) 148 CLR 636. *Chen v Minister for Immigration and Ethnic Affairs* (1994) 48 FCR 591 held that there was to be an oral hearing for applicants seeking review before the RSRC.

[138] See Macklin, above n 110; Catherine Dauvergne, 'Evaluating Canada's New Immigration and Refugee Protection Act in Its Global Context' (2003) 41 *Alberta Law Review* 725.

[139] See François Crépeau and Delphine Nakache, 'Critical Spaces in the Canadian Refugee Determination System: 1989–2002' (2008) 20(1) *International Journal of Refugee Law* 50, 88–89; Jenni Millbank, '"The Ring of Truth": A Case Study of Credibility Assessment in Particular Social Group Refugee Determinations' (2009) 21(1) *International Journal of Refugee Law* 1, 30.

[140] Millbank, above n 139, 27.

refugee law. The anniversary of its handing down is celebrated annually by the advocacy community in Canada as Refugee Rights Day.[141]

The early years of refugee determinations before the IRB were exemplary, in terms of RSD processes, especially in relation to the oral hearing.[142] However, the influence of the Canadian Government and the executive on the IRB, and especially on refugee decision-making, proved to be an ongoing and significant issue. As with Australia, the lack of independence from government, particularly in the form of member appointments, undermined the standard of procedural fairness afforded to refugee applicants as well as perceptions of the oral hearing as granting applicants a meaningful right to be heard. In analysing the IRB's operation from 1989 to 2002, François Crépeau and Delphine Nakache explain the 'difficulties' associated with the IRB as an institution in that period. These difficulties included the exceptionally politicised nature of appointments to the IRB and the ways in which this affected the day-to-day functioning of the institution. Crépeau and Nakache observe that:

> [P]olitical patronage with regard to appointments and renewals infringe[d] on this basic principle of independence ... Similarly, although the right to be heard was clearly a vital strength of the Board system, it was frequently compromised by the disrespectful or biased attitudes of certain Board members, [and] the use of hostile and aggressive cross-examination techniques by certain Refugee Protection Officers ...[143]

Criticisms levelled at the IRB in the early 1990s also reveal that the Board was implicated in the state's increasing attempts to limit and discredit onshore refugee claims.[144] At that time, the Hathaway review was commissioned in response to allegations that refugee hearing officers had been 'meeting privately' to discuss cases of individual refugee claimants with members of the IRB; and to allegations that 'the IRB had taken steps to establish [the] Refugee Analysis Liaison Unit (RALU)' whose reports would be provided to refugee hearing officers to assist them in *contesting* applications for refugee status.[145] The Hathaway review fits within a broader literature that has tracked the extent to which relentless political interventions into the executive and administrative spaces of migration determination have compromised these spaces and members' ability to meet basic standards of independence, up until the present day .[146]

[141] Dauvergne, above n 126, 668–69. Dauvergne notes that the decision also became part of the *Charter* mythology more generally, because in it, the Supreme Court radically held that that *Charter* applied to every person physically present in Canada, rather than just to Canadian citizens; *Singh v Minister for Employment and Immigration* (1985) 1 SCR 177, 209.

[142] See Dauvergne, above n 2, 78–80.

[143] Crépeau and Nakache, above n 139, 57.

[144] Crépeau and Nakache, above n 139.

[145] James C Hathaway, 'Rebuilding Trust: A Report of the Review of Fundamental Justice in Information Gathering and Dissemination at the Immigration and Refugee Board of Canada' (York University, 1993) 1–2.

[146] Crépeau and Nakache, above n 139.

3.3 Reform and Deterrence in the New Century

This final section traces reforms to RSD beyond the introduction of the IRB and RRT in Canada and Australia, respectively. In Canada, lasting reform to the oral hearing came with the *Immigration and Refugee Protection Act* (*IRPA*), most of which came into effect in 2002.[147] The new legislation marked 'the culmination of close to a decade of public consultations about immigration law and policy and [presented] a comprehensive overhaul of the previous legislation dating from the mid-1970s'.[148] The Act reformed the two-member panel system, such that determinations would now be made by a one-member panel.[149] In reality, Dauvergne notes, this change essentially brought the legislation into line with existing practice since, by the time of the reforms' introduction in 2002, two-member panels had become rare due to resource allocations and constraints.[150]

While the hearing process established in response to *Singh* had initially been very highly regarded, various reforms, access-to-justice issues, and resource limitations had effectively diminished its overall quality.[151] The *IRPA* made provision for the introduction of a Refugee Appeal Division (RAD) within the IRB, to hear appeals of decisions of the RPD – although its implementation was delayed just as the *IRPA* came into force. The RAD (whose eventual implementation roughly ten years later is discussed below) was intended to improve the overall fairness of RSD in Canada through the introduction of on-the-papers merits review of first-instance decisions, where previously no merits review had existed. Although the reforms provided for 'the weakest possible merits review' available,[152] the new procedure was in response to the profession's call for increased fairness in RSD processes.

The ongoing 'unimplemented' status of the Refugee Appeal Division reflected the then-Government's lack of commitment to change the law. It was also an attempt to contain the availability of review and cost of first instance refugee decision-making as much as possible whilst complying with the *Singh* ruling. The failure to implement the RAD put even greater pressure on the oral hearing before the IRB, and until 2012, no merits review of the Board's initial findings was available. When the RAD was finally introduced in late 2012, it came with a further major overhaul of RSD that severely shortened the procedural timelines for refugee protection applications.[153] While the reforms under Bill C-31 left formal access to the hearing intact, they reduced the fairness of the hearing process as a whole by instituting

[147] SC 2001, c 27. See also the *Immigration and Refugee Protection Regulations*, SOR/2002-227.

[148] Dauvergne, above n 138, 726.

[149] *Immigration and Refugee Protection Act* SC 2001, c 27, s 163; *Immigration and Refugee Protection Regulations* SOR/2002-227, pt 8. Multiple member panels could still be constituted at the IRB chairperson's discretion.

[150] Dauvergne, above n 138, 728. Dauvergne notes that prior to the reforms, single member determinations were made possible 'with the consent of the applicant to do so', even though there were safeguards in place in relation to eliciting the applicant's consent.

[151] Ibid 733 (footnotes omitted).

[152] Ibid.

[153] Bill C-31, *Protecting Canada's Immigration System Act*, 1st Sess, 41st Parl, 2012 (assented to 28 June 2012), SC 2012, c 17 ('Bill C-31'). Bill C-31 amended a number of areas of Canadian refugee and migration law, including provisions enabling the mandatory detention of groups designated as 'mass arrivals' and limitations on access to permanent residency for accepted refugees: see Donald Galloway, 'Rights and the Re-identified Refugee: An Analysis of Recent Shifts in Canadian Law' in Susan Kneebone, Dallal Stevens and Loretta Baldassar (eds), *Refugee Protection and the Role of Law* (Routledge, 2014) 35.

shortened pre-hearing timelines that placed more pressure than ever on refugee applicants as they prepared their claims. Advocates critiqued the new timelines as a means of limiting access to onshore refugee protection, as the timelines make it enormously difficult, procedurally, to prepare and present a successful claim.[154] As well, like Australia's 'accelerated' review process for those arriving by boat addressed below, the RAD primarily determines review applications on the papers, places limits on the provision of new information and certain classes of claimants are denied any form of RAD review.[155]

The 'designated county of origin' (DCO) list was also introduced with the 2012 reforms. The DCO list even further accelerates processing timelines for people from states 'designated' by the Minister according to specific criteria, and until a successful legal challenge in 2015 it also barred access to the RAD for DCO entrants.[156] Both the DCO classification process and the consequences of the list, which implies certain countries are 'safe', have been strongly critiqued. As Macklin has argued, the list itself is animated by a logic that asylum seekers from certain states are 'opportunistic migrants exploiting the refugee system (including its slow pace) to circumvent more restrictive regimes for non-citizens'.[157]

The justifications offered for the Canadian reforms are in keeping with the history of the oral hearing and RSD reforms in Australia, whereby the hearing was seen just as much as a site that could efficiently 'catch' onshore refugee applicants who were not genuine refugees, as it was a safeguard of the procedural fairness of the onshore determination process. Indeed, soon after the reforms came into force, the (then) Citizenship and Immigration Canada (CIC) website declared that 'too much time and too many resources are spent reviewing these unfounded claims'.[158] The site further explained that refugee claimants from these countries will have their claims 'processed fast' which will ensure that those who need it 'get protection fast' and those with unfounded claims 'are sent home quickly through expedited processing'.[159] Speed and efficiency are not, on their own, negative features of RSD. However, in the case of Bill C-31, fast processing times are deployed with an explicit cynicism towards applicants. The need for speedy determinations is articulated alongside the assertion that many refugee claims are unfounded. And, in the examples discussed here, efficiency-focused reforms are attended by expansions of executive discretion to counter the

[154] See Angus Grant and Sean Rehaag, 'Unappealing: An Assessment of the Limits on Appeal Rights in Canada's New Refugee Determination System' (2016) 49 *UBC Law Review* 203; Canadian Bar Association, 'CBA Says Bill C-31 Raises Serious Concern about Excessive Ministerial Discretion. Press Release.' <www.cba.org/cba/news/2012_Releases/2012-02-22.aspx>.

[155] *Immigration and Refugee Protection Act*, SC 2001, c 27, sub-ss 110 (3)–(6). If there is a 'serious' credibility issue raised on appeal, the RAD may elect to hold a hearing. For details of all groups denied RAD access and analysis of the effects of exclusions, see Grant and Rehaag, above n 154.

[156] *Immigration and Refugee Protection Act*, SC 2001, c 27, ss 109–11; *YZ and the Canadian Association of Refugee Lawyers v The Minister of Citizenship and Immigration and the Minister of Public Safety and Emergency Preparedness* 2015 FC 892; see also Idil Atak, 'Safe Country of Origin: Constructing the Irregularity of Asylum Seekers in Canada' (2018) 56(6) *International Migration* 176; Cathryn Costello, 'Safe Country? Says Who?' (2016) 28(4) *International Journal of Refugee Law* 601.

[157] Audrey Macklin, 'A Safe Country to Emulate' in Helen Lambert, Jane McAdam and Maryellen Fullerton (eds), *The Global Reach of European Refugee Law* (Cambridge University Press, 2013) 102.

[158] Citizenship and Immigration Canada, 'Designated Countries of Origin' <www.cic.gc.ca/english/department/media/backgrounders/2012/2012-11-30.asp> (archived at December 2015).

[159] Ibid.

alleged abuse of RSD systems.[160] As Donald Galloway argues, the 2012 reforms constituted a 'radical and revisionary shift in [Canadian] refugee law and the processes of refugee status determination', such that the legal concept of the refugee is altered 'as radically as it would be by substantive redefinition'.[161] The truncation and acceleration of RSD processes, and limited nature of administrative review, place great faith in the IRB, which is presented as reliable, efficient and effective, while construing protection visa applications as insincere, exploitative and burdensome.

The reforms both reflect and produce a culture of gatekeeping and disbelief within refugee status decision-making in Canada. The oral hearing in Canada was introduced to provide applicants with the 'fundamental right' to be heard before a decision-maker and to provide a form of independence in refugee decision-making. Its introduction, though, came alongside a number of reforms aimed at limiting onshore refugee arrivals. The CRDD's creation has been followed by a steady contraction of the opportunity for applicants to be heard during the oral hearing. This included the removal of dual-member decision-making panels, considered 'best practice' at the time.[162] The tightening of RSD processes has been justified, amongst other things, as countering 'abuse of the system'.[163] As this chapter has highlighted, justification for the entire suite of reforms to Canadian RSD was simultaneously based on notions of economy and efficiency, and on discourses of asylum seekers as bogus and abusing the system.

In Australia, although the RRT was amalgamated with the AAT in 2015 and operated within the AAT's Migration and Refugee Division (MRD), there is no comparable history of substantive reform of RSD timelines and processes for refugee applicants arriving 'regularly'. This is because, since at least the mid-1990s, Australian Government action in relation to onshore refugees has been directed almost exclusively towards onshore refugees who arrive 'irregularly' and particularly those who arrive by boat.[164] These asylum seekers' statutory right to onshore RSD has been removed in full.[165] Protection claims must be made either at designated places of 'offshore processing' or under a series of 'alternative' RSD processes that have at certain times permitted applications to the RRT and at other times entirely removed the RRT as an avenue of review.[166] During the period that asylum seekers were still

160 The process of placing certain countries on the DCO list, for example, is an entirely discretionary act, based on the Immigration Minister's view of whether countries of origin meet broad threshold criteria: *Immigration and Refugee Protection Act*, SC 2001, c 27, s 109.1.

161 Galloway, above n 153, 38–39.

162 Notably, Hambly, Gill and Vianelli have returned to the notion of multi-member RSD panels at the appeal stage as improving both the quality and fairness of refugee decision-making: Hambly, Gill and Vianelli, above n 135.

163 Citizenship and Immigration Canada, 'Making Canada's Asylum System Faster and Fairer: Additional Designated Countries of Origin Announced' (Media Release, 30 May 2013) <www.cic.gc.ca/english/department/media/releases/2013/2013-05-30.asp>.

164 See especially Michelle Foster and Jason Pobjoy, 'A Failed Case of Legal Exceptionalism? Refugee Status Determination in Australia's "Excised" Territory' (2011) 23(4) *International Journal of Refugee Law* 583; Jane McAdam and Kate Purcell, 'Refugee Protection in the Howard Years: Obstructing the Right to Seek Asylum' (2008) 27 *Australian Year Book of International Law* 87; Anthea Vogl, 'Over the Borderline: A Critical Inquiry into the Geography of Territorial Excision and the Securitisation of the Australian Border' (2015) 38 *University of New South Wales Law Journal* 114.

165 *Migration Act 1958* (Cth) s 46A. An 'unauthorised maritime arrival' (UMA) may only validly apply for a visa if the Minister personally permits it, known as a Ministerial 'lifting of the bar' in Australian RSD.

166 See Foster and Pobjoy, above n 164.

regularly reaching Australia by boat, the government also implemented 'enhanced screening' of asylum seekers at sea;[167] however this kind of maritime screening has been less prominent in light of highly effective boat interdiction and turn-back policies.

The most enduring development in contemporary RSD for those arriving by boat in Australia, however, was the introduction of a 'fast tracked' process for maritime arrivals in late 2014, and its operation alongside Australia's offshore processing policy, which entailed the determination of certain claims in Papua New Guinea or Nauru.[168] 'Fast track applicants' included people who arrived by boat to seek asylum between 2012 and 2014, and who were not forcibly transferred to Nauru or Papua New Guinea under Australia's 'offshore processing' regime.[169] The RSD process that applied to them was both 'separate and inferior' to the process for asylum seekers who arrived by plane or who were not otherwise part of this cohort.[170] Most significantly, alongside all 'unauthorised maritime arrivals', they were denied the right to apply for protection unless the Immigration Minister personally lifted a statutory bar and provided individual applicants with written permission to apply for a visa.[171] As well, neither *de novo* merits review and nor a further oral hearing were available for negative first instance 'fast-track' decisions. Instead, a separate review body within the AAT, the Immigration Assessment Authority (IAA), undertook 'on paper' review of original decisions and evidence, unless exceptional circumstances could be demonstrated.[172] In language very similar to the Canadian reforms, the IAA was not required to consider 'new' information that had not presented in the initial departmental hearing.[173] And while the Minister was required to refer all 'reviewable fast track' decisions to the IAA as soon as 'reasonably practicable', review could be denied if the Minister believed changing or reviewing the decision was contrary to the national interest.[174] Unsurprisingly, the IAA's introduction and the absence of an oral hearing on review was found to increase the

[167] See Alex Reilly and Rebecca La Forgia, 'Secret "Enhanced Screening" of Asylum Seekers: A Democratic Analysis Centring on the Humanity of the Commonwealth Officer' (2013) 38(3) *Alternative Law Journal* 143.

[168] *Migration and Maritime Powers Legislation Amendment (Resolving the Asylum Legacy Caseload) Act 2014* (Cth) sch 4. While I do not address the offshore processing arrangements in detail, access to any form of domestic RSD was denied for the asylum seekers arbitrarily transferred to Papua New Guinea and Nauru and eventually access to RSD in Papua New Guinea and Nauru was granted to those incarcerated in offshore detention. See Sara Dehm, 'Outsourcing, Responsibility and Refugee Claim-Making in Australia's Offshore Detention Regime' in Siobhan McGuirk and Adrienne Pine (eds), *Asylum for Sale: Profit and Protest in the Migration Industry* (2020) 47. Note the amendments, introducing fast track assessments, commenced in 2015.

[169] *Migration Act 1958* (Cth) ss 5(1), 473BB (in time at 2022); precise dates are arrival on or after 13 August 2012 and before 1 January 2014. A more limited category of 'excluded fast track review applicants' do not have access to any form of administrative merits review: *Migration Act 1958* (Cth) s 5 (1) (in time at 2022).

[170] Sara Dehm and Anthea Vogl, 'An Unfair and Dangerous Process' (Academics for Refugees, October 2017) 13 <https://academicsforrefugees.wordpress.com/research-reports/>.

[171] *Migration Act 1958* (Cth) s 46A(1), (2).

[172] *Migration Act 1958* (Cth) s 473DB (in time at 2022). Circumstances include where the IAA is satisfied that the new information was not known to the applicant or could not have been provided to the department at the time of the applicant's original hearing. An applicant could be invited to an interview to give, or provide comment on, new information, but the opportunity to respond orally was at the absolute discretion of the IAA: ss 473 DC, 473DE.

[173] *Migration Act 1958* (Cth) ss 473DB, 473DD (in time at 2022).

[174] *Migration Act 1958* (Cth) ss 473CA, 473DB (in time at 2022).

likelihood of 'serious legal errors' and departmental decisions being affirmed, as well as to significantly compromise procedural fairness in relation to assessment of testimony and credibility.[175]

In Australia, the so-called 'fast-tracking' of a select class of refugee claims, justified as a means by which to increase the efficiency of decision-making, took place as the operations and inefficiency of the AAT as a whole were under scrutiny. In 2022, this culminated in a major government review of the 'integrity and performance' of administrative review at the federal level. The review was motivated, inter alia, by concerns about the highly politicised selection process for AAT members, as well as immense backlogs and delays in case finalisations.[176] It followed an earlier statutory review of the AAT in 2019 prompted by similar concerns.[177] The caseload and 'intimidating backlogs' within the migration and refugee division were a focal point in both instances, as was the under-resourcing of migration and refugee decision-making.[178] Indeed in 2020–21, the median time for the finalisation of refugee protection visa review applications was 104 weeks, with a backlog of approximately 57,000 cases on hand at the end of 2021.[179] The 2022 review report's major and controversial recommendation was that the Attorney-General 'disassemble the current [AAT] and re-establish a new, federal administrative review system' by 2023.[180] About six months later, in late 2022, the Government announced its plans to abolish the AAT. Even though at the time of writing, the AAT is set to be abolished, and a new federal tribunal and process for appointment of decision-makers will eventually be established, there has been no indication that the central importance of the oral hearing will be removed or reformed for refugee and migration decision-making. However, precise details of any and all possible reforms to Australia's federal administrative review process (and processing timelines) were yet to be announced at the time of writing.

Read together, the reforms described in this section in Australia and Canada substantially diminish the access to, and procedural fairness of, RSD processes for select groups. In Australia, the IAA's introduction continues a long history of systemic discrimination against and punishment of those seeking asylum by boat. None of these reforms, however, remove the oral hearing as such or its status as *the site* for testing the content and credibility of refugee applicants' claims. In fact, the Australian and Canadian reforms further entrench the first instance oral hearing as the primary event within RSD. There is significantly more pressure on applicants to articulate the fullest and most accurate version of their claim during the first oral hearing, since applicants do not necessarily have access to a further

175 Emily McDonald and Maria O'Sullivan, 'Protecting Vulnerable Refugees: Procedural Fairness in the Australian Fast Track Regime' (2018) 41 *University of New South Wales Law Journal* 1003; Linda Kirk, 'Accelerated Asylum Procedures in the United Kingdom and Australia: "Fast Track" to Refoulement?' in Maria O'Sullivan and Dallal Stevens (eds), *States, the Law and Access to Refugee Protection: Fortresses and Fairness* (Hart, 2017) 243.

176 Senate Legal and Constitutional Affairs, 'The Performance and Integrity of Australia's Administrative Review System' (Commonwealth of Australia, 2022).

177 Callinan, above n 95, 1.

178 Ibid; Senate Legal and Constitutional Affairs, above n 176. I note that similar backlogs and delays have plagued the IRB with acute processing delays for refugee claims in particular. Immigration, Refugees and Citizenship Canada's (IRCC) response to date has centred operational and technological factors, rather than institutional reform: Pratyush Dayal, 'Refugees Feel Forgotten as Canada's Immigration Backlog Sits at Nearly 2 Million Applications', *CBC News*, 1 May 2022.

179 Senate Legal and Constitutional Affairs, above n 176, [5.20], [5.32]. Callinan, above n 95.

180 Senate Legal and Constitutional Affairs, above n 176, [7.56].

hearing or even full merits review. Getting it right the first time has always been central to credibility assessment, which tests consistency across multiple retellings of one's story. For certain classes of refugee claimants, giving a credible account of one's claim at the very first instance is more imperative than ever, as no further opportunities to do so exist.

3.4 Conclusion

The introduction of a statutory oral hearing in both Australia and Canada significantly improved the fairness of RSD processing, and represented a shift toward enhanced statutory and administrative rights and justice in the assessment of refugee claims. Simultaneously, though, contemporary critiques of the oral hearing and credibility assessment align with the history of the hearing as a mechanism that aimed to sort 'genuine' refugee applicants from 'bogus' unauthorised arrivals. The burden placed upon a refugee's oral testimony, and on orality as a primary means for testing credibility, coincided with the introduction of a hearing before a semi-independent executive decision-maker in both jurisdictions. While the precise history of the oral hearing differs between Australia and Canada, its emergence in both countries took place within the context of government attempts to manage and control increasing onshore or in-country asylum seeking. In each instance, as the numbers of onshore asylum seekers increased, the government sought to preserve executive control over arrivals at the same time *as* establishing effective forms of integrity, independence and procedural fairness in RSD. This reinforces my argument that analysis of credibility determination must be undertaken in the context of enduring sovereign attempts to exclude refugee arrivals. This is the case even though the crude politics of refugee deterrence cannot fully account for the conduct of RSD and the processes of judgment that shape credibility determinations. This is more than evident in the following chapters, which move away from a history of RSD procedure and into the hearing rooms and oral exchanges that form the book's core study.

4

The Stock Narrative of Becoming a Refugee

This chapter marks the beginning of four core chapters, in which I interrogate how refugee testimony was presented, tested and assessed – or as Nando Sigona describes it, 'probed, scrutinised and dissected'[1] – during the oral hearings. In this chapter, I suggest that a stock story of refugeehood, which I call the 'stock narrative of becoming a refugee', structured decision-makers' testing of oral testimony during the hearings. This stock story, which recurred throughout my dataset, is one version of how, when and why 'genuine' refugee applicants decide to leave their home countries and seek refugee status in the refugee-receiving state. The stock narrative of becoming a refugee, stated in its simplest form, is as follows: genuine onshore refugees, when faced with serious persecution or danger of persecution, take decisive and immediate action to flee this persecution and/or the country of origin. They then travel as directly as possible to a place where protection can be sought, and having arrived there, seek the host state's protection at the earliest opportunity. They do not contemplate return to their home country and achieve closure in the resolution of their refugee status.

Literary theorist Peter Brooks defines stock stories as common, culturally accepted and sanctioned narratives about how and why things function in the world.[2] For those with the power to produce and endorse them, such stories are familiar, credible and correct reflections of how things take place, and of the world as it is. They operate by way of unacknowledged assumptions, beliefs and language. Like narratives themselves, stock stories not only constitute our understanding of the day to day; they also seek to establish 'the way things are supposed to happen'.[3] Richard Delgado first used the term 'stock story' in the context of law and literature scholarship to describe stories that 'are part of, and reinforce, the dominant discourse'.[4] The concept of counter-stories has been at the centre of much law and 'outsider storytelling' scholarship, which has tracked the way dominant narratives, expressed in and through various forms of legal authority, function to discredit 'marginal' or 'outsider' stories

1 Nando Sigona, 'The Politics of Refugee Voices: Representations, Narratives and Memories' in Elena Fiddian-Qasmiyeh et al (eds), *The Oxford Handbook of Refugee and Forced Migration Studies* (Oxford University Press, 2014) 369, 372.

2 Peter Brooks, 'Narrative in and of the Law' in James Phelan and Peter J Rabinowitz (eds), *A Companion to Narrative Theory* (Blackwell, 2005) 415.

3 Peter Brooks, 'Narrative Transactions: Does the Law Need a Narratology?' (2006) 18 *Yale Journal of Law & the Humanities* 1, 11.

4 Richard Delgado, 'Storytelling for Oppositionists and Others: A Plea for Narrative' (1989) 89 *Michigan Law Review* 2411, 2412.

told by people who are denied the power to determine norms of credibility and truth.[5] As critical race and feminist theorists have long argued, legal 'fact-finding' and laws themselves are often simply stock stories that conceal their status as such. They are carefully structured to 'exclude, silence and oppress "outsiders" – those not part of the dominant culture, particularly people of colour, women and the poor'.[6] In characterising the silencing of 'alternative' stories as linguistic oppression, Elinor Ochs and Lisa Capps write that, 'the roar of countervalent stories is ever present, on the edge of recognition',[7] and cite Toni Morrison's account of dominant narratives as a means to 'sanction ignorance and preserve privilege . . . a suit of armour polished to shocking glitter'.[8]

In listening to and analysing the hearings in this study, this stock narrative of becoming a refugee arose as an all too neat, explicit or implicit normative standard against which applicants were required to submit their testimony for judgment.[9] This specific narrative structured the hearings in at least three ways: the applicant's evidence 'fit' with this story and therefore was not the basis of further questioning; the applicant's evidence did not correspond with the stock story, leading to extensive questioning that either did or did not form the basis of a credibility finding in the written reasons; or, finally, the applicant's evidence did not correspond with the stock story, yet the applicant's articulation of an 'alternative' narrative of flight, and reasons for deviating from the norm, were accepted by the decision-maker after interrogation and questioning. In all but three of the observed hearings, the decision-maker addressed, to varying degrees, the applicant's story of flight, transit and arrival against the stock story.

This narrative, and decision-makers' questioning in relation to it, ties the hearings in this study together in a way that the content of each applicant's claim did not. The claims in my dataset do not cohere around a particular kind of claim or a specific Refugee Convention ground. Insofar as the Refugee Convention definition of a refugee provides a legal and evidentiary framework, the question of why and when the applicant left their home country (at the very least) must be addressed in an application for refugee status. I have selected this story as my focus here because it demonstrates the narrativity required of refugee applicants. It reveals the way in which stock stories, and the expression of events in a narrative form, do not necessarily accord with the experiences of onshore refugee applicants; and, crucially, establish requirements of refugee applicants that move beyond domestic and international law.

As such, this chapter also explores to what extent the prescriptive stock narrative of becoming a refugee is embedded within the legal definition of a refugee and the domestic laws governing who is entitled to protection. In Section 4.1, I set out the stock narrative of

5 Ibid. For a tracing of these concepts outside of law and literature's engagement with them, see Michael Bamberg and Molly Andrews (eds), *Considering Counter-Narratives: Narrating, Resisting, Making Sense* (John Benjamins, 2004).

6 Lisa Sarmas, 'Storytelling and the Law: A Case Study of *Louth v Diprose*' (1993) 19 *Melbourne University Law Review* 701, 703; see also Kim Lane Scheppele, 'Foreword: Telling Stories' (1989) 87 *Michigan Law Review* 2073; Patricia J Williams, *The Alchemy of Race and Rights* (Harvard University Press, 1991).

7 Elinor Ochs and Lisa Capps, 'Narrating the Self' (1996) 25(1) *Annual Review of Anthropology* 19, 33.

8 Toni Morrison, *The Nobel Lecture in Literature 1993* (Knopf, 1994) 14.

9 The use of 'becoming' here is at odds with the formally 'declaratory' nature of refugee status under international law and its domestic enactments, whereby RSD processes confirm a status already in existence rather than constitute it: UNHCR, *Handbook on Procedures and Criteria for Determining Refugee Status under the 1951 Convention and the 1967 Protocol Relating to the Status of Refugees* (HCR/IP/4/Eng/REV1, 4th ed, 2019) Clause 28.

becoming a refugee in detail and analyse its presence within existing legal and procedural standards. Critically, while questions of past experience, flight and reasons for seeking refugee status must be addressed in the assessment of a claim for refugee protection, the normative expectations of onshore refugees embedded within the stock tale far exceed the legal basis for refugee protection. Section 4.2 is devoted to exposing how this story, with its distinct narrative form, was demanded of refugee applicants during the oral hearings. Section 4.2 also explores how applicants responded to this demand for narrativity. As with each of the book's remaining chapters, this section demonstrates that the demand for narrative is a burden placed upon refugee applicants' speech during the hearing itself; one that frequently interrupts, limits or disciplines the way in which an applicant is able to present testimony – but which applicants nonetheless navigate, respond to and/or contest as part of their oral claim, with varying degrees of 'success' depending on the narrative resources available to them.[10]

4.1 Becoming a Refugee in Domestic and International Law

In the stock story of becoming a refugee, the demand for beginnings, middles and ends manifests crudely. The stock narrative relates to how the applicant behaves in their country of origin when faced with risk or danger; the course of travel from one's home country to the refugee-receiving state; and how and when the applicant behaves in the receiving country and seeks refugee protection after having arrived. The narrative is marked by the imagined linear sequence of persecution, flight and status-seeking. Like all stock stories, the narrative itself slips almost imperceptibly between the claim that this is how genuine refugees *do* behave in the world and that this is how they *should* behave. Crucially, the narrative's resolution must be the applicant's willing, complete and unequivocal seeking of refugee status and entry into the subject position of a recognised refugee.

As Jan Blommaert explains, in documenting the narrative inequality experienced by African asylum seekers in Belgium, 'without recourse to long and detailed narratives about home, escape and travelling, asylum seekers cannot make their motives and causes for seeking asylum fully understood'.[11] He identifies the 'home narrative' (which I would describe as the beginning of the stock refugee narrative) as a 'particular type of densely contextualising sub-narrative' required of refugees.[12] In the structure of such 'home stories', refugees must first give 'contextualizing accounts' of their past lives and home societies and departure, such that 'displacement becomes a matter of identity' and the narrative's 'temporary and spatial elements are used to construct "refugeeness"'.[13] Further, as I observed repeatedly in the oral hearings, the required narrative closure which anchors 'the whole preceding [home] story' is found in the present – and specifically, in the act of seeking asylum and the status of being in exile.[14] One problem here, amongst others, is that 'the

[10] See Katrijn Maryns and Jan Blommaert, 'Stylistic and Thematic Shifting as a Narrative Resource: Assessing Asylum Seekers' Repertoires' (2001) 20(1) *Multilingua* 61.

[11] Jan Blommaert, 'Investigating Narrative Inequality: African Asylum Seekers' Stories in Belgium' (2001) 12(4) *Discourse & Society* 413, 414.

[12] Ibid 413.

[13] Ibid 434.

[14] Ibid 435.

violence endured by the refugees [does not] end with migration; it is embedded in the structures of most receiving societies'.[15]

Like the narrative form itself, the stock story of becoming a refugee – particularly its invocation of an immediate crisis, direct causality and certain resolve to flee and become a refugee – is a tool of both inclusion and exclusion. As a normative measure, it can efficiently render certain stories (and refugee applicants) as lacking credibility and authenticity or, alternatively, as credible and genuine. As the hearing excerpts demonstrate, the story is often a remarkably poor fit with the experience of refugee applicants. As a stock story, it relies on concealed assumptions and demands clear linear causality and moral closure. And significantly, as Marita Eastmond has noted, it actively propagates the idea of 'the refugee experience' as 'a uniform condition and ... the tendency to think of refugees as an undifferentiated, essentialized and universal category quite irrespective of the different historical and political conditions of displacement'.[16]

4.1.1 *Critiquing the Refugee Story's Content*

The stock narrative of becoming a refugee is not found in legal definitions of refugee status in either Australia or Canada, or in the Refugee Convention. The Refugee Convention definition requires that the refugee must 'be outside of his or her country of origin' and that this must be the case 'owing to a well-founded fear of persecution' on the basis of one or more of the five Convention grounds.[17] The definition does not set out exactly when or how a refugee must have left their country of origin, or the relationship between the timing of departure and the events giving rise to a well-founded fear.[18] However, for asylum seekers within state territory without lawful status, the Refugee Convention does establish an obligation to 'present themselves without delay to the authorities and show good cause for their illegal entry or presence'.[19] The relevant article addresses delay in seeking to regularise one's status, and by extension creates an obligation for this group of refugees not to postpone making an asylum claim or demonstrating to authorities another 'good cause' for unlawfulness.

The applicant in both Australia and Canada must have a 'subjective' and 'objective' fear of persecution, but this subjective fear may exist even if the applicant does not act in relation to it, immediately or at all. The UNHCR Handbook also acknowledges this fact in stating: 'An evaluation of the subjective element [of a well-founded fear] is inseparable from an assessment of the personality of the applicant, since psychological reactions of different individuals may not be the same in identical conditions'.[20] As Hilary Evans

15 Laurence J Kirmayer, 'Failures of Imagination: The Refugee's Narrative in Psychiatry' (2003) 10(2) *Anthropology & Medicine* 167, 181.

16 Marita Eastmond, 'Stories as Lived Experience: Narratives in Forced Migration Research' (2007) 20(2) *Journal of Refugee Studies* 248, 253.

17 Refugee Convention, as amended by the 1967 Protocol Relating to the Status of Refugees, art 1A.

18 For consideration of a related but distinct question, of whether or not the harm faced needs to be imminent to qualify for protection (the authors strongly argue it does not), see Adrienne Anderson et al, 'Imminence in Refugee and Human Rights Law: A Misplaced Notion for International Protection' (2019) 68(1) *International & Comparative Law Quarterly* 111.

19 Refugee Convention art 31(1).

20 UNHCR, above n 9, 11; Hilary Evans Cameron, 'Risk Theory and "Subjective Fear": The Role of Risk Perception, Assessment, and Management in Refugee Status Determinations' (2008) 20(4) *International*

Cameron so aptly puts it, 'the refugee definition says that a refugee must fear danger; it nowhere says that she must be a cautious person' who flees danger immediately.[21]

Aspects of the narrative of becoming a refugee have informed, and been informed by, domestic refugee law and the credibility criteria in certain jurisdictions. Notably, in Canadian and Australian jurisprudence 'delay' in making a claim upon arrival *may* be interpreted as negatively affecting the credibility of the claim.[22] However, the significance of delay will depend on the particular case and an applicant's credibility cannot be disputed solely on the basis that a claim was not made immediately, a principle that is also borne out in credibility guidance that makes allowances for late disclosure of gender-based harms, as addressed below.[23] A further, substantive legal basis for (and arguably product of) this narrative is the 'safe third country' rule that operates to some extent in both Australia and Canada.[24] The rule in principle requires refugee applicants to lodge their claim in the first country of arrival where effective protection could be sought,[25] thus

Journal of Refugee Law 567, 573. For a discussion of problems with requiring the applicant to demonstrate a 'subjective' element of fear, separated from the question of whether the applicant faces an actual risk of persecution, see James C Hathaway, 'Michigan Guidelines on Well-Founded Fear' (2005) 26 *Michigan Journal of International Law* 492; James C Hathaway and William S Hicks, 'Is There a Subjective Element in the Refugee Convention's Requirement of Well-Founded Fear?' (2004) 26 *Michigan Journal of International Law* 505.

21 Evans Cameron, above n 20, 573. Cf, though, Canadian and Australian jurisprudence below.

22 *Selvadurai v Minister for Immigration and Ethnic Affairs* (1994) 34 ALD 347; *Huerta v Canada (Minister for Employment and Immigration)* (1993) 157 NR 225, 227. Though where delays are inordinate and without explanation and go to the subjectivity of fear, this may constitute grounds for rejecting a claim: *Espinosa, Roberto Pablo Hernandez v MCI* [2003] FC 1324. See too Administrative Appeals Tribunal Migration and Refugee Division, 'Guidelines on the Assessment of Credibility' (2006, updated 2015) 7.

23 Ibid.

24 In Australia: *Migration Act 1958* (Cth) ss 36(3), 91N. Section 91N limits protection obligations for anyone who has spent seven days in a country where they hold a right to re-enter and reside, and which is declared by the Minister to provide access to protection. Although there seems to be 'some acknowledgement that the measures were more of a political gesture [against forum shopping] than a practical constraint on asylum seekers' due to the difficulties of enforcement: Mary Crock and Laurie Berg, *Immigration, Refugees and Forced Migration: Law, Policy and Practice in Australia* (Federation, 2011) 416; see also *WAGH v MIMIA* (2003) 131 FCR 269. In Canada, claimants may not be referred to the IRB if they came directly or indirectly from a designated country. The US is a designated country under the *Canada–US Safe Third Country Agreement* (5 December 2002) <www.cic.gc.ca/english/department/laws-policy/safe-third.asp>. See also *Immigration and Refugee Protection Regulations*, SOR/2002-227, r 159.3; *Immigration and Refugee Protection Act*, SC 2001, c 27, s 101(1)(e). In Europe, under the Dublin III Regulation, the state where the applicant was first permitted to enter European territory is a key determinant of responsibility for processing the claim: *Regulation (EU) No 604/2013 of the European Parliament and of the Council of 26 June 2013 Establishing the Criteria and Mechanisms for Determining the Member State Responsible for Examining an Application for International Protection Lodged in One of the Member States by a Third-Country National or a Stateless Person (Recast)* [2013] OJ L 180/31. Though on attempts at reform and the 'new' European Pact on Immigration and Asylum see 'Special Collection on the "New" Migration and Asylum Pact' (EU Immigration and Asylum Law and Policy) <https://eumigrationlawblog.eu/series-on-the-migration-pact-published-under-the-supervision-of-daniel-thym/>.

25 Luisa Feline Freier, Eleni Karageorgiou and Kate Ogg, 'The Evolution of Safe Third Country Law and Practice' in Cathryn Costello, Michelle Foster and Jane McAdam (eds), *The Oxford Handbook of International Refugee Law* (Oxford University Press, 2021). See also Audrey Macklin, 'Disappearing Refugees: Reflections on the Canada-US Safe Third Country Agreement' (2005) 36 *Columbia Human Rights Law Review* 365, 372. For a related development in Canada excluding those who have *made* a refugee application in certain states, see Idil Atak, Zainab Abu Alrob and Claire Ellis, 'Expanding Refugee

codifying at least one element of the stock story, that the refugee must make a claim at the earliest possible opportunity.[26]

There is no Refugee Convention provision that directly supports safe third country rules, and their legality is contested under international law in light of their burden-shifting nature and their potential to lead to 'chain' *refoulement* of asylum seekers.[27] With respect to the narrative of becoming a refugee, safe third country rules certainly encapsulate an expectation that asylum seekers' journeys are linear; that seeking refugee status is the determinative element of all travel and that choice or agency in selecting where to seek asylum displaces narratives of authenticity, victimhood and need. As Macklin puts it, the premise guiding Canada's safe third country agreement with the United States – that refugees ought to apply for protection wherever they arrived first – assumes that to do otherwise would be 'an opportunistic abuse of the international regime of refugee protection' and that '[a]sylum-seekers are the world's supplicants – and beggars cannot be choosers'.[28]

Elements of this narrative were also spelt out explicitly in one IRB screening form that was in use at the time of my observations, but which has since been revised.[29] The screening form, which was given to applicants after the submission of the paper-based application form, was designed to communicate matters that should be addressed in the oral hearing. Under the general heading 'Issues' was a subheading 'Subjective Fear'. Under this heading, each of the following 'issues' appeared next to a check box: 'delay in departure', 'delay in claiming', 're-availment' (meaning returning to country of origin), 'failure to claim elsewhere' and 'previous claim elsewhere'. The form indicated that any highlighted issues were to be considered 'central to the claim', implying that the applicant might be required to address any one of the selected issues before the IRB. The form itself imported a standard into refugee status decision-making that is not otherwise expressed in a domestic statute.[30]

Two of the earliest studies to address the expectation that applicants should take immediate steps to flee when faced with serious persecution are Robert F Barsky's study

Ineligibility: Canada's Response to Secondary Refugee Movements' (2021) 34(3) *Journal of Refugee Studies* 2593.

26 Although a detailed examination of the legality of this principle vis-à-vis international refugee law standards is beyond the scope of this chapter, see especially Michelle Foster, 'Responsibility Sharing or Shifting? "Safe" Third Countries and International Law' (2008) 25(2) *Refuge* 64.

27 See Susan Kneebone, 'The Legal and Ethical Implications of Extra-Territorial Processing of Asylum Seekers: The Safe Third Country Concept' in Jane McAdam (ed), *Forced Migration, Human Rights and Security* (Bloomsbury, 2008) 129.

28 Macklin, above n 25, 381.

29 Immigration and Refugee Board of Canada, 'Screening Form' (on file with author). The form was issued in accordance with Immigration and Refugee Board, 'Guideline 7 Concerning Preparation and Conduct of a Hearing in The Refugee Protection Division: Guidelines Issued by the Chairperson Pursuant to Section 159(1)(h) of the Immigration and Refugee Protection Act' (2003, updated 2012, Immigration and Refugee Board Ottawa). None of these issues are mentioned in the official Canadian refugee application forms.

30 Though for the relevance of delay in applying for protection within credibility guidelines and Canadian jurisprudence, see above n 24.

of why, when and where people make Refugee Convention claims, and Cécile Rousseau et al's interdisciplinary study of RSD in Canada, both conducted in the late 1990s and early 2000s.[31] Their insights, alongside the key plot points in the stock story of becoming a refugee, have endured. Rousseau et al's landmark Canadian study in the early 2000s, found that decision-makers misunderstood 'daily life in a country racked by war or other conflict'[32] and that they demonstrated a very poor understanding of the political complexities of violence.[33] Simplistic assumptions shaped decision-makers' understandings of how applicants experienced and responded to war and crisis: 'Board Members often seem to posit war as a Manichaean situation where clearly defined groups function in opposition to or in alliance with one another, and where an individual, if truly persecuted, will immediately flee.'[34] Barsky's study of refugee applicants' reasons for departure presented evidence that the timing of and motives for refugee applicants' decisions to flee were infinitely more complex than could be captured in a linear narrative of persecution, direct flight and the immediate submission of a Refugee Convention application:

> The flight, and the choices made ... [by refugee applicants], refract varying degrees of claimants' expedience and fear, pragmatism and ignorance, gullibility and knowledge, degrees which depend on the role of intermediaries, prior knowledge, profile, country of origin and, of course, chance.[35]

The refugee stock story, with its expectation of immediate flight in response to clear and present danger, is necessarily connected to a broader imagining of an applicant's home country, of what it is like to live there and how people there behave. In Rousseau and Foxen's interviews with seventeen former Board Members of the IRB, some members reported that the 'sources' against which they compared refugee applicants' evidence came from their own daily lives, including from holidays to the applicant's country of origin, popular culture or literary texts; and from other stories they had heard and believed.[36] Along similar lines, Evans Cameron also examined RSD decision-makers' orthodox expectations of immediate or imminent flight. She elucidates how decision-makers' narrative expectations conflict with psychological evidence about how actors assess and respond to risk:

[31] Robert F Barsky, *Arguing and Justifying: Assessing the Convention Refugees' Choice of Moment, Motive and Host Country* (Ashgate, 2000); Cécile Rousseau et al, 'The Complexity of Determining Refugeehood: A Multidisciplinary Analysis of the Decision-Making Process of the Canadian Immigration and Refugee Board' (2002) 15(1) *Journal of Refugee Studies* 43.

[32] Rousseau et al, above n 31, 54; see also Kirmayer, above n 15.

[33] Rousseau et al, above n 31, 61.

[34] Ibid.

[35] Barsky, above n 31, 23.

[36] Cécile Rousseau and Patricia Foxen, 'Constructing and Deconstructing the Myth of the Lying Refugee: Paradoxes of Power and Justice in an Administrative Immigration Tribunal' in Els van Dongen and Sylvie Fainzang (eds), *Lying and Illness: Power and Performance* (Het Spinhuis, 2005) 70–73. I explore the implications of these subjective sources of narrative and reasoning further in Chapter 5.

> psychologists, sociologists, anthropologists, economists and historians have studied how human beings perceive and respond to danger ... Before adjudicators could even potentially infer from these [responses to alleged danger] that a claimant was not afraid, or is lying, they must consider the psychological and cultural factors influencing the claimant's risk perception, assessment, and management.[37]

Evans Cameron, in a model that maps effortlessly onto the narrative of becoming a refugee that I am tracing here, identifies three assumptions about refugee behaviour (or as she calls them, 'articles of faith') that are handed down by refugee judges: that those who fear for their lives in their homelands will not delay in leaving; that they will ask for protection immediately in the first safe country that they reach; and that they will never return to their homeland for any reason.[38]

Evans Cameron explains exactly why a standardised response to risk is an unreasonable expectation by drawing on a range of psychological and anthropological concepts. Specifically, she shows that response to risk (and therefore, the decision to flee) depends upon how familiar the risk is, how appealing the prospect of responding is, whether the risk was initially perceived as controllable, whether the applicant has a high personal tolerance of risk, whether the applicant possesses optimism bias and what previous experiences the applicant has with the type of risk in question.[39] Attention needs to be paid to cultural factors that influence the applicant's risk management strategies. When the stock narrative of becoming a refugee is applied to an individual refugee, much-needed nuance is lost because the stock narrative posits a simple persecution–flight nexus. Indeed, there is such an extreme variance in personal responses to risk and harm that no assessment of credibility or truth should be based on how an applicant has reacted to fear or danger.[40] In short, the narrative of becoming a refugee not only accords poorly with compelling literature about human behaviour in response to harm; but in addition, the very notion that a standard response to risk exists *at all* is problematic, as is the expectation that there is a direct, causative and linear link between harm and flight.

While response to risk is, as noted, not an explicit element of the Refugee Convention definition, Gregor Noll correctly argues that the applicant's personal risk assessment and moment of departure is relevant to RSD because of the Refugee Convention requirement that the applicant hold a well-founded fear of persecution that is both subjective and objective.[41] The need to demonstrate subjective fear imports a procedural requirement into RSD, namely that the applicant must present an account of their personal perception of potential harm. Fear thus becomes the

[37] Evans Cameron, above n 20, 568.
[38] Ibid 567.
[39] Ibid 568.
[40] As Barsky notes, the assumption also discounts the very specific regional and national factors, including aspects of a particular conflict, that influence decisions about departure: Barsky, above n 31.
[41] Gregor Noll, 'Evidentiary Assessment under the Refugee Convention: Risk, Pain and the Intersubjectivity of Fear' in Gregor Noll (ed), *Proof, Evidentiary Assessment and Credibility in Asylum Procedures* (Martin Nijhoff, 2005) 141, 145–46.

applicant's 'personal risk assessment',[42] and the host state applying the Refugee Convention must take into account the applicant's own emerging sense and understanding of risk.[43] Consideration of subjective fear, though, does not equate to a demand that refugee applicants assess risk and respond to it immediately. However, if the applicant's own risk assessment is trusted and this assessment is recognised as being variable, then the narrative thrust of the stock story of becoming a refugee loses its force and the purported universality of the story is undermined. As the hearing excerpts reveal, questioning about the timing and date of departure was frequently used to gauge and judge subjective fear, and *how* (and how genuinely) applicants were responding to risk.

Evans Cameron's identification of refugee decision-makers' 'second article of faith' – that refugee applicants will ask for protection immediately in the first safe country that they reach – is another core event in the stock narrative of becoming a refugee. Indeed, a recurrent issue in the determination of refugee claims is the question of when (or at what point) the applicant sought refugee status, and whether the timing of this choice is consistent with the story of persecution upon which the claim is based. Millbank critiques this element of the stock narrative, observing that 'a fundamental but untested assumption of refugee adjudication is that claimants in genuine fear of persecution will make their claim at the earliest possible opportunity and as fulsomely as possible'.[44] She demonstrates that the assumption of immediate disclosure simply does not hold for applicants making claims on the basis of sexuality. Instead, delay in disclosure is a common and recognised response to feelings of shame or difficulties discussing one's sexuality, and refugee applicants may actively postpone making a claim to avoid discussing the basis of their feared persecution.[45]

International and domestic guidelines on refugee law and gendered harms clearly stipulate that expectations of early disclosure and immediate application, particularly as they relate to claims based on sexual violence (where delay in disclosure is a well-documented aspect of such claims) should not be applied.[46] The difficulties that claimants face in disclosing sexual harm, including high levels of trauma, shame and fear both within RSD and beyond it, are well-established.[47] The guidelines recognise that disclosure and the process of presenting testimony pose a serious challenge to certain classes of applicant,

[42] Ibid 144.

[43] See Thomas Spijkerboer, 'Stereotyping and Acceleration: Gender, Procedural Acceleration and Marginalised Judicial Review in the Dutch Asylum System' in Gregor Noll (ed), *Proof, Evidentiary Assessment and Credibility in Asylum Procedures* (Martin Nijhoff, 2005); and for an argument in favour of limiting the subjective requirement of a 'well-founded fear', see Hathaway, above n 20.

[44] Jenni Millbank, '"The Ring of Truth": A Case Study of Credibility Assessment in Particular Social Group Refugee Determinations' (2009) 21(1) *International Journal of Refugee Law* 1, 13.

[45] Ibid 14–15.

[46] See Administrative Appeals Tribunal Migration and Refugee Division, 'Guidelines on Gender' (1996, updated 2015); Immigration and Refugee Board of Canada, 'Chairperson Guideline 8: Procedures with Respect to Vulnerable Persons Appearing Before the IRB' (2006, updated 2012).

[47] Debora Singer, 'Falling at Each Hurdle: Assessing the Credibility of Women's Asylum Claims' in Efrat Arbel, Catherine Dauvergne and Jenni Millbank (eds), *Gender in Refugee Law: From the Margins to the Centre* (Routledge, 2014) 98; Jane Herlihy and Stuart W Turner, 'Asylum Claims and Memory of Trauma: Sharing Our Knowledge' (2007) 191(1) *The British Journal of Psychiatry* 3.

and specifically, that survivors of gender-based harm often do not make prompt and full disclosure of the harms they have suffered.[48] While the reforms and guidelines addressing gender-related persecution are far from perfect, and have been inconsistently and unevenly implemented,[49] they are significant insofar as they 'give not only legal but also procedural guidelines to decision-makers in relation to dealing sensitively and appropriately with women's narratives of persecution'.[50] Still, as Millbank rightly notes, guidelines excusing late disclosure do not remove the requirement of immediate disclosure, but rather provide a means of explaining and excusing the otherwise anomalous delay in disclosing.[51] So, such guidelines work to reinforce the normative quality of the story, but with certain exceptions.

Why are refugee applicants expected to know, as soon as they land in a 'safe country', that making an application for protection is the optimal decision; that they will never return to their country of origin; and that it is in their best interests to become a refugee applicant as soon as possible?[52] This expectation assumes that refugee applicants have predetermined plans and a deep-seated certainty about their decisions. The requirement of certainty about the potential of future harm, and relatedly of never returning home, is much more burdensome than the legal test of a 'real chance' used to determine whether applicants will face persecution if returned home in the future. In Canada, the legal test governing the objective limb of the well-founded fear of persecution requirement is whether a 'reasonable chance' of persecution exists – that is, a less than 50 per cent chance of persecution but more than a minimal or mere possibility – rather than a finding that persecution is inevitable.[53] Similarly, in Australia, the test is whether there is a 'real chance' that the applicant could be persecuted on Convention grounds.[54] Given these standards, why must the applicant exhibit absolute certainty that they must flee and seek protection at the earliest opportunity?

Alongside the expectation that refugees seek immediate protection is the presumption that applicants will never return to their home country. This expectation is that if applicants sincerely hold a 'well-founded' fear of persecution, they will not return to the source of that persecution. Put in terms of narrative form, this is an unrealistic expectation of narrative closure and of the story 'ending'. Here the applicant is once again denied agency regarding

[48] Helen Baillot, Sharon Cowan and Vanessa E Munro, 'Seen but Not Heard? Parallels and Dissonances in the Treatment of Rape Narratives across the Asylum and Criminal Justice Contexts' (2009) 36(2) *Journal of Law and Society* 195, 201.

[49] See, e.g., Nicole LaViolette, '"UNHCR Guidance Note on Refugee Claims Relating to Sexual Orientation and Gender Identity": A Critical Commentary' (2010) 22(2) *International Journal of Refugee Law* 173.

[50] Baillot, Cowan and Munro, above n 48, 201.

[51] Millbank, above n 44, 14.

[52] A related question is: why are applicants, who strategically apply for visas not related to protection (such as educational or work-related visas) in order to escape a country of origin, questioned about this decision, on the basis that it indicates something other than a single motivation for leaving? The use of non-protection visas to enter a receiving state was interrogated during several of the oral hearings, even where the applicant testified that the visa in question was the only means by which they could leave their country: *Flores* [2013](IRB); *Pillai* [2013](RRT); *Mena* [2014](RRT).

[53] *Adjei v Canada (Minister of Employment and Immigration)* (1989) 2 FC 680; *Ponniah v Canada (Minister of Employment and Immigration)* (1991) 13 Imm LR (2d) 241.

[54] *Chan Yee Kin v MIEA* (1989) 169 CLR 379, 389, 398, 406–7. The High Court of Australia held that the chance of harm could be 'real' even where the likelihood of its occurrence was less than 50 per cent and that a 'real chance' could be as little as 10 per cent. Later, though, the High Court (while endorsing *Chan*) held that percentages of likelihood are irrelevant to the task of determining whether the fear of persecution is well-founded: *MIEA v Wu Shan Liang* (1996) 185 CLR 259.

decision-making and the ability to assess risk. The assumption is that refugee applicants who are 'genuine' are those who do not take a calculated risk and return home prior to applying for refugee status.[55] Evans Cameron argues that we all take certain risks if such risks allow us to access something that we want or that is very important to us. Further, she refers to literature showing that 'if you want to take a particular risk very badly, this will not only affect how you weigh the pros and cons; it will also make you perceive the risk itself as less dangerous than it is'.[56] In regards to refugee applicants' decisions as to whether to risk returning home, 'the appeals of home are obvious: family and friends, personal property, community, cultural identity, status, financial security'.[57]

The above examination of the narrative of becoming a refugee highlights the expectations and assumptions about refugee behaviour that are embedded in this particular stock story. It bears emphasising that this story of refugee behaviour could very well take on a different form: that 'genuine' refugees stay in their home countries for as long as possible despite immense danger; that they endure high levels of fear and harm up to the point of departure; and that when they arrive in a 'safe' country, they do everything they can to return home and to avoid permanent migration and delay an application for status until the last viable moment. Legally, at least, there is nothing to say that this alternative narrative cannot belong to an otherwise genuine refugee.

4.1.2 Critiquing the Refugee Story's Form

It is hard to imagine a neater or more straightforward tale of causation in relation to seeking refugee status than that of the stock story outlined above. The key events in the story occur one after the other: the refugee does not hesitate upon leaving, does not 'go back' on this original decision to leave, and does not equivocate about the decision to seek refugee status upon arriving. The story is one guided by certainty, resolve and immediate need, not by ambivalence, chance or tentative risk assessment. The events in the narrative are fixed and causally linked, and the timing is linear. The requirement of a particular narrative *form* is apparent in that any sense of haphazardness or disorder to the sequence of events, or the interruption of direct causation, may be cited as evidence of the implausibility of the story. Refugee applicants are expected to take decisive action in response to danger, and it is assumed that the fear of persecution is either the primary or the sole cause of departure. In addition, it is expected that the decision to seek refugee status flows directly from the decision to leave, and that narrative closure is achieved for 'genuine' refugees through the determination of their claims.

The remainder of the chapter returns to Ewick and Silbey's definitional elements of narrative – the selective appropriation of past events; a temporal, causal ordering of those events; and characters and events that are related to each other in some form of

55 Note, the Refugee Convention cessation clauses apply to a refugee who has 'voluntarily re-established himself [*sic*] in the country which he left or outside which he remained owing to fear of persecution': art 1C(4). However, this clause has consistently been found to require more than mere temporary return to one's country of origin: Guy S Goodwin-Gill and Jane McAdam, *The Refugee in International Law* (Oxford University Press, 4th ed, 2021) 164–65.

56 Paul Slovic et al, 'Affect, Risk, and Decision Making' (2005) 24(4, Suppl) *Health Psychology* S35, 36.

57 Evans Cameron, above n 20, 571.

emplotment and narrative arc[58] – to bring these elements to bear on the stock narrative of becoming a refugee as it appeared in the dataset. The narrative of becoming a refugee not only meets the minimum conditions required of the model Anglo-European narrative form that I describe in Chapter 2 but exemplifies them. Indeed, it exemplifies the narrative form in three respects: namely, its temporal ordering of events; the exceptionally linear causal relationships between events within this story; and the extent to which the events form a clear structure that is identifiable as a plot.

4.2 Becoming a Refugee in the Oral Hearings

This section explores how the narrative of becoming a refugee manifested in the hearings and the narrative burden placed on each applicant. While each decision-maker's assessment of evidence against the stock narrative entered the final decision in diverse ways, a version of this narrative was put to the applicant in twelve out of fifteen hearings.[59] Where the applicant was asked to explain a story of flight that was at odds with the story of becoming a refugee, the applicant was required to account for the deviations in their own narrative and to carefully explain the causal connections between events about which they gave evidence.[60] It is worth noting that the stock narrative of becoming a refugee is but one of a number of stories in relation to their evidence that applicants are expected to navigate in the RSD hearings. Where necessary, I contextualise each applicant's presentation of evidence in relation to this particular stock narrative.

4.2.1 The Rostami *Hearing*

The *Rostami* hearing took place before the IRB and involved a female applicant from Iran. Ms Rostami had made a claim on the basis of her membership of a particular social group and her religion.[61] The international travel she had undertaken before leaving Iran, but after her 'problems' (as the Member referred to them) had begun, was the subject of a lengthy exchange between herself and the Member. Ms Rostami's route to Canada was also addressed at some length. In the first instance, the onus was on the applicant to explain

[58] Patricia Ewick and Susan S Silbey, 'Subversive Stories and Hegemonic Tales: Toward a Sociology of Narrative' (1995) 29 (2) *Law & Society Review* 197, 200.

[59] The narrative was implicitly or explicitly present in 12 of the 15 included hearings. In five of the seven Canadian hearings (*Rostami* [2013](IRB); *Bhatti* [2013](IRB); *Flores* [2013](IRB); *Perera* [2013](IRB); *Valdez* [2013](IRB)), the decision-maker raised the narrative of a becoming a refugee, including questions of decision and timing of departure, the travel route to Canada, and any interim trips before departing. In the *Flores* [2013](IRB) hearing, the applicant was required to explain the timing of and reasons for departing Cuba. In the *Perera* [2013](IRB) hearing, the applicant was required to explain why he left when he did, his route, why he went via South America and why he did not claim protection in the United States en route to Canada. The applicant's travel route and reasons for flight were not raised in the *Jabbar* [2013](IRB) hearing and were only mentioned but not interrogated in the *Valdez* [2013](IRB) hearing. In six of the eight Australian hearings (*Adere* [2012](RRT); *Jadoon* [2014](RRT); *Mena* [2014](RRT); *Zeidan* [2014](RRT); *Pillai* [2013](RRT); *Zahau* [2012](RRT)), the decision-maker invoked the narrative of becoming a refugee, including questions of decision and timing of departure, the travel route to Australia, and any interim trips before departing. The decision-maker did not raise these topics in the *Malik* [2013](RRT) or the *Mbassi* [2012](RRT) hearings.

[60] These are the *Rostami* [2013](IRB); *Adere* [2012](RRT); and *Bhatti* [2013](IRB) hearings.

[61] See Appendix.

why she had not applied for refugee status prior to her final departure from Iran. The Member's style in this hearing was direct, and at some points this directness verged on brusqueness and impatience.

The exchanges included from the *Rostami* hearing capture an applicant being bound to explain why, as someone claiming to have a well-founded fear of persecution, she had not left Iran as soon as she possibly could, and why – if she truly feared for her life – she would return to Iran having managed to depart on at least one occasion. The exchange below took place at the very start of the Member's questioning of the applicant:

MEMBER: When did you decide to leave Iran?
APPLICANT: When the problems with my husband began. I wanted to leave ... to separate and because in Iran all rights to divorce belong to a man and I wanted to divorce and I wanted...
MEMBER: [*Cutting off applicant.*] Okay, one question. You were married in 2000 and six months after that was still 2000 or 2001?
[*No answer. Both interpreter and applicant seem not to understand the question.*]
MEMBER: Maybe I'll ask another question. Since the beginning of your problems, which were approximately six months after your marriage in 2000, what countries have you visited?
APPLICANT: Up to now?
MEMBER: Yes
APPLICANT: [*Applicant speaking very quietly, mumbling.*] Turkey, Dubai.
MEMBER: Turkey was when?
APPLICANT: I do not remember the date, also to Syria.
MEMBER: Any other places you have visited since you had problems after you married?
APPLICANT: The ones I just told you...
MEMBER: You indicate you had visited Switzerland in 2011 and that in 2012 you stopped in Turkey and France.
APPLICANT: Yes.
MEMBER: For example, in 2011, your intention in going to Switzerland was what?
APPLICANT: I wanted to leave Iran, and I asked someone to arrange a visa for me, and my intention was to come to Canada.
MEMBER: Did you believe at the time that your life or personal security was at risk?
APPLICANT: [*Emphatic.*] Yes, always.
MEMBER: Why did not you request to stay in Switzerland and go back to Iran?
APPLICANT: Because the person who I paid to arrange a visa told me not to stay in Switzerland and that the best place was Canada and he had bankers' cheques from my father that he would keep if I could not get to Canada.
MEMBER: Can you explain the banker's cheques? How did that work?
APPLICANT: It's sort of a guarantee and if I stayed in Swiss [*sic*] he would [take the cheques] and put it in his bank, and so I had to go back.
MEMBER: Did you talk to the authorities about how you could stay in Switzerland or make a refugee claim in Switzerland?
APPLICANT: No.
MEMBER: Why not?
APPLICANT: [*Applicant now speaks louder and more clearly.*] Because I did not know anyone and I did not know anywhere and I could not take a walk and besides that, our arrangement was that I would not stay in Swiss [*sic*].

The Member implies without directly stating that the applicant should have made an application in the first country she reached, and at the earliest opportunity, in accordance with 'safe third country' rules. What is noteworthy about the above exchange is that the applicant counters the Member by asserting another story, an explanation for why she had not made a claim at the earliest possible opportunity, instead returning to Iran despite an existing fear and despite having already reached a third country.[62] Ms Rostami's explanation brings into view other actors, namely those arranging her passage out of Iran, whose actions and behaviour she was not able to control. In the RSD hearings, an applicant's re-entry into the country where persecution had allegedly taken place, and the ability to pass through state border authorities, was frequently interpreted as indicating that the applicant was not in danger or sought by authorities.[63] In Ms Rostami's case, the decision-maker possibly did not make this assumption about her re-entry because her claim pertained to persecution by non-state actors, from whom she alleged the Iranian state was unable and unwilling to protect her.[64] As such, there was no reason why she would have been 'known' to the authorities or why it would have been difficult for her to leave the country.[65]

When Ms Rostami had left Iran for good, she had stopped with her smugglers in both Turkey and France while en route to Canada. In the following extract, which came almost directly after the extract above, the Member questions the applicant about other countries she had visited after leaving Iran but before arriving in Canada.

MEMBER: Okay. [*Pause.*] On the way to Canada, you indicate you stayed in Turkey and France. In Turkey, your arrival date was [XXX] and the departure date was [XXX]. Why is it that you did not . . . try to stay? Did you make a request to make a refugee claim in Turkey?

APPLICANT: Umm, I went to Turkey illegally, and also the arrangement I had made with the guy was to take me to Canada, and all the time I stayed inside the hotel room that he appointed to me, and all the time our arrangement was that I would not go out. . .

MEMBER: In France you indicate you arrived in Paris on [XXX]. Did you request to stay longer in France or to make a refugee claim in France?

APPLICANT: [*Louder, clearer.*] No, there also, I did not leave the house I was in. The arrangement I had made with this person was that he would take me to Canada.

MEMBER: Did you think about making a refugee claim?. . .

APPLICANT: No, because I wanted to get to Canada. I had a friend in Canada. I did not leave the house to ask anyone; I did not leave the home at all. That person I paid also said 'do not leave the house' because if the police see me and arrest me he would have no responsibility towards me anymore.

62 The decision-maker returns to the story about the 'blank cheques' paid to the smuggler later in the hearing, and the applicant is questioned about this point at length.

63 And of course, this is a further stock narrative about how things operate in countries that are 'other' or unknown to the decision-maker.

64 The notion that not only refugee applicants but also persecutors act 'rationally' and with a single intention has been critiqued in relation to the 'nexus' requirement in the Refugee Convention definition, namely that the feared persecution is 'for reasons of' race, religion, nationality, membership of a particular social group or political opinion. I return to the idea that authorities behave consistently and logically in Chapter 7, which addresses the genre of refugee testimony. On this point, see also Jane Herlihy, Kate Gleeson and Stuart Turner, 'What Assumptions about Human Behaviour Underlie Asylum Judgments?' (2010) 22(3) *International Journal of Refugee Law* 351, 259.

65 The requirement to explain international 'holidays' or 'trips' that had occurred after persecution had begun but before the applicant had fled was also present in the *Zeidan* [2014](RRT) and *Mena* [2014] (RRT) hearings.

MEMBER: [*Pause.*] Why were you convinced the person you had paid could successfully get you to Canada?

APPLICANT: Umm, because I had heard about him and also other people he had helped and the person who told me said he is alright, he is a good person, and I can trust him to do what he says. . .

This entire subject, and the Member's concerns about the applicant's route out of Iran and her international travel prior to departure, does not feature in the written decision. IRB decisions are considerably more concise than those of the RRT. They often deal with the claim in a comparatively cursory manner; the written decision in Ms Rostami's case before the IRB, for example, is only six generously spaced pages long. The applicant's above explanations are remarkable in that she has clear, certain reasons for not leaving Iran as soon as possible, and she outlines why they do not contradict or undermine her existing fears. Ms Rostami displays a certainty and belief in her own narrative here, and she is also able to construct this story against the stock story that the decision-maker presents. She points out that these decisions had been taken out of her hands to some degree, as she had been following the orders of the smuggler. However, she asserts her own agency in choosing to obey the smuggler rather than, as the decision-maker suggests, making an unplanned application for protection in Switzerland, Turkey or France. This aligns with Barsky's observation that 'persons who are persecuted are generally devoid of the information required to claim refugee status ... They therefore rely upon chance, the advice of (often self-serving) intermediaries or hearsay to make life-threatening decisions.'[66] Given the often-central role of smugglers and other intermediaries in arranging passage to a Convention-signatory state, their erasure from the stock refugee story shifts the burden back onto the applicant to explain their role and influence.

The applicant's departure from Iran en route to Canada is addressed in the decision as follows, in the section entitled 'Allegations':

> The claimant then had her father make arrangements to leave Iran for Canada in [XXX]. She first tried to go to Canada via Switzerland, but could not go further than Switzerland due to problems and could not stay in Switzerland ... Fearing her ex-husband would harm her and fearing persecution related to her husband denouncing her, she decided to travel to Canada illegally.[67]

The decision makes no further mention of the applicant's route to Canada and no explicit finding about credibility or plausibility is based on the factual finding about departure. Here, the applicant's successful rebuttal of the stock refugee story as a normative standard reinforces both the form and content of the stock narrative. In spite of extensive questioning about Ms Rostami's 'refugee story', the Member ultimately found in her favour.[68]

[66] Barsky, above n 31, 235.

[67] *Rostami* [2013] (IRB Decision and Reasons) [10].

[68] Ibid [26], [31]; and see Appendix.

4.2.2 *The* Adere *Hearing*

Mr Adere's application for protection in Australia, an application to which his wife was attached, was based on the danger he faced in his home country of Ethiopia on account of both his actual political opinion and his imputed political opinion. In the *Adere* hearing, significant exchanges occurred between the decision-maker and Mr Adere about why he had not left Ethiopia earlier, in direct response to the persecution he alleged on the basis of his political opinion and his work within an NGO. Another aspect of the *Adere* case was that when Mr Adere and his wife had left Ethiopia, they had departed on student visas, as they had previously been accepted into a short-term course of study in Australia. They then decided not to return to Ethiopia. The decision-maker expressed 'concern' that the couple's study plans revealed that a fear of persecution may not have been the sole or main reason for departure, and that therefore they did not have a well-founded fear of harm or a credible claim to protection.

The decision-maker first raised these concerns in a discussion of the applicant's decision to leave, examining when he had made this decision and why he had not made it sooner. Mr Adere gave evidence that he had been abducted and extrajudicially imprisoned, and that during his abduction his family began to organise a visa that would allow him to flee Ethiopia permanently. However, after he had been released, he had chosen not to complete the final forms required for this visa, as at that stage he had not wished to leave. The decision-maker questioned the applicant at some length about this:

MEMBER: Did you ultimately get that visa [that was organised by your family]?
APPLICANT: No.
MEMBER: Why is that, do you know?
APPLICANT: I do not know; because I did not submit all the documents that I should.
MEMBER: So, why would you not submit the documents?
APPLICANT: [*Silence*]. . .
MEMBER: Would your wife get a visa if she [had] applied to visit the UK?
APPLICANT: Yes. Because we have been there.
MEMBER: Okay, so I suppose my question is, you did not submit the visa documents because you did not want to leave your wife, why would not your wife also apply for a visa so you would both leave together?
APPLICANT: I do not think she would agree to leave.
MEMBER: Why would she not agree to leave, do you think?
APPLICANT: We both loved what we were doing in Ethiopia. We were passionate about the community work. Going back and leaving the country and being an asylum-seeker was not what we want[ed]. In Germany we also volunteered in refugee centres. We did not want to be like that. I do not think any person would choose that situation, honestly speaking. I have travelled a lot and I have seen the people were desperate with a lot of issues and problems and I used to enjoy to go there and chat, to give them hope.
MEMBER: I'm going back to your story on [XXX]. You were released that day because you said your father bribed the authorities, [or] someone. You went home, had a shower, you had your fingerprints done [for your visa] . . . Why would you have your fingerprints done if you did not want to leave?
APPLICANT: I did not want to disappoint my family; you know, in our culture you have to do pretty much everything that your family says.
MEMBER: Ok, so why did you not then provide the documents that you needed to do, to get the visa?
APPLICANT: Honestly speaking, half of me did not want to go, did not want to be there, because the way they wanted was to be an asylum-seeker and get refugee status, and really, it was not

> a thing that I wanted, but I just wanted to show that I listened, but at the same time I did not submit all the documents because I did not want to leave the country, I did not want to be a refugee.

Two features of Mr Adere's hearing openly disrupt the linear causality and the victimhood implied in the story of becoming a refugee: the evidence he supplies that he and his wife did not want to become refugees, and the fact that they made active decisions not to apply for refugee status despite the harm that they potentially faced. The decision-maker, faced with these narrative disruptions, had a tone of incredulity when he questioned the applicant as to why he would not finalise a visa application when he believed that it would be successful and he would be able to escape the danger he faced on this visa. Such incredulity correlates with Jane Herlihy et al's finding, upon a detailed thematic review of appeal decisions in UK asylum system, that 'credible individuals were assumed to act in accordance with their fears'. Indeed, a core theme that Herlihy et al identified was UK decision-makers' assumptions 'that people behave "rationally" in the face of danger'.[69]

The decision-maker also questioned an apparent contradiction in Mr Adere's evidence, namely that the applicant undertook some but not all of the requirements for the visa application. Mr Adere clearly explained that he did this because he wanted to please and obey his family – but once again, the applicant's own decision-making process and complex narrative of departure is assessed against a far simpler story and crude narrative structure.[70] Some of the affective complexity facing the applicant is revealed when he says: 'Honestly speaking, half of me did not want to go.' The statement, which implies a sense of grappling with the decision, and even making a decision to maybe leave and then 'going back' on this decision, seems to the decision-maker to signify an excess of agency. Mr Adere's testimony disrupts the narrative of becoming a refugee required of the applicant, and the linear drive of the story towards seeking refugee protection.

As shown in the following extract, the decision-maker continues to question the applicant's lack of a clear reason for leaving Ethiopia and the lack of a direct persecution-departure nexus. As mentioned, the applicant and the applicant's wife left Ethiopia on a student visa in order to complete a course in Australia:

MEMBER: You said you'd applied [for the course] in January, and obviously these processes take time, because you have to get accepted into a program, which takes some time; that seems to be a longer term plan for you and your wife to study in Australia, before this most recent event of detention and interrogation occurred ... I mean, were you fleeing

[69] Herlihy, Gleeson and Turner, above n 64, 358.

[70] Assumptions about how families function, and a flattening of the complex relationships within families in assessing plausibility, is a theme in literature critiquing RSD. For example, Herlihy et al note that one thread running through the decisions they examined 'was assumptions about how families behave following traumatic events, including who decides which family member gets to flee the country and who looks after whom': ibid 258. Rousseau et al also note that decision-makers frequently had simplistic understandings of culture and of family relations that play a part in governing applicant behaviour, particularly when these relationships are 'not like' their own families or relationships: Rousseau et al, above n 31, 62–63.

the country because of its circumstances or just coming to Australia for a program that you have been interested in for some time?

APPLICANT: Yes, we have been interested in the course, in community development school . . . It was the best thing that could have happened; that's why we took it.

MEMBER: It does seem to me that, people, and this obviously does happen where people legitimately have a well-founded fear of harm in their own country if they think that something is likely to happen to them or they are of adverse attention or interest to the authorities, and sometimes flee the country by any means either lawfully or unlawfully. **It seems to me that what you have done is not so much fleeing, but have waited for a course that you have been looking for some time to actually be approved, and when you were able to go on that course you have actually left the country for reasons associated with educational career rather than fleeing the country because of concerns about what was happening there. So I suppose what I'm really trying to get a sense of is this: when you left Ethiopia on that occasion, were you leaving because of concern about what had happened to you in the past, or was it solely for education and career?** (emphasis added)

APPLICANT: I think that I had learned my lesson due to all incidents that had happened to me . . . I learned my lesson at that time.. . .

MEMBER: It may be open to me to find that the reason why you and your wife left the country in July was either predominantly or even solely because of the opportunity to come to Australia to study, not for any reasons associated with things that were happening in Ethiopia.

APPLICANT: [*Silence*]

As the above excerpt shows, the applicant's testimony is expected not only to demonstrate a clear decision to leave, but that the decision was made for a clear and singular purpose. It appears that the decision-maker is demanding the applicant resile from his position that his motivations for leaving could be mixed, and that more than a 'fear of persecution' could motivate the particular decisions he made.[71] In Evans Cameron's analysis of refugee applicants' responses to risks in their home country, she writes:

> Claimants often explain that they delayed in leaving their country, or chose to return home, because they pinned their hopes on a 'mirage.' They hoped that the agents of persecution would eventually lose interest in them. Faced with two unpleasant options – live in danger or live in exile – they imagined a third, more optimistic, possibility: with time, the problem will resolve itself.[72]

It would be overwriting Mr Adere's own narrative with yet another narrative to impose Evans Cameron's account of common responses to risk. Nonetheless, I suggest her description better accords with the evidence Mr Adere presented than the narrative imputed by the decision-maker's questioning, which very much accords with the stock story of becoming refugee. In Mr Adere's evidence, we see the stock

[71] Herlihy et al also make the important point that an early application relies on the assumption that asylum seekers are fully armed with information about the host country's application process – and that this may not accord with an applicant's experience of arrival, particularly in the context of diminishing access to legal aid and refugee-related social services: Herlihy, Gleeson and Turner, above n 64, 359–60.

[72] Evans Cameron, above n 20, 574.

story rolled out via questioning and the applicant attempting to navigate his way through this narrative. We also see the extent to which he attempts to construct a different narrative of flight, and that this narrative is either misheard, reconstructed or ignored.

The *Adere* application for review was unsuccessful. The Tribunal found that Mr and Mrs Adere were not credible witnesses and that their claims lacked plausibility.[73] After presenting a range of findings about the plausibility of the applicants' evidence, the decision-maker addressed their narrative of departure as follows:

> The Tribunal concludes that if [the applicant] was the subject of the significant mistreatment, detention and interrogation he claimed, and had the opportunity to pursue a visa which would enable him to leave the country to avoid further harm, he would not simply have abandoned such an application. It has considered his explanation, that he did not wish to leave the country or his wife, but does not accept [that] this provides a plausible explanation, and is more consistent with the actions of a person who did not have a genuine fear of harm in Ethiopia at the time . . .[74]

In the majority of the other oral hearings, the narrative of becoming a refugee was present in both explicit and subtle ways, and particularly in the structure and content of questioning. In the *Adere* hearing, the narrative as a 'standard' or stock story is explicit. According to the stock story, the applicant should have left the country of persecution at the earliest possible opportunity. In the *Adere* matter, any ambivalence about leaving – what the applicant describes as 'half' feelings – undermines the narrative thrust and the plausibility of the claim that harm was feared.

The *Adere* hearing also provides an example of a decision-maker requiring the applicant to explain side-trips or departures from the country of origin, where such trips took place after the applicant had reason to fear persecution but were not made for the purpose of seeking protection. In the decision-maker's questions about this point, the applicant was required to explain his non-refugee-related departure from, as well as return to, his country of origin. When Mr Adere was questioned along these lines, he provided an explanation for his deviation from the narrative of becoming a refugee:

MEMBER: One of the things that the delegate referred to was the fact that you travelled quite extensively in and out of Ethiopia prior to coming to Australia, and at that time the Delegate noted that if you had wanted to, you could have sought asylum in Germany or the UK or other countries you may have visited, you could have sought asylum there but you did not do so. Why was that?

APPLICANT (IN PERSON): If I had a chance, I would have explained this to her, that nobody chooses to be an asylum seeker. [*Pause.*] Honestly, I was living for other people; that's what I used to do. I had the chance to live in Germany, in a European country, anywhere I want, but honestly that wasn't the priority of my life . . . We want to live a better life, you know, sometimes people, we choose what is viable for us . . . That wasn't me, that wasn't something that I wanted to do.

[73] *Adere* [2012] (RRT Decision and Reasons).
[74] Ibid [112]–[113]. Note, this awkward wording is reproduced as it was expressed in the written decision.

The applicant goes on to explain how and why it became necessary for him to leave Ethiopia. The applicant stated that he 'could have lived anywhere' prior to his decision to flee, but that he chose not to do so. This completely disrupts the form and normative content of the narrative of becoming a refugee, and demonstrates an excess of both agency and mobility for the victimised subjecthood required of refugee applicants.

4.2.3 The Bhatti *Hearing*

The *Bhatti* hearing took place before the IRB and involved a male applicant from Pakistan.[75] Mr Bhatti's claim was based on his imputed homosexuality (and therefore his membership of a particular social group) as well as his imputed conversion from Islam to Christianity. After the Member had completed the formal introduction to the hearing, his questioning immediately turned to why and when the applicant had left Pakistan, as well as the route that he had taken in order to arrive in Canada. The Member required Mr Bhatti to explain why he had stopped in the United States but had not sought asylum there.[76] Directly after this, the Member's questioning goes on to address the applicant's brief stopover in the United States and his decision to travel over the border to Canada in order to make his application there:

MEMBER: [*Heightened inquisitorial tone and inflection; emphasis on 'why' and on 'Canada'*] And why did you come to Canada?
APPLICANT: A friend of mine said it would be best in Canada because in the States they were catching all the people and sending them back.
MEMBER: Who is this friend?
APPLICANT: His name is [XXX].
MEMBER: Where does he live?
APPLICANT: In [US state].
MEMBER: And what does he do?
APPLICANT: He is in construction.
MEMBER: So you were in the States; you had your friend there, so why not claim in the States?
APPLICANT: He told me after 9/11 that the situation for Muslims is not very good, and if they catch them, they deport them.
MEMBER: [*Incredulous, disbelieving tone*] So the guy works in construction and he said that there's not one Muslim in the States since 9/11.
ADVOCATE: That is not what my client said.
MEMBER: Well, he can clarify.
APPLICANT: Actually, he told me about this and introduced me to one of his friends ...
MEMBER: So let us repeat the question, or the answer actually.
ADVOCATE: [*interjecting*] So what exactly did your friend say?
APPLICANT: My friend said they give you rights and listen to you in Canada and not in the States.

75 *Bhatti* [2013](IRB).

76 See above n 24 (safe third country rules). Note, however, that the formal US–Canada Safe Third Country Agreement did not apply due to the applicant's mode of entry into Canada.

In the above exchange, the Member responds with open sarcasm when Mr Bhatti details why he did not make a claim prior to arriving in Canada. Despite the Member's scepticism toward Mr Bhatti, the Member delivered a positive *ex tempore* decision on the application. There was no mention of the applicant's stopover in the United States, except for the Member's mentioning of the missing United States visa in the applicant's passport. The primary reason that the applicant was so quickly afforded the benefit of the doubt in this matter was that this applicant, unlike others, had a large amount of documentation directly supporting his claim and evidencing persecution, including newspaper articles and government documents about the applicant. The Member described the amount of the applicant's documentation of his persecution as 'voluminous' and 'considerable'.[77] The documentary evidence possibly outweighed the failure of the applicant's narrative to be read as plausible, which is a remarkably rare occurrence in RSD.

4.3 Who Is the Acceptable Refugee? Implications of Form and Content

The stock refugee story referred to throughout this chapter could also be described as a particular 'plot' that is sanctioned as plausible and 'true' due to the normative meanings or purposes it imparts. One norm established by the narrative of becoming a refugee – as told from the perspective of a refugee-receiving, Refugee Convention-signatory state – is that good or 'genuine' refugees are defined by their refugee status. And relatedly, that they seek protection as victims with no other available options, rather than as complex, active subjects seeking to control their own futures. Dauvergne has argued that in the absence of a liberal justice standard for admitting migrants or outsiders, liberal nations rely on a 'humanitarianism consensus' in order to shape and constrain migration law. She argues that when we are humanitarian, 'we bestow, as a gift, something on others who have no rightful claim to it'.[78] Where 'humanitarianism' governs migration law, and refugee law in particular, the state gives permission to non-citizens to enter as 'needy outsiders'.[79] This kind of humanitarianism accords with the story of becoming a refugee, and with a particular narrative arc whereby the receiving state benevolently saves the refugee applicant. In this story, the state is able to mark itself as good, while still avoiding fixed duties that might be demanded as part of 'justice' or 'rights' narratives as between state and migrant.[80]

The stock narrative of becoming a refugee allows the state to cast the refugee applicant as a victim whom it helps or saves.[81] This framing is preferable to perceiving

[77] *Bhatti* [2013] (IRB Decision and Reasons) [11]–[12].

[78] Catherine Dauvergne, *Humanitarianism, Identity, and Nation: Migration Laws of Australia and Canada* (UBC Press, 2005) 72.

[79] Ibid.

[80] Ibid.

[81] See especially Liisa H Malkki, 'Speechless Emissaries: Refugees, Humanitarianism, and Dehistoricization' (1996) 11(3) *Cultural Anthropology* 377. Malkki's anthropological work demonstrates the way in which a 'dehistoricizing universalism' creates a context in which refugees are not approached as historical actors but 'as mute victims': ibid 378.

the refugee as a rights-bearing subject who undermines the state's absolute sovereignty by imposing the obligation of *nonrefoulement*, regardless of the applicant's conformity with rigid narratives of 'authentic' refugeehood. What is noteworthy and often overlooked in the narrative of becoming a refugee is that the refugee is presented as both desperate *and* certain in the decision to leave and in the subsequent decision to seek refugee protection from the state. The refugee's agency is limited in that they 'had to' leave in response to harm, then immediately apply for refugee status as a matter of necessity, and cannot return to the country of origin. And yet, applicants must also display a degree of empowered individualism in that they leave, arrive and seek status with a sense of purpose and conviction. These acts must evince agency, but only the agency to act in a direct, linear trajectory, always moving forward towards inclusion in the host state and never sideways or backward – and thus, in the manner of a neat, chronological narrative.

In a critique of credibility assessment in RSD that recalls Dauvergne's notion of the benevolent state, Gregor Noll argues that evidentiary assessment in RSD can be understood in comparison to Roman Catholic auricular confession practices, whereby applicants undergo rituals of confession, repentance and absolution.[82] Noll maintains that applicants are subject to the grace of the decision-maker, whose credibility assessment 'reproduces the assessment of remorse' in Roman Catholicism. This view of the applicant as sinner-perpetrator allows the state to 'neutralise the political agency of asylum-seekers and to recast them as mere impostors or "victims-to-be-saved"'[83] Contrite sinners are rewarded with absolution, which opens up the path to the re-inclusionary sacrament of communion. Similarly, the ideal refugee applicant behaves like a penitent delivering confession and is rewarded with inclusion and entry into the state.[84] Crucial to this comparison of Roman Catholicism to RSD is the narrative of the applicant as penitent who seeks resolution or closure via the granting of refugee status.[85] Positive asylum determinations, which represent the culmination of the story of becoming a refugee, are about re-inclusion into the system of nation-states.[86] Noll labels this culmination 'reconciliation', but it might just as well be called a resolution. Mapping each of these analyses onto the story of becoming a refugee

[82] Gregor Noll, 'Salvation by the Grace of the State? Explaining Credibility Assessment in the Asylum Procedure' in Gregor Noll (ed), *Proof, Evidentiary Assessment and Credibility in Asylum Procedures* (Martin Nijhoff, 2005) 197.

[83] Ibid 197.

[84] Ibid 201.

[85] Ibid 204.

[86] Jennifer Beard and Noll elaborate on this argument, writing that

> recognition of a refugee is not given by right on factual grounds but demands the applicant undergo a form of spiritual conversion or transformation, 'in the form of a movement and elaboration of the subject by the subject' into a condition beyond doubt: the formation of a credible legal subject, who gives an account of facts *internal* to herself. The refugee must *testify*, prove herself . . . not as a seeing body but as a body erased of any inscriptions of doubt.
>
> (emphasis in original)

Jennifer Beard and Gregor Noll, 'Parrhēsia and Credibility: The Sovereign of Refugee Status Determination' (2009) 18(4) *Social & Legal Studies* 455, 471; citing Michel Foucault et al, *The Hermeneutics of the Subject: Lectures at the Collège de France 1981–1982* (St Martin's Press, 2005) 15–16.

provides the story with a clear meaning. The point of closure comes with the bestowal or denial of refugee status, and this decision resolves the 'complication' of the applicant leaving their own sovereign and citizenship status.

A critical reading of the story of becoming a refugee highlights a motif that structures the appraisal of credibility more generally, which is that of the regulation of the 'genuine' refugee's exercise of agency and autonomy. Such a reading also highlights the contradictions that structure legitimate forms of refugee agency. The refugee must be forced to leave, thus displaying little or no agency in the initial decision. Having been forced to leave, the applicant must not display ambivalence; instead the applicant must confidently make a decision to become a refugee at the earliest possible opportunity. The expectation that refugees act resolutely and apply for status as soon as they arrive in the host country or in a 'safe third country' reinforces the fact that the applicant's 'refugeeness'[87] and need for refugee status must drive the narrative over and above all other considerations or concerns held by the applicant, or indeed any other actor in the refugee story.

4.4 Conclusion

In the narrative of becoming a refugee, the story is resolved with the making and then the determination of a claim for protection. However, this 'natural' endpoint might not appear as such to the applicant, who may choose to appeal or challenge deportation orders if the claim is unsuccessful, or who may view the granting of refugee status as a further plot point in a longer story of persecution, suffering and recurring trauma. The applicant may also see the granting of formal protection as a small event in the larger story of resettlement and other major life events, especially as applicants may experience ongoing discrimination or other fearful circumstances within their new community.[88] Indeed, this stock story forecloses the possibility that the 'end' of the story could be the return to one's country of origin. The stock story also fails to account for how the granting of refugee status may be not just the beginning of new relationships in the receiving state, but also the continuation of a life enmeshed in prior relationships with people in one's country of origin.[89] Eastmond offers a

[87] See especially Trish Luker, 'Performance Anxieties: Interpellation of the Refugee Subject in Law' (2015) 30 (01) *Canadian Journal of Law and Society* 91; see also discussions of 'refugeeness' in Marie Lacroix, 'Canadian Refugee Policy and the Social Construction of the Refugee Claimant Subjectivity: Understanding Refugeeness' (2004) 17(2) *Journal of Refugee Studies* 147. On the contradictory approaches to the 'authentic' refugee's agency, see Simon Behrman, 'Between Law and the Nation State: Novel Representations of the Refugee' (2016) 32 *Refuge: Canada's Journal on Refugees* 38.

[88] On the impossibility of complete closure in narrative, see Martin McQuillan (ed), *The Narrative Reader* (Psychology Press, 2000) 5; and on the difficulties of resettlement, see: Teresa Puvimanasinghe et al, 'Narrative and Silence: How Former Refugees Talk about Loss and Past Trauma' (2015) 28(1) *Journal of Refugee Studies* 69. Rousseau et al also note: 'Many authors have moved beyond traditional unilinear notions of adaptation and acculturation; some, for example, have shown that situations of marginality, alienation and poverty in the host culture impact negatively on refugee well-being more than actual experiences of violence and torture in the home country': above n 31, 50.

[89] And as Barsky notes: 'No study of refugee movement would be complete without some mention of the determining role that chance plays in the entire process. From being in the wrong place at the wrong time, to meeting an agent, to reading a particular newspaper article, any event has the potential to influence a refugee's choice of country': Barsky, above n 31, 186.

particularly sharp description of the problem with a demand for narrative in the refugee context:

> While 'predicament, human striving, and an unfolding in time toward a conclusion is central to the syntax of all human stories', in many refugee situations, the outcome is far from given. Refugees are in the midst of the story they are telling, and uncertainty and liminality, rather than progression and conclusion, are the order of the day.[90]

In the next chapter, I argue that in addition to being required to contend with certain 'stock' narratives in the hearings, such as the one addressed here, refugee applicants are also required to address expressions of the decision-maker's own subjective, narrative-based and normative world. The narrative expectations of individual decision-makers are especially difficult for the applicant to navigate because they are often highly subjective, idiosyncratic and at times impulsive. While this chapter has demonstrated that the narrative of becoming a refugee is, in both form and content, one of the 'stock stories' that guide credibility determinations, in Chapter 5 I trace narratives that cannot be sensibly be labelled 'stock stories', for they reflect the decision-maker's highly subjective and at times unpredictable understandings of the world. What links each of these contentions about how evidence is tested and appraised during the hearings is that these narrative standards are central to credibility assessment. And, while such standards are neither necessarily 'visible' nor obvious to the applicant, the applicant must nonetheless grapple with, interpret and respond to them, all within the confines of the unfamiliar, multilingual and adjudicative setting of the RSD oral hearing.

[90] Eastmond, above n 16, 251 (citations omitted).

5

Narrative Contest as Structuring the Oral Hearing

As I sat quietly at the back of the hearing rooms of the RRT or IRB, or in an office carrel carefully relistening to a hearing's audio recording, to my relative surprise I heard decision-makers present their own narratives to applicants. Sometimes these narratives were detailed and developed. At other times, they were explicitly of the 'what I would have done' variety or simply proposed a different arc of events or a different course of action, either in relation to the applicant or someone else who featured in their testimony. These narratives went beyond asking for further information or explanation. Instead, they involved decision-makers presenting an alternative, hypothetical account of how events would have taken place, if the story (and by implication the applicant) were credible. Refugee applicants, in turn, were required to contend with, appraise and explain these narratives against their own. In these encounters, which I term 'narrative contests', refugee applicants were required to respond to a decision-maker's own imagined counter-narrative of events, setting out how the story could or indeed *ought* to have taken place.[1] Applicants were either required to account for why their narrative differed from that expressed by a decision-maker, or in certain instances, capitulate or surrender to a decision-maker's view that an experience could not have taken place as the applicant described.

In these moments of narrative contest, much is demanded of the applicant: to hear the decision-maker's alternative narrative; address the issues it raises; explain why events did not take place as the decision-maker imagines they should have; and, finally, to incorporate the decision-maker's concerns (expressed as counter-narratives) into their existing evidence. This chapter tracks how, during these exchanges, applicants were required to demonstrate immense narrative competency as they presented their testimony. That is, applicants had to contend with imagined counter-scenarios presented by decision-makers, as well as their own narratives. Crucially, this chapter also demonstrates that as applicants navigated these exchanges, certain applicants displayed high levels of agency and resistance vis-à-vis

[1] I note that I use the term 'counter-narrative' in a different manner to those writing in the field of legal storytelling. The term 'counter-story' was first used in the context of law and literature by Richard Delgado, who applied the term to the stories told by outsiders or marginalised groups to challenge dominant narratives. As noted in Chapter 2, Delgado argues these counter-stories are told by 'outgroups' and 'challenge the received wisdom'. They are 'competing versions [of reality] that can be used to challenge a stock story and prepare the way for a new one': Richard Delgado, 'Storytelling for Oppositionists and Others: A Plea for Narrative' (1989) 89 *Michigan Law Review* 2411, 2414–15. A closer comparator is the concept of narrative competition as expressed by Richard Weisberg in his analysis of narrative in contested trials: Robert Weisberg, 'Proclaiming Trials as Narratives' in Peter Brooks and Paul Gerwirtz (eds), *Law's Stories: Narrative and Rhetoric in the Law* (Yale University Press, 1996) 71.

decision-makers' vast power to direct the hearing and co-produce evidence – a theme that runs throughout this book and that I address in detail in the following chapter.

As addressed in Chapter 1, a critical and important body of work has traced the imposition of certain culturally specific, 'Western', racialised and colonial narratives upon refugee applicants in the context of credibility determinations, especially but not only in relation to claims based on gender-based harms or sexual orientation. My findings in this study sit alongside such scholarship. I argue that the expression of decision-makers' views during the oral hearing and related narrative contests often took place at such a high level of subjectivity – and reflected such profoundly personal experiences about the way the world works – that it is difficult to neatly pin these expectations to larger narratives that may be determined by the class, gender or cultural position of the decision-maker, *even as* these factors are and were always at play. Subject position, personal history and experience each influence and shape the decision-maker's – and applicant's – view of the world. However, in certain moments during the hearings, when the decision-maker and applicant were in conflict, the decision-maker's own normative views were best understood as shifting, idiosyncratic and at times even impulsive.

Macklin provides a memorable example of this: in recalling her work as a refugee decision-maker, she observes that her own life experience and understanding of her own physical body as a 'veritable showcase of the effects of clumsiness' led her to accept there was nothing unusual 'about acquiring various random scars on one's body in the course of normal life'. By contrast, her 'agile and nimble' colleague put great stock in physical marks and scarring as compelling evidence of torture.[2] This chapter demonstrates that a decision-maker's various and entrenched presumptions can be determinative either of a claim or of the shape of oral evidence and its testing, even where the final decision omits these oral contests. While Rousseau et al characterise these moments as 'misunderstandings' rather than conflicts, they too emphasise their capacity to determine a person's fate, even as all parties may be 'oblivious to the cultural processes leading to such clashes'.[3] Indeed, the counter-narratives and the basis upon which decision-makers raised them were not necessarily apparent to applicants, who were nonetheless given little option but to contend with them.

My argument here recalls one of the core concerns of the credibility literature: the problem of decision-maker subjectivity.[4] Particularly illuminating here is Hanna Wikström and Thomas Johansson's contention that credibility assessments function as a form of 'normative

[2] Audrey Macklin, 'Truth and Consequences: Credibility Determination in the Refugee Context' in International Association of Refugee Law Judges (ed), *The Realities of Refugee Determination on the Eve of a New Millennium: The Role of the Judiciary* (International Association of Refugee Law Judges, 1998) 134, 140.

[3] Cécile Rousseau et al, 'The Complexity of Determining Refugeehood: A Multidisciplinary Analysis of the Decision-Making Process of the Canadian Immigration and Refugee Board' (2002) 15(1) *Journal of Refugee Studies* 43, 52.

[4] For literature that has shaped this field, see Macklin, above n 2; Michael Kagan, 'Is Truth in the Eye of the Beholder? Objective Credibility Assessment in Refugee Status Determination' (2002) 17 *Georgetown Immigration Law Journal* 367; Jenni Millbank, '"The Ring of Truth": A Case Study of Credibility Assessment in Particular Social Group Refugee Determinations' (2009) 21(1) *International Journal of Refugee Law* 1; Jane Herlihy, Kate Gleeson and Stuart Turner, 'What Assumptions about Human Behaviour Underlie Asylum Judgments?' (2010) 22(3) *International Journal of Refugee Law* 351.

leakage'.[5] They argue that when decision-makers assess 'different' socio-cultural narratives, their assessments represent a form of 'normative leakage', meaning that unspoken 'class and gender norms as well as postcolonial reasoning *implicitly* become a part of the [credibility] assessments'.[6] Their description of decision-makers' normative but inexplicit modes of reasoning reflects a concern that I share, about the often shifting and uncontained nature of decision-makers' views during hearings.[7] Building upon Thomas Spijkerboer's argument that decision-makers' normative standards are 'hard to make explicit, and most often they are not',[8] Wikström and Johansson observe that normative standards are frequently 'used but not acknowledged' by decision-makers.[9] In a similar vein, Macklin discusses the 'gut feeling' fallacy: 'the unquestioned assumption that our gut is a uniquely trustworthy arbiter of truth'.[10] Even the Australian 'Guidelines on the Assessment of Credibility' set out that '[w]hat is capable of being believed is not to be determined according to the Member's subjective belief or gut feeling about whether an applicant is telling the truth or not'.[11]

In tracing these encounters, and framing my analysis more generally, this chapter also sets out the limited international and domestic law, policy or guidelines that govern the testing of evidence – and credibility – *during* the oral hearing. As such, this chapter is divided into two parts. In Section 5.1, I set out the relevant law and policy that apply to the presentation of testimony in RRT and IRB oral hearings, in order to establish the very minimal nature of the rules that govern the reception and testing of evidence *during* the hearing. Section 5.2 then analyses various oral hearings in the dataset, to demonstrate that evidence was frequently tested via narrative contests in which applicants were required to respond to and address decision-makers' normative, and at times idiosyncratic and shifting, narrative-based understandings of the world. I present two specific hearings in detail to explore the narrative contests that took place between the applicant and the decision-maker.[12] Section 5.2 also explores how the knotty credibility criterion of 'plausibility' forges a direct link between credibility assessment and the narrative form.

5 Hanna Wikström and Thomas Johansson, 'Credibility Assessments as "Normative Leakage": Asylum Applications, Gender and Class' (2013) 1(2) *Social Inclusion* 92.

6 Ibid 100 (emphasis added).

7 Wikström and Johansson, above n 5.

8 Thomas Spijkerboer, 'Stereotyping and Acceleration: Gender, Procedural Acceleration and Marginalised Judicial Review in the Dutch Asylum System' in Gregor Noll (ed), *Proof, Evidentiary Assessment and Credibility in Asylum Procedures* (Martin Nijhoff, 2005) 67.

9 Wikström and Johansson, above n 5, 93.

10 Macklin, above n 2, 139. 'Instinct' and 'a feeling' are also terms that are used to describe the bases for subjective credibility assessments: Kagan, above n 4, 377.

11 Administrative Appeals Tribunal Migration and Refugee Division, 'Guidelines on the Assessment of Credibility' (2006, updated 2015) [9].

12 While this chapter focuses on two hearings before the RRT, the findings here also apply to a majority of the Canadian hearings. For the Canadian hearings, some form of narrative contest took place in all hearings except the *Flores* [2013](IRB) hearing. The *Jabbar* [2013](IRB) hearing featured only a small number of narrative contests between the Member and applicant, primarily addressing why the applicant's persecutors (the Taliban) would have behaved in the way the applicant described. Narrative contests in relation to more than one topic took place in all of the hearings before the RRT, except the *Zeidan* [2014](RRT) hearing.

Recalling what Robert Thomas identified as the most stubborn problem of refugee assessment, namely 'the decision-makers' own presence of self',[13] I argue that it is when decision-makers articulate their own, more compelling version of an applicant's narrative that the decision-maker's presence is most acutely felt during the hearing. Macklin argues that decision-makers must interrogate themselves in order to determine the basis for their findings with respect to plausibility and credibility.[14] My observations of the hearings resonate with Thomas' and Macklin's concerns. Thomas and Macklin both point to the need for decision-makers to be aware of how, why and when they pose *particular* counter-narratives to applicants during the hearing and to interrogate the normative basis for their sense of how the story goes, or indeed should have gone.

5.1 Legal Framing of the Oral Testimonial Encounter

This section maps the legal and procedural standards that govern the oral hearing in Australia and Canada. The minimal restrictions that apply to the hearing itself recall Barsky's claim that very little of the oral hearing can be explained or understood merely by reference to the formal law and procedures that govern its conduct. Indeed, to examine the refugee hearing only through pre-given legal standards is to reduce the process to its barest bones and even actively impede our understanding of how the oral hearing functions.[15] It is for this reason that Barsky draws on critical discourse analysis and theory to examine 'the rules, conventions and the procedures which legitimate and to some degree determine a particular discursive practice' within the hearing; it is also why I draw on narrative-based standards and conventions in the analysis that follows.[16]

Decision-makers are afforded an extremely wide discretion in testing and judging refugee applicants' evidence. This is due in large part to the unique nature of RSD, which generally involves cross-cultural communication, a primary reliance on uncorroborated applicant testimony, the presentation of traumatic or distressing events and predictions about future events. Standard rules of procedure and evidence would function poorly in this context, to say the least. The inquisitorial nature of the hearing, low evidentiary standards of proof and the lack of formal evidentiary rules represent an attempt to address the challenges of 'bare' testimony within RSD; the limited availability of other forms of evidence; the highly speculative nature of refugee determination; and the high stakes of refugee decision-making.[17] However, I suggest here that

13 Robert Thomas, 'Assessing the Credibility of Asylum Claims: EU and UK Approaches Examined' (2006) 8(1) *European Journal of Migration and Law* 79, 84.

14 Macklin, above n 2, 139.

15 See Robert F Barsky, *Constructing a Productive Other: Discourse Theory and the Convention Refugee Hearing* (John Benjamins, 1994) 8.

16 Ibid 10.

17 The *UNHCR Handbook*, discussed in detail below, describes the decision-making context especially plaintively:

> The relevant facts of the individual case will have to be furnished in the first place by the applicant himself [*sic*]. It will then be up to the person charged with determining his status (the examiner) to assess the validity of any evidence and the credibility of the applicant's statements.

UNHCR, *Handbook on Procedures and Criteria for Determining Refugee Status under the 1951 Convention and the 1967 Protocol Relating to the Status of Refugees* (HCR/IP/4/Eng/REV1, 4th ed, 2019) 43 ('the Handbook').

one effect of the existing informal standards and broad decision-maker discretion – which ostensibly aim to ameliorate the challenges of RSD – is to enable decision-makers' subjective views and impulses to profoundly influence how evidence is tested and the determination of refugee applicants' credibility.

These findings are echoed in Nick Gill et al's in-person study of 240 matters before Britain's First Tier Tribunal (Immigration and Asylum Chamber), which analysed the implications of broad procedural discretions afforded to judges in asylum hearings.[18] This research tested the assumption that where procedural discretion is available to judges, its effect is to help litigants to 'participate fully in the legal process', especially litigants classed as vulnerable.[19] Notably, the authors found that judges used their procedural discretion 'less frequently to redress vulnerabilities of appellants' than they did in ways that were indifferent to these vulnerabilities or exacerbated them, or exercised discretion according to factors not relevant to redressing an applicant's disadvantages or barriers to participating in a hearing.[20] These findings 'cast doubt over the tactic of allowing broad procedural discretion so that judges are able to redress appellant disadvantages in specific cases'[21] and are strongly supported by my analysis of the Canadian and Australian oral hearings in the dataset. The limited constraints on both decision-makers' procedural discretion and oral hearing procedures also set the stage for and enable what Laura Smith-Khan, Marie Jacobs and Katrijn Maryns have carefully analysed as the co-production of refugee testimony by multiple actors *including* decision-makers, even though such testimony and evidence is ultimately attributed in its entirety to the applicant.[22]

The evidentiary and procedural standards governing the hearing do not compel the 'cultures of disbelief' and scepticism described in Chapter 1. Nor, it should be noted, does every decision or decision-maker reproduce cultures of doubt and suspicion in their approach to applicants and their evidence.[23] However, existing standards of procedure certainly do not considerably constrain decision-maker subjectivity and its expression during the oral hearing, nor dictate how decision-makers must or even should shape the conduct and terms of the hearing. As this chapter demonstrates, the testing of evidence during the oral hearing exists as a central problem for RSD, alongside the existing credibility criteria and its inherent normativity. As the following section demonstrates, existing standards fail to both guide decision-makers' approaches to evidence during the hearing as well as to provide applicants with a bare minimum sense of the basis on which their testimony will be tested.

[18] Nick Gill et al, 'The Limits of Procedural Discretion: Unequal Treatment and Vulnerability in Britain's Asylum Appeals' (2018) 27(1) *Social & Legal Studies* 49.

[19] Ibid 6.

[20] Ibid 22.

[21] Ibid 23.

[22] Marie Jacobs and Katrijn Maryns, 'Managing Narratives, Managing Identities: Language and Credibility in Legal Consultations with Asylum Seekers' (2022) 51(3) *Language in Society* 372; Laura Smith-Khan, 'Why Refugee Visa Credibility Assessments Lack Credibility: A Critical Discourse Analysis' (2019) 28(4) *Griffith Law Review* 406.

[23] For a rare overview of the different approaches decision-makers take to running the oral hearing, see Canadian Council for Refugees, 'The Experience of Refugee Claimants at Refugee Hearings at the Immigration and Refugee Board' (2012) 38–44 <http://ccrweb.ca/files/irb_hearings_report_final.pdf>.

5.1.1 *International Refugee Law and RSD Procedure*

As has been regularly observed, principles, rules or standards governing the process of RSD are absent from the Refugee Convention and the 1967 Protocol.[24] *The UNHCR Handbook on Procedures and Criteria for Determining Refugee Status* (the Handbook), first published in 1979 and updated several times, is the key international source of guidance on RSD procedure and the minimum standards under international refugee law for assessing refugee claims.[25] While the Handbook's section on procedural aspects of RSD is relatively short (a meagre four pages), it directly addresses the encounter between the decision-maker and the applicant and the question of evidentiary assessment within RSD. The Handbook is the founding source of much of the language governing credibility assessment in Refugee Convention-signatory countries, particularly as it exists within domestic guidelines and jurisprudence on the determination of credibility, and this is the case in Australia and Canada.[26] Even though the document itself is not directly referred to in domestic statutes, the criteria of plausibility, internal and external consistency and coherence, as set out in the Handbook, frame credibility assessment in both jurisdictions.[27]

In contemporary refugee law, evidentiary assessment takes place as part of the determination of an applicant's overall credibility. However, credibility is only mentioned three times in the section of the Handbook dealing with fact-finding.[28] Instead, as discussed in Chapter 1, the Handbook focuses on establishing the 'benefit of the doubt' as the standard governing refugee testimony assessment (although this is not presented as the standard of

[24] As the UNHCR Handbook notes, 'the determination of refugee status, although mentioned in the 1951 Convention (cf Article 9), is not specifically regulated': UNHCR, above n 17, 41.

[25] UNHCR, above n 17. For an overview of the context and history of the Handbook's production, see Chapter 1. For other UNHCR guidance on RSD processes, see Executive Committee of the United Nations High Commissioner for Refugees, 'Determination of Refugee Status' (EXCOM Conclusion No 8 (XXVIII), 12 October 1977); UNHCR, 'Global Consultations on International Protection: Asylum Processes (Fair and Efficient Asylum Procedures)' (EC/GC/01/12, 31 May 2001); UNHCR, 'Building in Quality: A Manual on Building a High Quality Asylum System' (September 2011).

[26] In the decision *Chan Yee Kin v Minister for Immigration & Ethnic Affairs* (1989) 169 CLR 379, the High Court of Australia accepted the Handbook as a guiding but not binding document within Australian refugee law; see also *Chan v Canada (Minister of Employment and Immigration)* [1995] 3 SCR 593 (Canada). In the UK, Lord Steyn characterised the Handbook as 'high persuasive authority' which is 'much relied on by courts and tribunals': *R v SSHD, ex parte Adan and Aitseguer* [2001] 2 AC 477, 608.

[27] Immigration and Refugee Board, 'Assessment of Credibility in Claims for Refugee Protection' (Legal Services, 2004); Administrative Appeals Tribunal Migration and Refugee Division, above n 11. The Canadian document addressing credibility assessment is approximately 100 pages long, is not an official 'guideline' and deals in detail with multiple aspects of credibility assessment. By contrast, the Australian Credibility Guidelines are nine pages long, sparsely referenced and contain general statements and principles with regards to credibility assessment.

[28] UNHCR, above n 17. The Handbook states that once the applicant has furnished the facts of their case, it is then up to the decision-maker 'to assess the validity of any evidence and the credibility of the applicant's statements': at [195]. It also states that where it is difficult to produce supporting evidence, 'if the applicant's account appears credible, he [*sic*] should, unless there are good reasons to the contrary, be given the benefit of the doubt': at [196]. Lastly, the Handbook sets out that the benefit of the doubt should only be given where the decision-maker is already satisfied as to the applicant's general credibility: at [204] and see discussion in-text. These cursory references to credibility largely assume that it has already been positively established, and demonstrate the Handbook's lack of guidance when credibility is in doubt.

proof as such).[29] The 'benefit of the doubt' principle recognises the limited access that refugee applicants may have to other forms of proof, and the fact that some statements may not be susceptible to proof at all.[30] The section of the Handbook entitled 'Establishing the Facts' repeats in a range of ways that the requirement of supporting evidence should not be 'too strictly applied', and that where no solid evidence is available, the applicant should not be penalised and instead should be encouraged to give all possible evidence in 'a climate of confidence'.[31] The document goes on to emphasise that 'it is hardly possible for a refugee to "prove" every part of his [*sic*] case and, indeed, if this were a requirement the majority of refugees would not be recognised'.[32] However, under international law, the burden of proof nonetheless rests 'in principle' on the refugee applicant, although the adjudicator shares 'the duty to ascertain and evaluate all the relevant facts'.[33] However, this duty may be met 'to a large extent' through the decision-maker being 'aware the objective situation in the country of origin concerned [and] being aware of relevant matters of common knowledge' and by verifying facts already alleged.[34] Once again, the refugee applicant has the burden of establishing the truth of their claim and the facts relevant to it but UNHCR has recognised that the decision-maker should 'lighten' this burden and ultimately 'shares' in the responsibility of substantiating facts relevant to the application.

Read as a whole, the Handbook posits a setting where the broad discretion of decision-makers is exercised in such a manner that evidence is interpreted in good faith and with an operating presumption that testimony is credible. In this imagined setting, the applicant's character is not being tested, so 'untrue statements by themselves are not a reason for refusal of refugee status'.[35] In addition, decision-makers should seek to find 'an explanation for any misrepresentation or concealment of material facts'.[36] The Handbook sets out that evidentiary assessment must not take 'isolated incidents out of context' and that decision-makers should evaluate any apparent inconsistencies or untrue statements 'in the light of all the circumstances of the case'.[37] These statements in the Handbook give an impression of the hearing as a space that is open, receptive and inclined to overlook small inconsistences, and which favours a holistic assessment of the applicant's testimony in a manner that is sensitive to the effects of trauma on memory, narrative and expression.[38]

[29] On this terminology, see UNHCR, 'Note on Burden and Standard of Proof in Refugee Claims' (1998).

[30] UNHCR, above n 17, 44.

[31] Ibid 39.

[32] Ibid.

[33] UNHCR, above n 29, [6]; UNHCR, above n 17, [196], [210].

[34] UNHCR, above n 29, [6]. This conflicts with the Handbook's earlier and much broader statement of the duty, that the decision-maker may need to 'use all means at his [*sic*] disposal' to produce evidence in support of the claim: ibid [196].

[35] UNHCR, above n 17, 39. This principle is supported by Bohmer and Shuman's research into the diverse reasons that motivate people with genuine protection needs to lie during refugee decision-making processes or other encounters with host state authorities: Carol Bohmer and Amy Shuman, *Political Asylum Deceptions: The Culture of Suspicion* (Palgrave Macmillan, 2018).

[36] UNHCR, above n 17, 39.

[37] Ibid.

[38] In its 'Note on Burden and Standard of Proof,' published in 1998, UNHCR reiterates that consideration should be given to the fact that 'due to the applicant's traumatic experiences, he/she may not speak freely; or that due to time lapse or the intensity of past events, the applicant may not be able to remember all factual details or to recount them accurately or may confuse them'. The Note warns that 'insubstantial

The Handbook's guidance does little to structure decision-making where credibility is in doubt. In fact, under the Handbook's guidance, 'the benefit of the doubt' is only applied to an applicant's testimony *once* they have been found to be credible.[39] In the Handbook's main qualification of the benefit of the doubt principle, we are told that the benefit should only be given when 'all available evidence has been obtained and checked and when the examiner is satisfied as to the applicant's general credibility'.[40] This qualification seems to me to reflect the beginnings of a culture of disbelief within RSD, leading to a troubling paradox for refugee applicants. The core concessions that the Handbook makes – interpreting the refugee applicant's testimony in light of the challenges they might face in presenting it – only apply once credibility has already been determined in the refugee's favour.[41]

As also noted earlier, the content of credibility assessment is described, though not formally defined at the international level, via the criteria that 'the applicant's statements must be coherent and plausible, and must not run counter to generally known facts'.[42] The Handbook states that any allowance made for a lack of evidence 'does not, however, mean that unsupported statements must necessarily be accepted as true if they are inconsistent with the general account put forward by the applicant'.[43] Thus, the Handbook provides the overarching criteria of coherence, consistency and plausibility that have become absolutely central to domestic RSD.[44] It does little, however, to explain the content of such standards, or most notably for the purposes of this chapter, how such standards should be appraised or tested – either during the oral hearing or outside of it.[45]

As noted in Chapter 1, there have been a series of practical and thoughtful engagements with how credibility assessment should be conducted since the publication of the Handbook, one of which is the UNHCR's 'Beyond Proof – Credibility Assessment in EU Asylum Systems' report (Beyond Proof report).[46] The Beyond Proof report was motivated by the need for a more harmonised approach to credibility assessment within the EU, as well as by the UNHCR's identification, in the exercise of its supervisory responsibility, of 'a trend across [EU] Member States whereby first instance negative decisions . . . often seem to result from the fact that key elements of the applicant's statements are not accepted as credible'.[47]

vagueness or incorrect statements' should not be decisive factors when determining credibility: UNHCR, above n 29, 3.

39 UNHCR, above n 17, 44.

40 Ibid 39. For a domestic and unambiguous restatement of this principle in Canada, see *Chan v Canada (Minister of Employment and Immigration)* [1995] 3 SCR 593.

41 UNHCR, ibid.

42 Ibid. This description is repeated in UNHCR's Note on Burden and Standard of Proof: UNHCR, above n 29, 3.

43 UNHCR, above n 17, 44.

44 Immigration and Refugee Board, above n 27, [1.1]. Administrative Appeals Tribunal Migration and Refugee Division, above n 11, [9], [28].

45 See Millbank, above n 4, 5–6.

46 UNHCR, 'Beyond Proof: Credibility Assessment in EU Asylum Systems: Summary Report' (May 2013) 7 ('Beyond Proof Report'). See also International Association of Refugee Law Judges, 'Assessment of Credibility in Refugee and Subsidiary Protection Claims under the EU Qualification Directive – Judicial Criteria and Standards' (2013); Hungarian Helsinki Committee, 'Credibility Assessment in Asylum Procedures – A Multidisciplinary Training Manual' (Volumes 1 & 2, 2015, 2013).

47 UNHCR, above n 46, 7. And for a detailed and lucid review of the history of initiatives in relation to credibility assessment and gender, see Debora Singer, 'Falling at Each Hurdle: Assessing the Credibility of Women's Asylum Claims' in Efrat Arbel, Catherine Dauvergne and Jenni Millbank (eds), *Gender in Refugee Law: From the Margins to the Centre* (Routledge, 2014) 98.

The Beyond Proof report reinforces the identification of credibility assessment as the 'core task' of RSD, but is unique because it addresses exactly *how* credibility is tested *during* applicant interviews and oral hearings.[48] Alongside a 'multidisciplinary training manual', the report attempts to identify and amend many of the incorrect but entrenched normative practices that have guided credibility assessment. As a mere report it is of course not binding on RSD conducted by the UNHCR, let alone on domestic practice – but it does reflect the urgent need for a more predictable approach to credibility assessment both within and outside of the oral hearing.[49]

5.1.2 Domestic Law and RSD Procedure: Australia and Canada

In Australia, as noted, the formal standards of evidence do not apply to the Tribunal when conducting RSD.[50] Similarly, in Canada, all hearings before the Board must be dealt with 'as informally and quickly as the circumstances and the considerations of fairness and natural justice permit',[51] and the RPD is not bound by 'any legal or technical rules of evidence'.[52] As well, in both Australia and Canada it is the decision-maker who governs exactly how the hearing will proceed and therefore selects which events will be addressed during the hearing and in what order. From start to finish, as long as certain procedural fairness standards are met, exactly how evidence is tested is at the decision-maker's discretion.

In line with international guidance, in Canada the burden of proof is shared between the applicant and decision-maker,[53] and encompasses the IRB member's 'responsibility to identify the facts and arguments that may help the claimant meet the definition of a refugee'.[54] As Evans Cameron explains, in one matter the member incorrectly concluded that it was 'not the duty of the panel to sift through the documentary evidence and make a case for any claimant when the claimant himself [*sic*] fails to make his own case'.[55] On the contrary, on appeal, the Federal Court found 'that this is "precisely" the Board's duty'. By contrast, in Australia the *Migration Act* makes clear that the burden of proof rests on the refugee applicant. The *Migration Act* sets out that it is the responsibility of the refugee applicant to specify all particulars of their claim for refugee protection, and to provide sufficient evidence to establish the claim.[56] The Australian Credibility Guidelines for AAT decision-makers do however set out that refugee applicants are often unable to support claims through documentary or other proof, and that the tribunal should have due regard to

48 Canadian Council for Refugees, 'The Experience of Refugee Claimants at Refugee Hearings in the New System' (April 2014) <http://ccrweb.ca/sites/ccrweb.ca/files/refugee-hearing-report-2014.pdf>.

49 As noted in Chapter 1, although the UNHCR has stated its intention to produce updated guidelines on credibility assessment, there were no new UNHCR credibility standards at the time of writing: UNHCR, above n 46, 8–9.

50 *Migration Act 1958* (Commonwealth) s 420.

51 *Immigration and Refugee Protection Act*, SC 2001, c 27, s 162(2).

52 *Immigration and Refugee Protection Act*, SC 2001, c 27, s 170(g).

53 *Gutierrez v Canada (Minister for Immigration and Citizenship)* 2011 FC 1526.

54 Hilary Evans Cameron, *Refugee Law's Fact-Finding Crisis: Truth, Risk, and the Wrong Mistake* (Cambridge University Press, 2018) 81.

55 Ibid. *Kathirkamu v Canada (Minister for Immigration and Citizenship)* 2003 FCT 409.

56 *Migration Act 1958* (Cth) s 5AAA.

other information such as expert evidence and country information, which can assist its decision-making.[57]

The most significant procedural limitations, however, on how the hearing is conducted operate as a result of the standards governing procedural fairness, and specifically, the 'adverse inference' rule before the AAT or the 'fair hearing' rule before the IRB.[58] In Australia, adverse inferences or findings must be put to the applicant and the applicant must be given the opportunity to respond.[59] As the Australian Credibility Guidelines set out, the applicant must be 'made aware of the case against him or her . . . [T]he Tribunal is under a duty to ensure that an applicant has an opportunity to be heard on the issues to be decided'.[60] The IRB must also give the applicant the opportunity to make representations generally, either in person or through a representative.[61] While none of these rules determines *how* evidence will be put to the applicant nor how it should be put by the applicant, they constitute the most protected aspect of the applicant's right to be heard within RSD processes.

The Australian Credibility Guidelines state that '[a]pplicants are best able to present their case at a hearing which respects the dignity of the applicant and is conducted in a fair and non-intimidating manner'.[62] Members are expected to 'ask appropriate questions in a courteous, non-threatening or non-intimidating manner'[63] with no additional guidance as to what may be considered appropriate.[64] In the testing of evidence, the Member must not intimidate applicants or constantly overbear an applicant who is giving evidence – though there is a high threshold as to what will be considered intimidating or an unacceptable level of interruption.[65]

In Canada, IRB Members are required not to display 'excessive zeal' in an attempt to find contradictions in an applicant's testimony during the hearing[66] but may question applicants extensively or energetically.[67] Before it was updated in 2020, the IRB guidance on credibility also noted that there may be circumstances where the questioning is 'excessive or overly

[57] Administrative Appeals Tribunal Migration and Refugee Division, above n 11, [6], [38].

[58] In Australia: *Kioa v West* (1985) 159 CLR 550; *Minister for Immigration and Border Protection v WZARH* (2015) 256 CLR 326. In Canada: *Baker v Canada* [1999] 2 SCR 817.

[59] The MRD must give the applicant 'clear particulars of any information that the Tribunal considers would be the reason, or a part of the reason, for affirming the decision that is under review' and this may be done during the oral hearing or in writing: *Migration Act 1958* (Cth) ss 424AA, 424A.

[60] Administrative Appeals Tribunal Migration and Refugee Division, above n 11, [17].

[61] *Immigration and Refugee Protection Act*, SC 2001, c 27, s 170(e). The IRB is also, in limited circumstances, required to afford the applicant and other witnesses the opportunity to clarify evidence and to explain perceived inconsistencies or contradictions: *Gracielome v Canada (Minister of Employment and Immigration)* (1989) 9 ImmLR (2d) 237 (FCA); though for a more recent reading down of this principle see Immigration and Refugee Board, above n 27, [2.5].

[62] Administrative Appeals Tribunal Migration and Refugee Division, above n 11, [15].

[63] Ibid.

[64] Though note that the MRD Guidelines on Gender, under the heading 'Credibility', set out that questions establishing credibility should be directed towards the applicant's 'realisation and experience of sexual orientation and gender identity rather than questions that focus on sexual acts': Administrative Appeals Tribunal Migration and Refugee Division, 'Guidelines on Gender' (1996, updated 2015) [21].

[65] In *Re Refugee Review Tribunal; Ex parte H* (2001) 179 CLR 425 the High Court of Australia held that the RRT Member's constant interruptions to the applicant's evidence and constant questioning of credibility formed the basis of a reasonable apprehension of bias in the decision-maker.

[66] *Attakora v Canada (Minister of Employment and Immigration)* (1989) 99 NR 168 (FCA).

[67] *Rajaratnam v Canada (Minister of Employment and Immigration)* (1991) 135 NR 300 (FCA).

aggressive or the interventions are improper', which will include 'demonstrating an unfavourable attitude'; however, this text was removed from the updated version.[68] Nonetheless, jurisprudence in Canada and Australia requires that credibility (and plausibility) findings are based on the available evidence, though the standard for challenging credibility findings on judicial review in Australia is higher than in Canada.[69] In Canada, there is clear authority in that adverse findings of credibility must 'not be based solely on conjecture or speculation' and that it is 'not appropriate for decision-makers to base their assessment of credibility on their own ideas about how events actually took place or should have taken place'.[70] Such authority is directly relevant to the findings in this chapter, but was markedly absent from most decision-makers' testing of evidence. Further, where plausibility assessments are 'highly speculative and a claimant has not been given an opportunity to address them, a reviewing Court will give the conclusion little weight'.[71] However the IRB's credibility guidance also states that 'the panel is entitled to evaluate the testimony on the basis of reasonableness, common sense and rationality and may reject *unrefuted* evidence if it is not consistent with the probabilities of the case as a whole'.[72] While this jurisprudence imposes a considerable (though at times contradictory) constraint on credibility findings, but it does not strictly constrain what may be put to an applicant or the basis for interrogating plausibility during a hearing.[73] Significantly, neither the Australian Credibility Guidelines nor the IRB's guidance document were referenced in the oral hearings or in the non-standardised sections of the written decisions in either jurisdiction.

I do not suggest here that a better framing or expression of credibility criteria will lead to perfect decision-making; or that yet further guidelines will lead to perfectly conducted hearings (even if they are uniformly followed). Indeed, even the existing standards, such

[68] Immigration and Refugee Board, above n 27, [2.6.4]. *Yusuf v Canada (Minister of Employment and Immigration)* [1992] 1 FC 629 (CA); *Kumar v Canada (Minister of Employment and Immigration)* [1988] 2 FC 14 (CA). Though, once again, the threshold for breaching these standards is high. For example, the Member in *Yusuf* made 'sexist, unwarranted and highly irrelevant observations'. There is a gendered element to the successful appeals, in that 'inappropriateness' often relates to sexist comments or insensitive responses to allegations of sexual assault: *Reginald v Canada (Minister of Citizenship and Immigration)* [2002] 4 FC 523 (TD).

[69] *Canada (Minister of Employment and Immigration) v Satiacum* (1989) 99 NR 171 (FCA); *Vallejo, Juan Ernesto v MEI* (FCA, no A-799-90). In Australia, the standard for challenging a credibility assessment is higher. A negative determination may be challenged on grounds of legal unreasonableness or making a finding in the absence of a 'logical, rational or probative basis'; courts, however, will not engage in merits review and will only find no logical basis if there is 'no logical connection between the evidence and the inferences or conclusions drawn': *Minister for Immigration and Citizenship v SZMDS* (2010) 240 CLR 611, [135]; and on the high bar for unreasonableness see *Minister for Immigration and Citizenship v Li* (2013) 249 CLR 332.

[70] Immigration and Refugee Board, above n 27, [2.2.5]. See also *Selvarasu v Canada (Citizenship and Immigration)* 2015 FC 849.

[71] *Arumugam Kandasamy v MEI* (FCTD, no IMM-1406-93) [32]; *Yu v Canada* (Citizenship and Immigration) 2015 FC 167.

[72] Immigration and Refugee Board, above n 27, [2.2.5] (my emphasis). See also *Ye v Canada (Citizenship and Immigration)* 2014 FC 1221.

[73] Connected, no doubt, to the fact that protection visa decisions in Australia are subject to a privative clause, which limits the availability of judicial review to decisions infected by jurisdictional error: *Migration Act 1958* (Cth) s 474. See further: *Plaintiff S157/2002 v Commonwealth of Australia* (2003) 211 CLR 476.

as they are, were not applied in the hearings I observed. However, in my analysis of the RSD oral hearings and transcripts, members' discretion in relation to how the hearing was run and how credibility and evidence were tested, was conspicuous and remarkable. Decision-makers' vast discretion and the minimal standards governing how the hearing is conducted enables decision-makers' presentation of counter-narratives to applicants, as well as the unexamined normativity and unpredictability that inevitably shapes such narratives.

5.2 Narrative Contest, Counter-Narrative and Resistance in the Hearings

5.2.1 The Mena *Hearing*

Ms Mena appeared before the RRT in Melbourne.[74] Ms Mena's country of origin was Egypt and her claim to protection was based on her fear of a forced marriage; her membership of the particular social group, young and unmarried women; her Christian religion; and her imputed political opinion. Like the majority of the hearings addressed in this book, the *Mena* hearing did not deal with every aspect of the applicant's claim that ultimately featured in the written decision, and the topics that were addressed were not discussed in any kind of discernible order. Instead, the hearing focused on select events and details within Ms Mena's testimony. In the hearing, some aspects of the applicant's testimony were raised for the explicit purpose of allowing the Member to put all adverse inferences to the applicant. However, not all topics that the Member raised were addressed for such a clear or explicit purpose. One such recurring topic and site of narrative contest was evidence of a shoulder injury that Ms Mena referred to in her testimony.

Ms Mena's Dislocated Shoulder

One incident relayed by Ms Mena during the hearing concerned an encounter with a taxi driver that culminated in her dislocating her shoulder. The Member addressed the alleged shoulder dislocation in detail, both when Ms Mena initially described the events surrounding it, and then again when the Member returned to the subject two further times during the approximately four-hour long hearing. The shoulder incident was also included in the Member's written reasons. Ms Mena's evidence was that the dislocation occurred when she escaped from a taxi in order to avoid a potential sexual assault by the male taxi driver. The exchange between Ms Mena and the Member regarding this incident is an example of the narrative contests described above. The discussions of Ms Mena's shoulder injury show the extent to which the Member, when testing the plausibility of the applicant's evidence, presents the applicant with a counter-evidence in narrative form.

The applicant in this instance was expected to respond to this hypothetical story of what should have happened by either accounting for the differences between the narratives and providing another, new narrative, or by accepting the Member's determination that the original narrative was implausible and embracing the alternative narrative suggested by the Member. The excerpt details both the incident and the Member's initial response:[75]

[74] *Mena* [2014](RRT).

[75] Directly preceding this exchange, the applicant was questioned about the details of her fear of being forced to marry her Muslim neighbour. Note that at some points in the exchange above, the applicant, who had a good command of English, interjected and presented her testimony directly to the Member.

MEMBER:	You mentioned in your written claims an incident with the taxi driver. Can you tell me when that incident took place?
APPLICANT:	On the [XXX] of May. It was on my sister's anniversary.
MEMBER:	Are we talking about 2011?
APPLICANT (IN PERSON):	Yeah. [*Inaudible comment*]
MEMBER:	I'm sorry.
APPLICANT (IN PERSON):	[*Plaintive/upset*] I wasn't lucky this year.
MEMBER:	I'm sorry?
APPLICANT (IN PERSON):	I wasn't lucky this year. I wasn't lucky this year.
MEMBER:	[*Interrupting*] Can you tell me what happened in that instant? I just need you to pause because I need to hear your evidence.[76]

After the Member directly interrupts Ms Mena's testimony because the Member needs to 'hear [her] evidence', Ms Mena attempts to explain the incident:

APPLICANT:	So it was my, uh, my sister had her two children and it was their birthday. She wanted to buy things for the birthday but she could not leave the house because she had, uh, three young, uh, ones. I told her do not go, do not take your children out because it's ... It wasn't safe. I will take a taxi and I will buy everything you need...
APPLICANT (IN PERSON):	Just one thing. It's not the kid's birthday. It's the anniversary for my sister.
APPLICANT:	Uh, it was anniversary, not the kid's birthday, my mistake. Uh, so when I was talking on the phone, I found that he [the taxi driver] turned left. So I told my sister, that's not the street I need. Uh, I know ... Uh, I do not need ... I do not know this street ... Uh, so, uh, I, I told the, uh, taxi driver. I told him, um, 'Please go back to the main street I know because I do not know this street and I cannot go back. So, if you can just drop me off at a shop, I will be there five minutes and you can drop me back. Uh, I just want to buy a cake.' And then he told me, uh, there is another word but I cannot remember, but they call it infidel. So he said, 'You infidel, you will not tell me how, uh, how to drive or how to ... Where to go.' ... He pushed the central lock so I started screaming. He tried ... He ... He was driving on the left and I was behind the right passenger. So he tried to, uh, stop me from screaming. He put his hands on my, on my face, on my mouth. Um, and it was on the highway. There were no cars. I, uh, in Egypt we do not have seatbelts. So I tried, I opened the window and I started screaming, and I put my arms, uh, outside, um, and told him stop and let me get out. He said no, I will educate you, and he started swearing. Uh, so, he tried to slow down, uh, to grab me because half ... Half of my body was outside. I was screaming so he, um, he opened the centre [*sic*] lock because he wanted to grab me. Um, and then at that time, he was driving at 15 or 20Ks. So I jumped from the car.

After the applicant presented this detailed account of what had taken place, the Member immediately asked about any injuries she may have acquired as she escaped the car:

[76] This is an example of an applicant's emotional or affective response being dismissed or redirected by the decision-maker.

MEMBER: Were you injured when you jumped out of the car?
APPLICANT: I felt that my, um, right, uh, shoulder was dislocated because I could not lift it up.
MEMBER: Did you go to hospital?
APPLICANT: My father had, uh, this, these symptoms before and he knew from, uh, um, he knew some exercises and some physiotherapy. How to, um, get it back to normal and from karate, I, uh, I knew, uh, some exercises to help with dislocated shoulder. Um, because if, when you are playing karate, you can use these exercises.
MEMBER: I understand that a dislocated shoul ... shoulder is excruciatingly painful and would definitely require hospital attention to put it back on its socket if nothing else.
APPLICANT: It wasn't dislocated. May, maybe it was cracked. I could not lift it up. I could, uh, move it to the front but not to the back and not, uh, I could not lift it up.
MEMBER: So did your father's physiotherapy help?
APPLICANT: Um, I did some exercises, but until now, I feel the pain if I sleep on this shoulder. Uh, I, I hear cracks and I cannot lift anything heavy.

The Member did not question the applicant about the details of the assault. What is lost in the written transcript of this dialogue is the insistence in the Member's voice when she states that a dislocated shoulder is 'excruciatingly painful' and would 'definitely require hospital attention to put it back in its socket if nothing else'. Equally lost is the speed with which the applicant accepts that her shoulder therefore had not been dislocated but instead had 'maybe' been cracked.

The above exchange raises two immediate questions. First, of all the details that might have led to further questioning in the hearing, why was a dislocated shoulder addressed? Second, what is the true nature of the alleged injury? Significantly, the Member's claim that medical attention is required for a dislocated shoulder – or rather, for all dislocated shoulders – is presented as a fact capable of an objective truth. This is a form of deductive reasoning: if a shoulder is dislocated, it must require hospital attention, and inversely, if a person does not go to the hospital, a shoulder cannot be dislocated. The Member's certainty here determines the outcome of the exchange.[77] Neither the applicant nor the Member is in a position to present 'expert' opinion on the treatment required for dislocated shoulders, but it is the Member's certainty that determines the truth of the applicant's claim. As Wikström and Johannson note, such judgments, if acknowledged at all, are often described as 'common sense', but they could equally be labelled 'discretion, stereotyping, or acting based on cultural norms/normative standards'.[78]

A close reading of the exchange about the shoulder injury reveals that the Member's narrative frame also redirects and shapes the evidence that is subsequently presented. By insisting that the shoulder was not dislocated, a fact which the applicant accepts,

[77] Although it is certainly arguable that those in Global North countries have greater access to medical assistance and therefore are more likely to attend hospital, not every similarly located person would go to the hospital in such circumstances. Given the fights I have with my own family trying to get them to seek basic medical advice, it is not my experience that the Member's response is necessarily that of, for example, a person living in Australia.

[78] Wikström and Johansson, above n 5, 95. On common sense reasoning in RSD, see also Laurence J Kirmayer, 'Failures of Imagination: The Refugee's Narrative in Psychiatry' (2003) 10(2) *Anthropology & Medicine* 167, 167–68.

the Member dictates that the story then proceed on the basis that the shoulder was 'maybe' hurt (as the applicant says, 'maybe it was cracked') but not dislocated. The applicant originally submitted that she had dislocated her shoulder, and her account was overwritten by the Member during the hearing.

The Member revisited the topic of the applicant's shoulder later in the hearing. As well, the applicant's advocate returned to the topic after having identified it as a source of doubt for the Member. In a final statement, Ms Mena's advocate addressed the extent to which Ms Mena's own, lay diagnosis may have affected the Member's assessment of Ms Mena's credibility:

ADVOCATE: Um, just really briefly to touch on the injury. I think it, it's possible that Ms Mena is overstating and self-diagnosing the dislocation. I think um, I certainly have a tendency to do that and we all do. Um, and, and it sounds as though it could have been jarred. I guess she's had no diagnoses of the injury when she fell out of ... she jumped out of the taxi, sorry.

Um, and so her explanation about the father um, knowing a way to do physio- to, to help her overcome that jarring and her also knowing that from her physical activity being involved in karate is I think a reasonable explanation for her loosening up that jarring...

MEMBER: Well, I would not accept on any evidence before me that her shoulder was dislocated.

ADVOCATE: No. So I just wanted to indicate that there was actually no diagnosis of dislocation um, as an untrained person with no medical training, she's given herself that diagnosis but that's not actually an assertion that it was diagnosed as being dislocated and then not having any medical treatment. It's just her own feeling about it.

In this exchange, the advocate also generates a series of counter-narratives, all of which accept the Member's assessment, and explain the deemed 'implausibility' of the dislocation. The 'dislocation' is replaced with the possibility that the shoulder 'could have been jarred'. The dislocation is also explained as a 'self-diagnosis' and therefore implicitly wrong. Finally, in an attempt to bridge the gap between the earlier claim of dislocation and the later concession that it was 'maybe cracked' or possibly 'jarred', the advocate describes Ms Mena as overstating her injury, remarking, 'I certainly have a tendency to do that, and we all do.' This final statement represents an attempt to persuade the Member to accept a further narrative, that 'exaggeration' is a common response to one's own illness or ailment. The new narrative reinscribes plausibility as a standard that can reasonably be based upon common sense, which is informed by common experience.[79]

The question of the dislocated shoulder appears in the Member's written reasons. There, we find another account of the injury, this time in the Member's words, as being 'like a dislocation'. However, we are informed that 'it was not actually a

[79] The Independent Asylum Commission's extensive study into RSD in the UK noted the frequent use of 'speculative arguments' about what the asylum seeker could have done, and that decisions about plausibility were made without considering the impact of 'different political, social and cultural contexts': Independent Asylum Commission, 'Fit for Purpose Yet? The Independent Asylum Commission's Interim Findings' (2008) 20.

dislocated shoulder, rather dislocation was her self-diagnosis'. In the Member's report of the hearing, the applicant did not go to the doctor because she had had injuries 'like this' before (i.e., not a dislocated shoulder) and knew how to treat them. The Member's final findings about the dislocated shoulder and any bearing they might have had on Ms Mena's credibility were included under the heading 'Consideration of Claims and Evidence' and the subheading 'Credibility'. In her conclusion about the shoulder, the Member wrote that, '[w]hile the Tribunal considers it indicates a tendency to exaggerate her evidence, the nature of the injury itself has little bearing on her claims'.[80] The Tribunal then finds that some, though little weight should be given to this aspect of the applicant's evidence when assessing the applicant's overall credibility.[81] Ultimately Ms Mena's application for review was unsuccessful. The Member found that there were issues which caused the Tribunal to 'hold serious concerns about the applicant's credibility' and these issues were based primarily on the Member finding 'inconsistencies' in Ms Mena's account of her evidence during the hearing.[82] The RRT did not accept Ms Mena's evidence as credible in relation to her primary claim that she would be subjected to a forced marriage if she returned to Egypt and found there was no 'real chance' of persecution on the basis of her religion, political opinion or her status as an unmarried Christian woman.[83]

The decision-maker's story or stories featured heavily during the hearing. The counter-narratives presented by the Member revealed significant details about the Member's own outlook and narrative-based world. The presentation of counter-narratives also compelled the applicant to respond to hypotheticals of the Member's invention, all of which related to the Member's own expectations about how anyone (or, actually, the Member herself) would have behaved.[84] In Dauvergne's assessment of the oral hearing as a site of identity construction, she observes that the decision-maker's identity emerges through the matrix of personal and role expectations that they express. But while the decision-maker can choose how to construct their identity, the applicant's identity is either controlled or assigned by others, or adopted in an attempt to gain access to status and protection.[85]

Observations that a decision-maker's identity, background and social position influence the decision-making process are of course not new. Indeed, such observations recall mid-twentieth-century legal realism, as well as critical race theory and feminist scholarship about the relationship between judicial decision-making and the social position, power and personal experiences of decision-makers, explored in Chapter 1.[86] However, my point here

[80] *Mena* [2014](RRT).

[81] Ibid.

[82] Ibid [38]. I have not addressed these inconsistencies in this chapter.

[83] Ibid [41]–[80].

[84] This is similar to Herlihy et al's findings in their review of UK asylum decisions and the assumptions about human behaviour that they contain. *All* of the determinations they reviewed 'contained assumptions concerning what judges considered people "would have done" in the situations described': Herlihy, Gleeson and Turner, above n 4, 258.

[85] Catherine Dauvergne, *Humanitarianism, Identity, and Nation: Migration Laws of Australia and Canada* (UBC Press, 2005) 101.

[86] See especially Patricia J Williams, *The Alchemy of Race and Rights* (Harvard University Press, 1991); Aileen Moreton-Robinson, 'Whiteness, Epistemology and Indigenous Representation' in Aileen Moreton-Robinson (ed), *Whitening Race: Essays in Social and Cultural Criticism* (Aboriginal Studies

is not that an objective assessment, free from the influence of the social context and the personal views of the decision-maker is possible. Rather, in the context of refugee hearings, when these views are presented to the applicant, the applicant is required to respond and at time account for the decision-maker's counter-version of events. Furthermore, despite the nominally non-adversarial setting, the applicant is expected to explain the discrepancies between the two or more versions of the story that 'ought' to have taken place – and critically these (re)negotiations alter the factual matrix *over the course of* the oral hearing and *remake* testimony that is finally presented for assessment.[87]

5.2.2 The Adere *Hearing*

The *Adere* hearing was one of the more adversarial hearings that I observed.[88] In the hearing, the points of contention between the decision-maker and the applicant did not pertain to significant elements of the definition of a refugee, as it is expressed in the Refugee Convention and domestic legislation. Evidence relating to core aspects of the definition was not even addressed at any length in the *Adere* hearing; there was little attempt to establish that the harm the applicant experienced was persecutory; and limited attention was given to whether the story was corroborated by secondary sources of evidence or country information.[89] The most intensive questioning of the applicant, Mr Adere, and of his wife, who appeared as a witness, focused on the plausibility of discrete and fragmented aspects of his story.

The questions I explore here relate to three different topics: a phone number, the behaviour of a hired driver, and a laptop. In each instance, the Member's questioning took the form of presenting a fully formed counter-narrative to the applicant, that is, the Member's own version of how things must or should have gone. The Member in this hearing demonstrated a tendency to universalise his own experience when seeking to determine plausibility and narrative causality, in order to correctly 'apprehend the authenticity or the duplicity of the story being told'.[90] As noted in Chapter 4, Mr Adere's country of origin was Ethiopia, and he was the primary applicant. His claim addressed the persecution he would face as a person working in a non-governmental organisation, and therefore as a member of a particular social group. His RRT hearing took place over the course of approximately three hours. Unlike the majority of other applicants, Mr Adere spoke in a mix of English and his native tongue, and for parts of the hearing, he did not use the services of the interpreter.

Press, 2004) 75; Reg Graycar, 'The Gender of Judgments: An Introduction' in Margaret Thornton (ed), *Public and Private: Feminist Legal Debates* (Oxford University Press, 2009) 262.

[87] The transactional nature of narrative is highlighted in Conley and O'Barr's work on the role that judges play in shaping the oral evidence of lay litigants and witnesses in lower-level courts: John M Conley and William M O'Barr, *Rules versus Relationships: The Ethnography of Legal Discourse* (University of Chicago Press, 1990).

[88] *Adere* [2012](RRT).

[89] Refugee Convention, as amended by the 1967 Protocol Relating to the Status of Refugees, art 1A(2).

[90] Cécile Rousseau and Patricia Foxen, 'Constructing and Deconstructing the Myth of the Lying Refugee: Paradoxes of Power and Justice in an Administrative Immigration Tribunal' in Els van Dongen and Sylvie Fainzang (eds), *Lying and Illness: Power and Performance* (Het Spinhuis, 2005) 67.

Mr Adere's Phone Number and the Hired Driver

One of the topics of extended dispute during the hearing concerned the abduction of the applicant from an Ethiopian airport after he had returned from an overseas trip, and his subsequent transportation to a rural prison. The applicant reported that at the time of the abduction, he did not know where he was being taken or why, and he had no time to contact his wife or family. He then reported that he yelled out his home phone number to the government-employed driver of the abduction vehicle, and requested that the driver tell his (the applicant's) wife where he was being taken. Mr Adere recounted that the government-employed driver did call Mrs Adere and inform her of his whereabouts, and consequently, his family was able to find him and help him get out of prison.

The Member took issue with several aspects of this part of the applicant's evidence. None of the Member's concerns focused on the applicant's experience of abduction or what happened to him while detained. First and foremost was the Member's view that if he (the Member) could not remember the number, despite having heard it twice during the applicant's oral testimony, then it was implausible that the government driver would recall it. In addition, the Member insistently expressed disbelief that a government-employed driver would contact the applicant's wife on the applicant's behalf. The counter-narratives here appear to be that people cannot ordinarily memorise phone numbers if they have only heard the number a couple of times and that government-employed drivers certainly do not assist government abductees. The expression of these counter-narratives took place as follows:

APPLICANT (IN PERSON): On the way to [XXX] prison I told the driver, I gave him my number, I told him this is my wife's number, please call her and let her know what happened to me.
MEMBER: So when you say the driver, was that a police driver?
APPLICANT (IN PERSON): I do not know. Could be a police driver or maybe they hired a car; a rental. . .
MEMBER: Okay, so, you say you asked the driver to ring your wife.
APPLICANT (IN PERSON): Yes.
MEMBER: And tell her what?
APPLICANT (IN PERSON): Tell her I'm in [XXX] prison.
MEMBER: What did the police say when you told the driver to do that?
APPLICANT (IN PERSON): I said this is the number, ring my wife. I screamed it. I wasn't hoping that he would tell her or call her. But he did.
MEMBER: There's some difficulty, Mr [XXX], that you have mentioned your wife's number twice now, and I have difficulty in remembering the number, but he remembered that, and he chose to make a communication with person as a result of a request from a somebody who was in custody. I just find it unusual that a driver, whether a police driver or a hired driver, would be able to do that.

Directly after this comment, the applicant tried to account for the situation by noting that he (the applicant) also found it 'surprising':

APPLICANT (IN PERSON): I was surprised too. I was in a desperate situation. [*Pause*] The only thing I could do was to tell the driver to do this.
MEMBER: I understand that you were in a desperate situation; I'm just having a difficulty being able to accept that in the circumstances that you have described, that you

will be able to say to a driver of a vehicle in which you have been detained, as you have just described to me, to yell out a telephone number once, and the driver remembered it although he had no interest in doing it, why would the driver want to communicate that?

APPLICANT (IN PERSON): It was a compassion [*sic*]; and the number wasn't long, it was just a 6-digits [*sic*] number. Honestly, I told him like, 4X-4X-1X, that's it.

The Member then repeated that, even though he had heard the number now four times, he still could not remember it. He then compared his own situation to the anonymous driver of the car, whom the Member concluded was in a worse and more difficult position than himself to memorise a phone number.

The Member again repeated the 'difficulties' he was having with the applicant's testimony. Rather than conceding the point or perhaps not responding at all, the applicant tried to reconcile his own story with the Member's expectations. Quite unexpectedly, the applicant tried to create an 'Australian' point of comparison for the Member, and attempted to explain a particular view of plausibility whereby unexpected things do happen because people can be unexpectedly compassionate:

APPLICANT (IN PERSON): For example, 1331 is a well-known number in Australia; if you yell out that number people will know it, and in my country a 6-digits [*sic*] number is not very long, people can remember. And also sometimes people do unexpected things; maybe he was hearing the conversation we had in the car, like I was trying to explain to them who we are and this and that, and I was yelling a lot of times, I was begging them to let me call my family, let me tell them, and out of compassion he was seeing how desperate I was to communicate with my family . . . just so, out of compassion he might do this. It is for me as well out of compassion people do unexpected things.

In the above exchanges the decision-maker presented clear counter-narratives and both invited and expected a response from the applicant. Here, in contrast to the *Mena* hearing, where the applicant conceded the Member's narrative, Mr Adere refused to do this and displayed a great deal of conviction in presenting his own narrative. As well, he tried to create a shared reality as between himself and the Member, similar to the advocate's attempt in the *Mena* hearing to ground plausibility in the common experience of exaggerating illness when engaging in self-diagnosis. Mr Adere was not merely required to present testimony in a narrative form; he had to make his story compelling by responding to the Member's own story or stories.

The Laptop

In this section, a narrative contest over a laptop demonstrates the extent to which the Member's highly subjective, idiosyncratic and seemingly impulsive views were presented to the applicant as a direct counter-narrative. The dispute about the laptop reveals the way in which applicants find themselves constructing a narrative around events in their testimony that they might not have anticipated a decision-maker would deem central or important. Another significant point about this laptop narrative is the materiality of the laptop itself, as a tangible object. In contrast to the

Refugee Convention's intangible requirement that the applicant display a 'well-founded fear' and an inability or unwillingness (due to fear) to avail oneself of state protection, Mr Adere's laptop and phone number, and Ms Mena's dislocated shoulder, are or signify concrete, physical things in the world. The role of 'material' facts and knowledge is at the heart of the challenges posed by processes of RSD and credibility determination. Indeed, the requirement that an applicant's evidence be 'externally' (as well as internally) consistent constitutes a requirement that evidence accords with independent country information: usually this means documents, 'reports' or material evidence that certain 'things' have happened. While the events surrounding the laptop and shoulder are hardly verifiable by reference to external sources, they do recall the problem of the law's preference for proof via *object*ive and tangible sources.[91]

The exchange about the laptop revolved around a raid that had taken place on the applicant's home after he had arrived in Australia on a student visa. In his testimony, Mr Adere recounted that government officials had come to his family home looking for evidence of his anti-government activity, and found his laptop. Mr Adere reported that although the authorities had found nothing of interest to them on his computer, this incident was critical in increasing his fear of returning to Ethiopia. Of relevance to the laptop exchange is that the applicant's original visa to Australia was granted on the basis that he and his wife were coming to complete a short, professional course of study. In questioning the applicant on the raid, the Member focused on his own belief that if he were in the applicant's position, leaving his country of origin to complete an educational course abroad, he would have taken the laptop:

MEMBER: I want to take you back to the [XXX] incident where you said your house was visited. You told me that they questioned and detained your father. Did they do anything else?

APPLICANT: They looked for documents related to me, but the only thing they could get was my previous work report.

MEMBER: Okay. They did not take anything else other than those documents?

APPLICANT: They took my laptop, but they could not find anything. So they dropped it. . . .

MEMBER: Okay. You're coming to Australia as a student on a course; would not you bring your laptop with you?

APPLICANT: I did not want to.

MEMBER: Why is that?

APPLICANT: I do not know, nothing special.

MEMBER: Most people these days, when they do courses they use laptops. So, you left your laptop at home?

APPLICANT: Yes. [In the professional school in Australia] mainly you do it by works, by action.

MEMBER: People quite often use laptops for things like emails, and communicating with family; things like that.

APPLICANT: We had email access in the [Australian] office . . . And our goal was to go back to Ethiopia in six months.

[91] See Robert Gibb and Anthony Good, 'Do the Facts Speak for Themselves? Country of Origin Information in French and British Refugee Status Determination Procedures' (2013) 25(2) *International Journal of Refugee Law* 291.

The Member then repeats his own narrative, that people travelling for work take their laptops with them:

MEMBER: Okay, my understanding is that you were here for six months; people usually take laptops with them to wherever they go. It's just a little unusual that people would leave a laptop, particularly if they are using it as a part of their work, that they would leave it when they are going on a training course for a 6-month period rather than simply pack it in their bag and take it with them?

APPLICANT: I use my laptop only to check my emails; that's it. In the office we had computers, not laptops.

The Member again returned to the topic of the left-behind laptop when questioning Mrs Adere, who had not been present during the questioning of Mr Adere:

MEMBER: You came to Australia to study; why would your husband leave his laptop in Ethiopia?

APPLICANT WIFE: Well, we did not bring all our stuff with us; we left our belongings there. One thing was our laptop. We left it there.

MEMBER: I would have thought people coming for studying would bring their laptop with them.

APPLICANT WIFE: I know that, but in our country we are not that much involved with laptops; we write on papers.

As noted in the previous chapter, the *Adere* application for review was unsuccessful due to the Member finding that Mr and Mrs Adere were not credible witnesses and that their claim lacked plausibility.[92] The laptop exchange is recorded in the final decision, with the Member noting that '[t]he Tribunal observed it seemed unusual that a person travelling to Australia for an extended study program would leave their laptop in their home country rather than bring it with them'.[93] In a later paragraph that also addresses evidence about the laptop, the Member finds that 'neither applicant was a credible witness' and asserts that he does not accept there was ever a raid on the applicant's home after the applicant's departure or seizure of the applicant's possessions.

In the written decision, the Member also directly addresses the topics of the phone number and the driver in relation to his finding that the applicants were not credible, writing that the Tribunal had

> some difficulty accepting the driver of a police vehicle would remember a number shouted to him, or that he would agree under those circumstances to telephone the family of a prisoner he was driving. It also expressed concern the driver would be able to remember a telephone number shouted under the circumstances described . . . (repetition in original)[94]

In reaching a conclusion that the applicant was never abducted or detained in a rural prison, the Member writes:

[92] *Adere* [2012] (RRT Decision and Reasons) [57].
[93] Ibid [104].
[94] Ibid [43].

> The Tribunal does not accept as plausible the assertion that a driver of a vehicle in which police were transporting a detainee or prisoner would involve himself in such activity [of calling the applicant wife], nor does it accept as plausible that a driver in those circumstances, even if willing to assist, could memorise and recall a telephone number yelled at him in the presence of two police officers whilst he was driving.[95]

Finally, the Member finds that evidence about the driver, prison and the telephone call to the applicant's wife was 'a story concocted to create a basis on which to claim past adverse treatment prior to departure from Ethiopia'.[96]

5.3 Conclusion

In Dauvergne's observations of refugee oral hearings, published over fifteen years ago, she noted how little 'we' or decision-making bodies know of the 'other'.[97] She observed that processes used to construct a refugee applicant's identity often reduced that identity to 'a pinpoint – a passport printed on the correct type of paper, a number registered in the correct way, a nursery rhyme recalled, the scars of a regime's favourite torture exposed'.[98] I would add to Dauvergne's remarks that these 'pinpoints' of identity are also plot-points in broader narratives. These plot-points often centre on material, tangible claims made by the applicant, in an attempt to resolve the question of plausibility in a way that is fixed, testable and knowable. Decision-makers answer the difficult question of what is plausible with reference to their own sense of the world. The *decision-maker's* narratives and counter-narratives, upon which plausibility assessments are based, only become apparent when decision-makers assess their 'own values, prejudices, orientation and perspective – and ask [themselves] *why* [they] choose to find a particular contradiction crucial'.[99]

In the hearing's narrative-based exchanges, the decision-maker and the applicant enter into a narrative contest, and it is frequently the applicant who must either explain their own narrative as plausible, or fall into line with the decision-maker's alternative version of how events could or should have taken place. Applicants were required to account for why their own narratives differed from the decision-makers' at times idiosyncratic, narrative-based views of the world and notions of what amounted to plausible evidence or behaviour. This reinforces the existing literature's concern with decision-makers' subjective impulses in credibility determination. Simultaneously though, it adds to these concerns by interrogating how this subjectivity manifests in the hearing, the burden it places on applicants seeking to present testimony, and its capacity to fundamentally remake the testimony that the applicant is seeking to present.

95 Ibid [105].
96 Ibid [106].
97 Dauvergne, above n 85, 118.
98 Ibid. Dauvergne goes on to state that 'the pinpoint is what it is to be other: to be reduced to almost nothing, a blank space against which we can imagine otherness': at 118.
99 Macklin, above n 2, 140.

The end of the Handbook's short section on fact-finding freely acknowledges that 'the examiner's conclusion on the facts of the case and his [*sic*] personal impression of the applicant will lead to a decision that affects human lives'.[100] The Handbook goes on to state that this fact obliges the examiner to 'apply the criteria in a spirit of justice and understanding'. My observations of the hearings, though, repeatedly affirmed that where the plausibility of evidence was in doubt, subjective impulses often were not attended by the sanguine 'spirit of justice and understanding' suggested by the Handbook.[101] The narrative contests described in this chapter reveal decision-makers' willingness to indulge their personal impressions and to share their own narrative-based views of the world. What is more, the adversarial nature of these narrative contests reveals a significant deviation from the law's framing of these hearings as inquisitorial – as existing, allegedly, for the benefit of the applicant or in light of their 'special position'.

This is not to say that all decision-makers in the dataset were openly adversarial, but certainly in instances where credibility was doubted, decision-makers frequently took on the role of testing the applicant's evidence not by working with the applicant to jointly 'discover' the truth, but by raising explicit counter-narratives to challenge the plausibility of certain pieces of evidence. One reason for the failure of the oral hearing to function as an inquisitorial forum is that when the norms of the adversarial system are taken away, 'inquisitorial norms do not simply flow in to take [their] place'.[102] Susan Kneebone made a similar observation of the RRT in the very early phases of its operation, noting that 'members and advisers are uncomfortable with an inquisitorial role in the hearing, and indeed tend to be confrontational in their approach to questioning'.[103] The norms of adversarial justice continued to characterise the RSD oral hearings that I observed. Indeed, that members and lawyers operate within common law systems, and may have little or no formal training in the procedures and values of inquisitorial processes, helps to explain the narrative-based contests described in this chapter.[104]

This finding – that the norms of adversarial systems persist within RSD – also frames the next chapter, which explores how individual decision-makers ran the hearings and asks whether and on what terms applicants were able to present their oral evidence during the hearings. One of the key observations made in the next chapter is that, once again, despite the 'informal' nature of the hearings and the broad discretion afforded to decision-makers, applicants were rarely assisted by decision-makers to present their claims. Instead, the applicants' capacity to present their testimony was thwarted by the hearings' fragmented and decision-maker-driven nature. As such, the chapter explores the RSD oral hearing as a 'narrative occasion' during which applicants are impeded rather than enabled to meet the demand for narrative that is the focus of this book.

[100] UNHCR, above n 17, 44.

[101] Ibid.

[102] Dauvergne, above n 85, 101. Dauvergne goes on to point out that 'since lawyers represent most claimants, and many tribunal members are legally trained, implicit norms of the adversarial system do tend to dominate the proceedings': at 99.

[103] Susan Kneebone, 'The Refugee Review Tribunal and the Assessment of Credibility: An Inquisitorial Role' (1998) 5 *Australian Journal of Administrative Law* 78, 94.

[104] Dauvergne, above n 85, 100. With the exception of private law in Quebec, Canada, which operates under a distinct civil law tradition.

6

'I'll Just Stop You There': Fragmentation of Refugees' Oral Testimony

For refugee applicants with access to legal advice or other forms of advocacy, the shaping and managing of their evidence and oral testimony begins long before their first or subsequent asylum hearings. In most instances, lawyers have already taken a strategic approach to managing their client's narrative which, as Jessica Hambly notes, often involves actively reshaping and 'translating' a client's complex and fractured account into a story that meets refugee law's substantive and technical requirements.[1] Jacobs and Maryns, in their analysis of legal consultations in the Belgian asylum procedure, argue that 'a particular language ideology is being articulated [by legal experts] which rates a detailed, chronological, and consistent account as more credible than an experiential, fragmentary story'.[2] Crucially, they also conclude that a recurring source of confusion for refugee applicants during oral interviews is the tension between the suggestion to asylum seekers that they are being granted 'an opportunity to tell their "story", and the underlying expectation of a factual reconstruction of events in the form of a report . . . [which is] ultimately assessed on "textualist" criteria of consistency and detail'.[3] In something of a similar vein, Laurence Kirmayer writes that, of course, an asylum seeker may articulate their testimony as 'a univocal, rational self [who] can give an unambiguous account of events and an honest reading of its own motivations, which can then be used to decide the refugee status of the person'.[4] However, he identifies two problems with this possibility: first, that such an account would be of an entirely fictive entity; and second, that it must be told in circumstances that effectively 'conspire against its appearance'.[5]

This chapter investigates the conduct of the oral hearings in order to explore to what extent, if any, applicants were able to present their evidence in a form that fulfilled both the credibility criteria and the demand for narrative. I argue that a close reading of the conduct and structure of the RSD hearings, undertaken throughout the book and in this chapter

[1] Jessica Hambly, 'Interactions and Identities in UK Asylum Appeals: Lawyers and Law in a Quasi Legal Setting' in Nick Gill and Anthony Good (eds), *Asylum Determination in Europe: Ethnographic Perspectives* (Palgrave Macmillan, 2019) 195, 201; and see Marie Jacobs and Katrijn Maryns, 'Managing Narratives, Managing Identities: Language and Credibility in Legal Consultations with Asylum Seekers' (2022) 51(3) *Language in Society* 372.

[2] Jacobs and Maryns, above n 1, 20.

[3] Ibid 13; see also Matthew Zagor, 'Recognition and Narrative Identities: Is Refugee Law Redeemable?' in Fiona Jenkins, Mark Nolan and Kim Rubenstein (eds), *Allegiance and Identity in a Globalised World* (Cambridge University Press, 2014) 311.

[4] Laurence J Kirmayer, 'Failures of Imagination: The Refugee's Narrative in Psychiatry' (2003) 10(2) *Anthropology & Medicine* 167, 179.

[5] Ibid.

especially, reveals that applicants were both expected to present evidence in a narrative form and actively impeded in their efforts to do so. Further, that a core impediment to applicants meeting the requirement for a chronological, consistent and coherent account of their evidence was the profound fragmentation and unpredictability of the structure and subject matter of the majority of hearings in the dataset.

The idea of fragmentation is useful in describing refugee testimony within RSD processes because it conveys my experience of the evidence being, at the end of almost all hearings I observed, 'broken up' or incomplete. The word *fragment* derives from the French *fragment* or the Latin *frangĕre*, both meaning to break.[6] The Oxford English Dictionary's first definition of the noun 'fragment' is '[a] part broken off or otherwise detached from a whole; a broken piece; a (comparatively) small detached portion of anything'.[7] A secondary, figurative definition of the term is 'a detached, isolated, or incomplete part' and a third is 'an extant portion of a writing or composition which as a whole is lost; also, a portion of a work left uncompleted by its author'.[8] The testimony I witnessed and heard during the oral hearings certainly did not consistently start at what might be labelled a chronological 'beginning' or end at an 'end', even though this was frequently how evidence was presented in the decision-makers' subsequent written decisions. In speaking of personal narratives as 'fragmented', I am not suggesting that applicants do have otherwise naturally complete and coherent narratives. Rather, the conditions of speech and the narrative occasion of the hearing functioned to fragment applicants' testimony in such a manner that made it difficult and, in some cases, impossible for applicants to meet the demand for narrative during the hearing, and to tell their stories in a plausible, coherent and orderly way.

In all but three of the observed hearings, decision-makers afforded applicants only a limited opportunity to speak and to be heard on their own terms.[9] In certain instances, decision-makers began by allowing applicants the opportunity to direct their own evidence, but then intervened and reverted to directing the hearing according to their own concerns, queries or whims. Further, where applicants did ultimately present evidence in a narrative form, I demonstrate that they did so in circumstances that were adverse to the expression of narrative-based testimony. Indeed, some applicants did the work of pulling together a narrative *in spite of* decision-makers' fragmenting interventions and question styles. Applicants either interrupted the decision-maker to present evidence the applicant believed to be important or – as explored in the previous chapter – persisted in presenting their version of events in the face of decision-makers' directions and interruptions. Critically, while decision-maker interruptions certainly were not always hostile, they did frequently stop the applicant from meeting the demand for evidence in a coherent narrative form.

Of course, remedying the hearing by giving applicants an uninterrupted opportunity to present evidence in a narrative form is something of a useless response to the book's core argument – that narrativity and the ability to construct narrative should neither be required

6 *The Oxford English Dictionary* (2nd ed, 1989), s.v. 'fragment'.

7 Ibid.

8 Ibid.

9 Based on the processes of fragmentation described below, seven out of the eight observed Australian hearings (*Adere* [2012]; *Malik* [2013]; *Mbassi* [2012]; *Mena* [2014]; *Pillai* [2013]; *Zahau* [2012]; and *Zeidan* [2014]) and five out of the seven Canadian hearings (*Bhatti* [2013]; *Perera* [2013]; *Rostami* [2013]; *Valdez* [2013]; and *Solemani* [2015]) fit the criteria I have used to describe a fragmented hearing. I address the hearings that do not meet these criteria below (*Flores* [2013](IRB); *Jabbar* [2013](IRB); and *Jadoon* [2014](RRT)).

of refugee applicants nor operate as a measure of an applicant's 'worthiness' as future refugee-citizens. I return to this point in Chapter 8. And yet, RSD procedures as simultaneously demanding narrative coherence and denying applicants the capacity to meet such demands reinforces the oral hearing and credibility criteria as operating as part of state apparatuses for refugee exclusion and deterrence.

In Section 6.1, and as my own means of disrupting expectations of linearity, I return to the opening of the oral hearing in each jurisdiction to examine the ways in which the hearings were explained to the applicants and how individual decision-makers set up the hearings. These 'opening statements' are critical as they frame the hearing and establish what the applicant can expect of the hearing. They also reveal the wide discretion that each decision-maker holds over how the hearings proceed. Section 6.2 then addresses my contention that the conduct of the hearings has led to fragmented and decision-maker-driven narratives. In order to explore how narrative fragmentation occurred in the hearings I observed, I discuss three distinct means of fragmentation: reverse-order questioning; changing the subject or subject switching during the hearing; and decision-makers' questions in relation to time, sequencing, precise dates of events.

The majority of hearings that did involve the fragmentation of evidence contrasted with three hearings in which the applicant's presentation of testimony was not impeded in the ways I describe here.[10] Instead, the form and tone of questions predominantly permitted the applicant to speak; the applicant was not questioned extensively about the timing and sequence of events; and rather than jumping without explanation from subject to subject, decision-makers 'signposted' to inform the applicant what was coming up next and, in some cases, clearly explained why they were asking particular questions.[11]

Finally, I note that in this small dataset, it was evident that applicants in the Canadian hearings were given a greater opportunity to articulate their evidence without the Member interjecting or redirecting the applicant to sequence the evidence or to recall particular dates or temporal details, such as time between events. In particular, in the two 'non-fragmented' Canadian hearings,[12] the applicants were more frequently able to address parts of their claim that pertained to the core requirements of the refugee definition under Canadian law (such as alleged incidents of past persecution), rather than respond primarily to the decision-makers' unpredictable concerns. Even though decision-makers still played a central role in directing the hearing, in these hearings and in the Australian *Jadoon* hearing, the decisions-makers' genuinely open questions related more closely to the narrative required of applicants in their written applications for refugee protection. As well as this, questioning did not lurch, out of chronological sequence, from subject to subject, and when the Member did change topics, this was signposted with comments such as: 'You mentioned earlier your involvement in [XXX] group, I am going to ask you about that...';[13] and 'You explained that you would not be safe in Jalalabad; can you now explain what would happen if you

[10] As noted, these were: *Flores* [2013](IRB); *Jabbar* [2013](IRB); and *Jadoon* [2014](RRT).

[11] On this point see Gill et al's observational study of judicial refugee decision-makers in the UK, which highlights the relationship between members' (discretionary) approaches to the hearing and an applicant's ability to participate in proceedings; in particular, the study identifies a suite of judicial actions that the authors argue are 'vulnerability-redressing' for refugee litigants: Nick Gill et al, 'The Limits of Procedural Discretion: Unequal Treatment and Vulnerability in Britain's Asylum Appeals' (2018) 27(1) *Social & Legal Studies* 49.

[12] *Flores* [2013](IRB); *Jabbar* [2013](IRB).

[13] *Flores* [2013](IRB).

moved to Kabul?'[14] These factors combined to significantly change the tone of the hearing and to provide, at least to some extent, applicants with an opportunity to meet the hearing's narrative mandate.

6.1 Setting Refugee Applicants Up: Opening the Oral Hearing

The opening of each hearing establishes, for all present, what kind of narrative occasion is about to take place. At this particular moment, decision-makers generally told applicants and others present the purpose of the hearing, what would be expected of them and the opportunities they would have to present their evidence. Although formal aspects of the hearing and its purpose are determined by the law and procedure governing RSD in Canada and Australia, the nature of the hearing as a narrative occasion was substantially determined by individual members, as both the 'framers' of the hearing and the applicant's primary audience. While it may seem 'out of order' to return to the beginning of the hearing at this point in the book, this approach, I hope, avoids presenting the hearing itself as an occasion with a neat beginning, middle and end. It is also important because the 'opening' of the hearing and the limited information provided to applicants was often implicated in the forms of fragmentation I describe below.

In terms of the structure and content of the opening section of the hearings, surprisingly little has changed since Barsky's observation of Canadian RSD hearings in the late 1980s. Barsky notes that while the opening of the hearing establishes the rules that will govern the hearing, simultaneously 'a whole realm of legal knowledge that is needed to understand how [the hearing] is initially construed is glossed over', as are the many discursive rules and norms governing what is 'sayable' or pertinent.[15] Indeed, in the specialised discursive and legal context of the hearing, decision-makers' descriptions of how it will run barely scratch the surface of the constraints and expectations that govern applicants' testimony. The opening statements nonetheless structure the applicant's expectations about the hearing that is to follow, and in both jurisdictions, that script was relatively standardised. The members' script and the topics addressed in the openings were based on an informal, non-mandatory template, which for Canada I accessed through Access to Information (ATI) and for Australia through Freedom of Information (FOI) requests. I requested access to all documents provided to decision-makers to guide their conduct of the hearing. However, the templates provided essentially addressed the 'opening' section of the hearing, with no direct script or guidance for 'the rest' of the hearing – an absence that becomes evident in the exchanges presented in the remainder of this chapter.[16]

In the observed hearings, decision-makers often presented one of two versions of the hearing to the applicant. The first version explained the hearing as a site where the decision-

[14] *Jabbar* [2013](IRB).

[15] Robert F Barsky, *Constructing a Productive Other: Discourse Theory and the Convention Refugee Hearing* (John Benjamins, 1994) 79, 98–102.

[16] These templates provide a suggested rather than mandatory script in both jurisdictions. They both broadly guided members to first introduce themselves; explain the role of the Board/Tribunal and the definition of a refugee; and outline how the hearing would run and the role of the interpreter: Migration Review Tribunal-Refugee Review Tribunal, 'Member Introductory Remarks at RRT Hearings' (not dated), FOI Request 15-0011 (on file with author); Immigration and Refugee Board, 'RPD New Member Training' (not dated), ATI Request A-0015-00798 / DSA (on file with author).

maker would ask 'further questions' about evidence they had already read, and the applicant would then be able to add 'anything' they wished to at the end. This version was frequently expressed to applicants appearing before the RRT. The second version, often featured in the IRB hearings, described the hearing first and foremost as a place where the decision-maker would address 'issues' within the applicant's evidence, and which would not necessarily give the applicant the opportunity to present any 'additional' evidence. In the hearings where applicants were told they would be able to present 'any' evidence they wished, the majority of these hearings did not meet this expectation.

In the *Adere* hearing, as with many of the RRT hearings, the RRT Member gave the applicant a rather informal and short outline of how the hearing would run. The below extract also provides an example of the applicant being told two things at once: that the applicant would be questioned on the decision-maker's terms because the Member has 'some understanding' of the claim, and that the applicant would be given the opportunity to speak:

MEMBER: I already have information that's available on the file ... so I have some understanding of the issues that you are raising and the claims that you have made. The purpose of this hearing is two-folded [*sic*]; it's my chance to ask you and your wife questions and to give evidence about matters in order to help make me to form a decision, and it's also your opportunity to tell me anything else that you think I need to know to properly understand your case.

This explanation, slightly modified by some decision-makers, was part of a longer, non-mandatory script, in which RRT Members explained the process of de novo review and the law in relation to refugee status and complementary protection.[17] In the above excerpt, the Member indicated that the applicant could present additional information but did not state that the applicant would be given an opportunity to present the claim in full, or independently of the decision-maker's knowledge. By contrast, the Member in the *Zeidan* application before the RRT explained the hearing as a far more open space for the articulation of testimony. The Member emphasised that the applicant should not feel restricted to the questions asked:

MEMBER: The role of the hearing is to give you an opportunity to put forward any information that you want me to be aware of before reaching my decision. So I have some questions based on the information that you already provided, but you should not feel restricted to those questions.[18]

The RRT Member in the *Pillai* hearing similarly described the hearing as a space that was created for the applicant 'to present all relevant evidence in support of your claim'. Applicants before the RRT were given the impression that the decision-maker would direct the hearing, but also, to a greater or lesser degree, that the applicant would be able to present 'all' evidence that they wished. As Section 6.2 reveals, such openness, despite being foreshadowed at the start of a hearing, was frequently not a

[17] Migration Review Tribunal-Refugee Review Tribunal, FOI Request 2015/0011, above n 17.

[18] After this statement, the applicant indicated that she did not understand what the Member had said, and the Member repeated the entire explanation in full.

feature of the hearings. Further, neither Mr Pillai nor Ms Zeidan were given the open opportunity to present their claims or 'all of their evidence' during their hearings.

In the IRB hearings, when the Members introduced the hearing, they often set out *specific* issues that the hearing would address and generally did not indicate to applicants that they would be given a chance to present 'their evidence'. The following extract from the *Jabbar* hearing provides a representative example:

MEMBER: So today's hearing will focus on the following issues, that is your credibility and the internal flight alternative, and this is how we are going to proceed. First, I will ask you questions, then your counsel may ask questions, and I could come back with some questions and then your lawyer will make submissions. If you ever do not understand, please say so.

APPLICANT (IN PERSON): [*Softly.*] Okay.[19]

In hearings before the IRB, these comments were also part of a standardised script to introduce the hearing.[20] In the *Perera* hearing before the IRB, the Member very specifically set out the particular issues that would be discussed, and her explanation of the hearing procedure was remarkably direct:

MEMBER: What I am going to do is list the issues that I will be focusing on. We will be looking at internal flight alternative, subjective fear, and being an ethnic minority, and persecution versus harassment or discrimination. And I will have some questions for you about the agent of persecution to try and understand who you fear in Sri Lanka and based on who you fear, I may have some questions on state protections.

What was common to descriptions in both jurisdictions is that in neither setting were applicants given a clear or thorough sense of what was about to take place and what exactly would be expected of them. Explanations were either so general as to not attempt to outline the hearing for the applicant, or the hearing itself did not neatly follow the 'map' provided by the decision-maker. This is significant given that, alongside the interpreter, an applicant is the primary speaker for the majority of the hearing. The shortest hearing that I attended ran for two and a half hours, and the longest was just over six hours. In each instance, the applicant was directly questioned for a minimum of half of that time.

Moving into the next section of this chapter, it is noteworthy that decision-makers' foregrounding did little to guide the applicants' testimony or to describe the nature of the exchanges that would follow. As Section 6.2 reveals, in both the IRB and RRT hearings, applicants had few opportunities to present the evidence that they wished to during the hearing. Equally, though, in both jurisdictions applicants *were* at times given an uninterrupted opportunity to present their testimony; however, the opening of the hearings did little to prepare applicants for this.

[19] As noted, the overall structure and content of the IRB hearing differs from the RRT hearing in that IRB hearings provide advocates with the opportunity to directly question their clients at the end of their evidence, and this opportunity is generally taken up.

[20] Immigration and Refugee Board, above n 16.

The end of the hearings, although not examined in detail here, was also standardised and included practical information about next steps, timelines and discussion of further submissions if and where necessary. Similar to many of the hearings I observed,[21] the Member at the end of the *Jadoon* hearing gave the applicant a chance for final comments after Mr Jadoon had been questioned at length about discrete and disconnected parts of his evidence:

> MEMBER: All right. Is there anything else you wanted to say to me?
> APPLICANT: No. That's all, I suppose.

Each time a comparable question was posed towards the end of questioning, the tone and timing of the question strongly indicated that the questioning of the applicant was coming to a close. As such, it was difficult to conceive of applicants at that particular moment articulating any significant or missed element of their evidence, and the question was generally asked in a manner that indicated the applicant's turn to speak was, in fact, at an end.

6.2 Demanding and Impeding Narrative: Three Forms of Fragmentation

This section analyses three interwoven means of fragmenting testimony during the oral hearing. Although each decision-maker had a unique style, the three features of the hearing that I describe here formed the basis of strong, recurring themes in the process of coding the hearings. A major finding that runs through each feature of the hearings is that when applicants did present evidence in a narrative form, they generally did so in circumstances that I argue were adverse to the expression of narrative-based testimony. The forms of fragmentation I discuss operate beyond the role of the interpreter and the process of translation, which require the applicant quite explicitly to 'break up' testimony, as addressed in Chapter 1.

6.2.1 Reverse-Order Questioning

Chapter 5 described the minimal governance over the conduct of the oral hearing, as provided by statute, regulation or administrative guidelines, and consequently, the wide discretion that decision-makers hold as to how the hearing proceeds. In Canada, one significant exception to the absence of uniformly applied standards governing the hearing process is the guideline on 'reverse-order questioning', which France Houle describes as 'one of the most controversial policy instruments issued by the IRB'.[22] IRB Guidelines and the RPD rules set out that during IRB hearings, the decision-

[21] For example at the close of the *Zahau* [2012](RRT) hearing:

> MEMBER: Did you want to say anything else, or would you like me to sum up what my issues are?

[22] France Houle, 'Thamotharem and Guideline 7 of the IRB: Rethinking the Scope of the Fettering of Discretion Doctrine' (2008) 25(2) *Refuge: Canada's Journal on Refugees* 103, 103.

maker is to question the applicant *in the first instance*, to be followed by the counsel for the applicant where an advocate is present.[23] This is the 'reversed' element of reverse order questioning, since in most adjudicative settings (and particularly in adversarial ones) the applicant is given the opportunity to present evidence before it is tested or interrogated. In the IRB Guideline that explains reverse-order questioning, the reform is justified as follows:

> Beginning the hearing in this way allows the claimant to quickly understand what evidence the member needs from the claimant in order for the claimant to prove his or her case.[24]

Reverse-order questioning is now standard practice. In all the Canadian hearings I attended, the reverse-order questioning guideline was followed.[25] However, reverse-order questioning was not always the norm.[26] According to Macklin, prior to 2003, the decision-maker may or may not have indicated specific areas of concern at the outset of the hearing. After this, '[c]ounsel for the asylum seeker would begin by posing questions to the claimant to enable her/him to recount the significant events leading up to the decision to seek asylum.... The decision maker might also pose questions directly to the claimant'.[27]

In hearings before the RRT, the Member is the only person who directly questions the applicant. Consequently, the questioning order is not 'reversed', since advocates are not given the opportunity to question applicants at all, even though they are generally permitted to make submissions at the close of the hearing.[28] All of the Australian hearings I attended proceeded in this way. Just as with the IRB oral hearing, applicants before the RRT are simply not given a chance to put their case first or in full. This is the case even though there is no statutory rule or direction for how the hearing will run in the various guidelines and directions governing the RRT.[29] This process is, however, an

23 Immigration and Refugee Board, 'Guideline 7 Concerning Preparation and Conduct of a Hearing in The Refugee Protection Division: Guidelines Issued by the Chairperson Pursuant to Section 159(1)(h) of the Immigration and Refugee Protection Act' (2003, updated 2012, Immigration and Refugee Board Ottawa). See also *Refugee Protection Division Rules*, SOR/2012-256, r 10.

24 Ibid [19]–[22].

25 The IRB Member may vary the order of questioning in exceptional circumstances: Immigration and Refugee Board of Canada, 'Chairperson Guideline 8: Procedures with Respect to Vulnerable Persons Appearing before the IRB' (2006, updated 2012); see also *Refugee Protection Division Rules*, SOR/2012-256, r 10(5).

26 Notably, two failed legal challenges to reverse-order questioning argued that it breached principles of natural justice and fettered RPD members' discretion in the conduct of the hearing: *Canada (Minister of Citizenship and Immigration) v Thamotharem* [2006] FCJ No 8 (QL); *Benitez v Canada (Minister of Citizenship and Immigration)* [2006] FCJ No 631 (QL).

27 Audrey Macklin, 'Asylum and the Rule of Law in Canada: Hearing the Other (Side)' in Susan Kneebone (ed), *Refugees, Asylum Seekers and the Rule of Law: Comparative Perspectives* (Cambridge University Press, 2009) 78, 97.

28 In some hearings, advocates sought permission, at the end of a Member's questioning, for the applicant to clarify certain issues; however, this was either done by requesting that the Member ask further questions, or by the applicant independently addressing particular issues.

29 Though the Australian Credibility Guidelines do note that '[t]he nature of Tribunal proceedings is such that it is the Member who asks questions of the applicant and other persons giving evidence':

entrenched procedural norm within the RRT and unlike in Canada, advocates appearing before the RRT did not previously have the opportunity to open the hearing or to 'lead' evidence in their clients' cases.

Audrey Macklin argues that the introduction of reverse-order questioning reforms in Canada are best explained as the result of two of the Canadian Government's concerns at the time. The first concern was efficiency. Macklin notes that although this was the rationale provided, no evidence was ever proffered to show that reverse-order questioning is in fact faster or more efficient than conventional questioning methods.[30] The second concern was the Government's desire to control and contain the 'audibility' of the asylum applicant within the hearing.[31] These motivations resonate with the history of the Canadian oral hearing and its introduction in the broader context of new and extensive refugee deterrence mechanisms and as a means, amongst other things, to sort 'genuine' refugees from 'bogus' claimants.

Here, once again, the differing norms in adversarial and inquisitorial settings, and the failure of the RSD oral hearing to realise either approach, become relevant. The approach to discovering 'the truth' or fact-finding in the adversarial system has generally involved allowing each party the opportunity to present its case in full and to define the relevant issues without undue interference by the other party and with only 'minimal intervention by the decision-maker'.[32] Witnesses are able to present their 'evidence-in-chief' first. Only once this has occurred may the other side, in cross-examination of witnesses, test or challenge the other party's evidence.[33] For all of the critiques of this approach, in the RSD oral hearing the fact is that applicants never get a chance to present what would be evidence-in-chief and yet are regularly cross-examined as if they had been given this opportunity. Nor does the oral hearing function in an informal, inquisitorial and non-adversarial manner; in the absence of an inquisitorial style of decision-making, both decision-making bodies fall back on adversarial norms and approaches to fact-finding and decision-making.[34] The theoretical advantages of an inquisitorial approach – in particular having an informal hearing and the decision-maker and applicant *jointly* endeavouring to ascertain the facts – are also absent from the hearing. Although the decision-maker actively intervenes, the nature of these interventions is frequently to test facts rather than to establish them.

As a procedural norm, reverse-order questioning is perhaps best thought of as an issue of who gets to direct the hearing. In both jurisdictions, it is the decision-maker who takes on

Administrative Appeals Tribunal Migration and Refugee Division, 'Guidelines on the Assessment of Credibility' (2006, updated 2015) [16].

30 Macklin, above n 27, 101.

31 Macklin assesses the Canadian legal system's treatment of onshore refugee applicants via the frame of whether 'asylum seekers' audibility is enabled or muted', and asks specifically if applicants can be heard within RSD procedures: ibid 78.

32 See Felicity Nagorcka, Michael Stanton and Michael Wilson, 'Stranded between Partisanship and the Truth: A Comparative Analysis of Legal Ethics in the Adversarial and Inquisitorial Systems of Justice' (2005) 29(2) *Melbourne University Law Review* 448.

33 Australian Law Reform Commission, 'Review of the Federal Civil Justice System (Federal Tribunal Proceedings)' (Issue Paper 24, 1998) [2.13]. Indeed, cross-examination and the competition among parties is presented by some as 'the greatest legal engine ever invented for the discovery of truth': John Henry Wigmore et al, *Evidence in Trials at Common Law* (Little, Brown, 1974) 32.

34 Catherine Dauvergne, *Humanitarianism, Identity, and Nation: Migration Laws of Australia and Canada* (UBC Press, 2005) 99–100.

this role. This norm, combined with the two other processes of fragmentation of the hearing described below, limits the applicant's ability to present testimony, and has profound implications for the structure of the hearing as a narrative occasion.

6.2.2 Changing the Subject

During the hearings, decision-makers frequently switched from one subject to another, without warning or explanation. It is difficult to overstate how extreme certain members' unexplained shifts between subjects were, and how challenging it was to predict or to follow the direction of certain hearings. The applicants and advocates were in no better position than myself with respect to knowing what would happen next. In this section, I examine the *Rostami* hearing before the IRB, which reveals how Ms Rostami was required to deal with the decision-maker's unexplained and abrupt shifts between entirely disconnected subjects. These 'subject shifts' limited the applicant's ability both to comprehend what the decision-maker was asking and to answer the question at hand; the subject shifts certainly did not result in the applicant presenting evidence in a chronological manner. The *Rostami* hearing before the IRB is particularly apposite to the discussion of subject shifting, as at almost no point in the hearing was the applicant given a chance to discuss, without closed questions from the Member, any elements of her claim that related to the Refugee Convention definition of a refugee, such as her persecution and its causes, her inability to seek assistance from the state or her inability to reasonably relocate within Iran. Indeed, at the end of the hearing, the Member asked the applicant's advocate how much time the advocate might need for questioning the applicant. Her advocate responded by stating the Member 'has not asked [the applicant] much about her life' – and so the advocate requested more time than would usually be required.[35] As with other final questioning by counsel before the IRB, though, the evidence led by her lawyer was not an opportunity for her case to be presented in full.

The *Rostami* hearing certainly did not start at the beginning of the 'narrative of becoming a refugee' discussed in Chapter 4. That is, the hearing did not begin by exploring the applicant's experience of persecution or harm. At the very outset of the *Rostami* hearing, the applicant's advocate informed the Member that the original version of a particular piece of documentary evidence (to do with the applicant's religious conversion from Islam to Christianity sometime prior) was not on the file. A short discussion then took place to organise a copy of the original to be sent to the IRB after the hearing. Following on from that discussion, the Member opened the hearing with a discussion of the applicant's religious conversion, which had taken place after her arrival in Canada:

MEMBER: Since we are already talking about religion, I would like to ask you a question about that. In your PIF [personal information form] you indicated you were Muslim. Do you still consider Islam is [*sic*] your religion or one of them?

APPLICANT: No.

MEMBER: Okay. What is your religion now?

APPLICANT: I am an Evangelical from the Protestant branch of new-born or born-again Christians.

[35] The Member replied to this by stating that he had clearly set out the 'issues' with her claim as he saw them.

MEMBER: Um, we'll get back to that later, but I will ask you some general questions now. When did you leave your country?
APPLICANT: Ummm, in the Iranian calendar, it would be [XXX].

Once the year that the applicant had left Iran was agreed upon, the Member asked an open question about the applicant's 'problems', but then interrupted Ms Rostami and redirected her to discuss a different aspect of her claim:

MEMBER: Ms Rostami, when did your problems begin in your country?
APPLICANT: About six months after we married, we had lots of fights, and really bad fights.
MEMBER: Wait, just to place this in context, when did you get married?
APPLICANT: 2000.
MEMBER: Continue, go ahead.
APPLICANT: Even when I divorced him, he would still harass me, and he kept calling me, following me, everywhere I went, and because he worked for the Government I had a feeling he was controlling everything I did, and sometimes I even felt he was controlling my phone. Due to this harassments [*sic*], I lost my job, and also a person I was in a relationship with because he worked for the Government, and I took part in election demonstrations in 2009, and I also thought . . . [*interrupted by the Member*]
MEMBER: Wait, did you lose a relationship with someone you were going to marry?
APPLICANT: Yes, it was this reason why we did not marry [*sic*].
MEMBER: Yes, but was it your intention to marry this man [who was] scared away by your ex-husband?
APPLICANT: Yes, my intention was to get married, but I was only with him six or seven, months and I wanted to get to know him more before I married, as I did not want the same experience as in the last marriage, and I wanted to get to [*pause*] to know him, to do things together.. . .
MEMBER: Umm, okay, we'll get back to that a little later. Who do you fear in your country?

This opening excerpt reveals the unpredictability of the conduct of the hearing for the applicant – and given the disjointed and impulsive nature of the Member's subject shifts, perhaps for the Member also.[36] The above dialogue took place in the first few minutes of the Member's questioning of the applicant, directly after the Member finished the opening formalities as set out in the hearing template. In those few minutes, the topics covered included the applicant's religion; the date she left her country; the 'problems' in her marriage; the actual date of her marriage; and whether her ex-husband had prevented her from pursuing a subsequent relationship. Indeed, it appears that the hearing began with the issue of religion because some documents about the applicant's religion happened to be absent. When the applicant began to explain her religion in greater depth, the Member redirected her to 'some general questions' and asked the closed question: 'When did you leave your country?'

[36] This corresponds with research conducted by the Canadian Council for Refugees (CCR), which found that 'most claimants described a question-answer format at their hearings' that did not necessarily follow the sequence of their claims. The report found that 'for some claimants, this model was not ideal because it gave the Board Member control over their narrative, and sometimes prevented them from saying what was important to them.' Applicants in the CCR study also described how a focus on 'facts' such as dates or addresses, fragmented and depersonalised their accounts: Canadian Council for Refugees, 'The Experience of Refugee Claimants at Refugee Hearings at the Immigration and Refugee Board' (2012) 38–39.

The previous excerpt ended with the Member asking the applicant whom she feared in her country. In response to this, the applicant listed that she feared both the government and her husband, and then attempted to explain why she feared her husband. The Member then asked her to stop talking about her husband and to explain her fear of the government:

MEMBER: What kinds of problems with the regime would you have? Harassment from your husband is what I am hearing so far.

APPLICANT: During the election of 2009 and after, I used to take part in demonstrations, and he was against it, and we would have terrible fights, and after he would beat me up.

MEMBER: I did not catch that.

APPLICANT: He would beat me up.

MEMBER: So that's your husband again. Can you tell me about problems you would have with the regime other than your husband?

APPLICANT: My husband works in the [XXX] in Iran and he would know when I left Iran, when I came back, and if he finds out that I changed religion, he would inform the Government, he would harass me again, call me and generally harass me.

The zigzagging course of this hearing reveals that the applicant, while required to give evidence, was not given the opportunity to direct how evidence was given or what would be addressed and when.[37] Ms Rostami did not discuss any evidence outside of the topics raised by the Member. Even when Ms Rostami began to answer the question about her religion at length, the Member stopped her. In a similar vein, in response to the question about when the problems in her marriage had begun, the applicant described these problems in some detail and arguably attempted to place these events within some form of a chronology. The Member, however, chose not to let this narrative continue and redirected her to a new subject.

[37] An 'x-ray' summary of the sequence of subjects in the Member's questioning in the *Rostami* hearing, following the questions above, is as follows: the details of the applicant's post-divorce relationship; whom the applicant feared in Iran; what would happen if the applicant returned to Iran; why the Iranian regime would know of the applicant; the date the applicant decided to leave Iran; why she left Iran; the date of the applicant's marriage; countries she had visited since her 'problems' with her husband had started; details of each country visited; details of an earlier attempt to flee Iran; the applicant's relationship with her smuggler/agent; why she chose Canada; details of her ex-husband's job; details of her ex-husband's employer; the relationship of her ex-husband's employer with the Iranian regime; her ex-husband's alleged stalking of the applicant; the applicant's employment history; the ex-husband's practice of making unwanted calls to the applicant; the applicant's place of residence in Tehran; the places of residence, employment and marital status of her siblings; details of her family home and the applicant's relationship with her parents; whether the applicant changed her telephone number or the family telephone number to avoid her ex-husband; the decision-maker's summary of her claim as he sees it; the applicant's seaside holiday post-divorce with her family; the location and content of the applicant's passport; pages destroyed in her passport; details of applicant's overseas travel prior to departing Iran (again); her ex-husband's knowledge of this travel; her name on an airport blacklist in Iran; the date of the applicant's divorce (again); her previous applications for a (non-protection-related) visa to Canada; how the applicant accessed her ex-husband's employment documents; the applicant's employment history; her allegations of harassment at a former place of employment; the inconsistent spelling of the applicant's husband's name in documents; the applicant's current religion; her current religious practice; and her view about the afterlife, according to her Christian religious beliefs.

To explore IRB and RRT decision-makers' control over the course and subject matter of applicant testimony, I also assessed the hearings through a schema of open versus closed questions. Alan Bryman defines open and closed questions broadly, describing a closed question as presenting respondents 'with a set of fixed alternatives from which they have to choose an appropriate answer' and open questions as allowing respondents to reply 'however they wish'.[38] Questions about 'personal', 'factual' or quantitative data can also be classified as closed, as they seek to elicit a fixed answer or particular fact.[39] By contrast, open questions may be defined as those which allow respondents to construct and determine an answer themselves, and which do not contain 'some implicit indication of categories such as yes/no responses, a number or quantity, or a single noun'.[40]

The dominance of closed over open questions in the majority of hearings in both jurisdictions was patent. Further, whether an open or closed question invited longer responses, or 'gave the floor' to the applicant, depended on the whim of the decision-maker. Notably, even when decision-makers posed open questions, the possibility of longer-form answers that allowed applicants to direct their own testimony, only arose when the decision-maker *permitted* a longer response. Not all open questions appeared to invite longer responses, and some closed questions permitted the applicant to give relatively open, detailed accounts of their evidence. That said, the majority of closed questions sought specific, closed replies and elicited short responses.

In order to test my impression that closed questions predominated over open ones in the observed cases, I undertook a quantitative exercise of tallying open versus closed questioning in the hearings.[41] One randomly selected hearing from each jurisdiction demonstrates the closed nature of most questions the applicant was required to address, *at the same time as* being judged against the credibility criteria of coherence, plausibility and consistence. In the *Pillai* hearing before the RRT, of the Member's 145 contributions that could be classed as questions, 96 questions were closed and 49 were open.[42] In the *Perera* hearing before the IRB, of 129 questions in total, 83 were closed questions and 46 were open.[43] The process of counting questions in the hearings revealed the decision-makers' substantial, constant and directive participation in the hearing. In reviewing the typed transcripts of most hearings, it is striking that in only a minority of instances were applicants' answers longer than the decision-makers' questions. Indeed, in some instances where the applicant began to answer an open question in detail, the decision-maker abruptly interrupted the applicant in order to redirect the answer-in-progress or to pose another question, sometimes on a new subject altogether. The following example from the *Pillai* hearing before the RRT demonstrates this practice. In the following extract, the Member posed an open question:

38 Alan Bryman, *Social Research Methods* (Oxford University Press, 2nd ed, 2004) 145.

39 Andrea Fontana and James H Frey, 'Interviewing: The Art of Science' in Norman K Denzin and Yvonna S Lincoln (eds), *Handbook of Qualitative Research* (Sage Publications, 1994) 361.

40 Jane Ogden and Danielle Cornwell, 'The Role of Topic, Interviewee and Question in Predicting Rich Interview Data in the Field of Health Research' (2010) 32(7) *Sociology of Health & Illness* 1059, 1063.

41 It was not always clear which questions and statements were open and which were closed. For example, sometimes the Member would put a proposition to the applicant, i.e., 'What if I said . . .' or 'In my view . . .' or 'It seems to me that . . .'. The implication was that the applicant should respond. I classified these inflected statements as open when they began with a 'what'.

42 *Pillai* [2013](RRT).

43 *Perera* [2013](IRB).

'Why did you decide to come to Australia?' When the applicant attempts to respond with details of his persecution, the Member responds: 'Sure, we will get to the details of why you left', and redirects the applicant by asking another open question. The Member then immediately redirects the applicant again by asking closed questions about other topics, including previous work-related trips out of Sri Lanka, the applicant's Australian visa and its duration, and then raises her retirement:[44]

MEMBER: Why did you decide to come to Australia, since you have been travelling around the world on numerous occasions as part of your professional career? Why did you decide to come to Australia in July [XXX]?

APPLICANT: I was working in [XXX] province as an assistant to [XXX]. At the time, there were a lot of life-threatening situations happening. So to take care of my life, I decided to come to Australia.

MEMBER: Sure, we'll get into the details of why you left. I am just wondering why you chose Australia as the country of destination?

APPLICANT: Because I was working under Mr [XXX], there was a lot of life-threatening situations, especially letter and telephone threatening [*sic*]. So I had to come out of Sri Lanka very quick. At the time, I had the visa for Australia; that's why I chose to come.

MEMBER: What type of visa was it? What period of time was it valid?

APPLICANT: One-year visa.

MEMBER: Okay. So you retired in February [XXXX]?

By contrast to an applicant attempting to speak at length but not being given the chance to do so, in some instances, applicants chose not to give extended responses even when decision-makers provided open invitations to speak. My observation was that this was either because of the predominance of closed questions surrounding more open ones (establishing a pattern of short and direct answers), or because the applicant could not or did not wish to give evidence on the topic raised by the open question. Members' open questions certainly did not always coincide with topics that the applicant wanted to or indeed was prepared to discuss. This is an observation that immediately recalls the narrative contests discussed in the previous chapter. The excerpts in Chapter 5 revealed that when a decision-maker is directly challenging the applicant's story, the questions are quite openly posed, inviting the applicant to 'explain' or 'account for' a particular course of action, asking why, what or how certain events took place.[45] However, it was often the case in these moments that the applicant had nothing further to add, or responded like Mr Adere to repeated demands to explain why something 'unexpected' happened: 'I do not know … I was surprised too.'[46]

[44] In the final third of the hearing, approximately two hours later, the Member returned to the question of the applicant's persecution for the first time. The topic was not addressed at length, and the applicant was not given an opportunity to explain the details of the 'life-threatening' situations he refers to above.

[45] In such circumstances, questions were often begun with openly contrary statements and in a disbelieving tone, i.e., 'But why would/would not you?' For example in the *Adere* [2012](RRT) hearing discussed in Chapter 5:

Member: [*To the applicant wife.*] You came to Australia to study; why would your husband leave his laptop in Ethiopia?

[46] *Adere* [2012](RRT).

In the *Pillai* hearing, a significant amount of time was spent on the applicant's claim that, as part of his work, he had produced a report that had caused him to be targeted by anti-government groups in Sri Lanka.[47] The Member posed numerous open questions about the 'methodology' that the applicant had employed to produce the report. I am unable to say how accurately the term 'methodology' was translated into Tamil (the applicant's mother tongue). However, the applicant did not appear to understand the repeated open questions about the 'methodology' of the report and at no point was his understanding of the term or its translation clarified by the Member, which raises a serious question about the nature of the translation of this rather technical term. The exchange directly raises the problem of the assumptions 'of absolute equivalence of meaning between languages' and of the interpreter as a mere conduit or invisible member of the 'triadic exchange' in asylum settings.[48]

The applicant's short answers were not satisfactory to the Member, who repeated questions related to methodology several times. After the applicant provided relatively short responses to the Member's inquiries, the Member pressed the applicant further, asking the following questions in quick succession:

MEMBER: Could you tell me about what working methodology you used to produce this report?
MEMBER: What was your brief?
MEMBER: How did you go about preparing the report?
MEMBER: But what was your methodology?

After the applicant failed to answer these open but interrogative questions to the Member's satisfaction, the Member went on to say,

MEMBER: I'm finding that you cannot express how you went about producing that report. And that's a concern for me, because if you were the author of the report I would expect you would be able to explain how you went about preparing it. So I am giving you an opportunity to give that evidence.

The applicant then identified some of the people whom he had contacted when he began writing the report, and he started to list the report's findings, which he alleged were a cause of his persecution. The applicant's responses here were short and did not directly address the question of methodology, to which the Member then returned, asking the following questions:

MEMBER: So tell me more about your methodology; what did you do to prepare the report? ... If you are producing a report on the issue of [XXX] in the region – tell me about what research you did?
APPLICANT: I was considering population, as well as [XXX], as well as [what was permitted under] the gazette.
MEMBER: Okay. Tell me more, please.

After the applicant had nothing further to add in response to these questions, the Member again began asking closed questions in quick succession, such as whom the

[47] Details are omitted here and in the following excerpts to preserve anonymity.
[48] Katrijn Maryns, 'Asylum Settings' in Franz Pöchhacker (ed), *Routledge Encyclopedia of Interpreting Studies* (Routledge, 2015) 22, 23.

applicant had contacted; when he had contacted them; and how he had made particular findings in the report.

The above excerpts reveal that open questions are not 'the answer' to the presentation of testimony in the oral hearing, particularly where the applicant is unwilling or unable to answer the questions. However, the predominance of closed questions (alongside the fact that open questions were not always posed in a way that invited open responses) evinces the decision-maker-directed nature of the hearings. Indeed, the Canadian Council for Refugees' 2012 report on the conduct of Canadian oral hearings found that applicants were often troubled by decision-makers asking questions that applicants perceived to be 'irrelevant' and their failure to address the substance of the applicants' claims:

> Some claimants complained that their hearings were negatively impacted by irrelevant or inappropriate questions. Others were deeply concerned that their Board Members failed to ask them about key aspects of their claim.[49]

This report points to another issue: the significance of decision-maker tone in the running of the hearing and in posing questions. In the hearings I observed, members' affective modes or tones of expression varied significantly. Beyond the open or closed nature of the questions being asked, the hearings revealed the deep significance of *how* decision-makers asked and responded to questions during the hearing.[50] The open questions extracted above, for example, were asked directly, forcefully, and repeatedly. In the hearings where applicants were able to present longer, uninterrupted tracts of testimony, questions (both open and closed) were asked in a tone that did not convey disagreement, impatience or dissatisfaction with an applicant's responses.

Within the dataset, three hearings were marked by a questioning style that permitted applicants to convey testimony on their own terms and in which decision-makers' direction of the hearing sounded and felt more like an examination-in-chief rather than an unpredictable cross-examination of evidence. In these hearings, applicants were asked open questions in a manner that roughly followed the sequence of their protection claims. They were given the chance to respond to most questions without being interrupted or redirected, even where their own answers were not chronologically sequenced. Where applicants provided uninterrupted testimony, it was often in

49 Canadian Council for Refugees, above n 36, 2. Claire Bennett made a similar finding in her interviews with women who had sought refugee status in the UK on the basis of their sexuality. In reflecting on their substantive interviews and court appearances, participants found the 'style of questioning, how the interview was conducted, . . . the inability to refuse any questions, and not being believed' to be stressful. Some women interpreted the style of questioning to be 'specifically designed to "confuse" or "infuriate" them': Claire Bennett, 'Lesbians and United Kingdom Asylum Law: Evidence and Existence' in Efrat Arbel, Catherine Dauvergne and Jenni Millbank (eds), *Gender in Refugee Law: From the Margins to the Centre* (Routledge, 2014) 138, 145.

50 The role of the interpreter is crucial here. In most instances, the Member's questions were interpreted and then delivered to the applicant by an interpreter. However, the Member in all the observed hearings spoke directly to the applicant. While my sense of the tone of questions is highly subjective, where tone was conveyed through the phrasing of questions or via the repetition of a particular question, I believe this was evident to the applicant *even though* the Member spoke in English. Tone was especially affected by members' responses to questions, and where a member responded by affirming a piece of testimony (e.g., by saying 'yes', 'thank you' or 'okay') as compared to where a member did not respond at all.

response to an affectively calm and inviting questioning style. Some examples of such questioning included: 'Can you tell me what happened in that instance?';[51] 'Tell me more about that group [of which the applicant was a member]';[52] 'Please explain to me why the Taliban would want to hurt you';[53] and 'You mentioned your [agents of persecution] are more powerful than before; can you explain that to me?'[54] These are all examples of questions that invited the applicant to speak freely about a particular piece of evidence. Additionally, where decision-makers acknowledged answers as heard (rather than as 'correct') with a comment, or some form of affirmative gesture, applicants continued to provide further, mainly uninterrupted testimony.

As noted above, closed questions in some instances also elicited long, narrative-based and applicant-directed responses. For example, in the *Flores* hearing before the IRB, the Member elicited several long-form answers from the applicant by posing mixed open and closed questions. In that hearing, the applicant alleged persecution on the basis of her political opinion and her status as an artist, and gave evidence of her inability to show her works in her country of origin due to government censorship. The Member posed several closed questions that elicited short replies, as well as both open *and* closed questions to which the applicant responded at length. An example of the latter is: 'Did at any moment in Cuba did [*sic*] the authorities say anything about your performances? ... I will be more specific, did [at] any moment the authorities say to you, [you] are not allowed to perform because of whatever?'[55]

Arguably, even a very small number of genuinely open questions, alongside open-ended prompts and closed questions, might allow the applicant to present their evidence in full and therefore have the opportunity to create a narrative through a series of extended responses. As noted, however, the manner in which open questions are asked determines whether an applicant is able to direct and control their own evidence. Certain open questions still elicited fragmented testimony, which lurched from topic to topic, across time, location and subject matter. In one view, the written application has already allowed the applicant to offer a narrative on their own terms, and that ought to be sufficient. However, given that one of the core functions of the oral hearing is to test credibility, and that credibility rests on the criteria of coherence, consistency and plausibility, the applicant should be given an opportunity to demonstrate these criteria during the hearing.

6.2.3 *Interrogating Time and Timing*

Questions related to time, dates and sequencing featured in all observed hearings. Such questions were disruptive and fragmenting, both where the applicant was able to confidently recall the date, year or sequence of events and where applicants were unsure of an accurate answer. As well as fragmenting the applicant's testimony, 'time questions' also clearly revealed decision-makers' demands for evidence in a narrative form. That is, they revealed an expectation that evidence could be expressed sequentially, with incidents both causally

[51] *Mena* [2013](RRT).
[52] *Flores* [2013](IRB).
[53] *Jabbar* [2013](IRB).
[54] Ibid.
[55] *Flores* [2013](IRB).

and temporally linked, even as the structure of the hearing directly impeded a sequential telling of events. In the hearings I observed, questions about dates and the order of events were often the subject of tense exchanges between applicants and decision-makers, and such exchanges were time-consuming elements of the hearing.

The timing of events is not crucial to providing evidence of persecution. Indeed, RRT and IRB guidelines and documents about evidentiary assessment in RSD explicitly set out that the failure to recall the chronology or dates of events should not necessarily be interpreted as discrediting the applicant, or the evidence as a whole. For example, as the Australian Credibility Guidelines set out, '[a] person may remember events that affected him or her most in emotional or physical terms but not necessarily in time sequence. Such confusion and forgetfulness do not necessarily imply that a person is not telling the truth . . . A person may forget dates, locations, distances, events and personal experiences due to a lapse of time or other reasons'.[56] Furthermore, as addressed in Chapter 1, research into the nature of autobiographical memory has formed the basis of repeated and strident critiques of the methods used to test asylum seeker credibility and testimony.[57] Some of the foremost concerns of this literature are the unreliability of and variation within autobiographical memory, and the disturbing and disordering effects of trauma on one's sense of time, timing and chronology. As Eastmond notes, extreme violence, displacement or trauma may create an experiential field 'in which narrative falters and fails', and in which extreme experiences both resist and destroy temporal and narrative ordering.[58] However, refugee applicants' failures to recall temporal details still form the basis of credibility determinations, despite clear psychological evidence that confusion regarding dates is not evidence of a lack of credibility. The hearings demonstrated that questions of time and sequence very much persist as a means of testing an applicant's evidence *during* the hearing.

Beyond the significant problems posed by the reliability of memory and the effects of trauma, which render questions about time and dates especially difficult for certain applicants to address, an individual's relationship to time is also a cultural phenomenon.[59] Different calendars and relationships with formal measures of time exist across cultures; some people have a sharper awareness of the year and month than others; and individuals' sense of what is a 'long' or 'short' amount of time is highly subjective. An extract from the *Adere* hearing exemplifies critiques commonly made of questions about time and dates as a basis for testing credibility:

[56] Administrative Appeals Tribunal Migration and Refugee Division, above n 29, [30]–[31]. See also Immigration and Refugee Board, 'Assessment of Credibility in Claims for Refugee Protection' (Legal Services, updated 2020) [2.3.6].

[57] See especially Hilary Evans Cameron, 'Refugee Status Determinations and the Limits of Memory' (2010) 22(4) *International Journal of Refugee Law* 469; Hannah Rogers, Simone Fox and Jane Herlihy, 'The Importance of Looking Credible: The Impact of the Behavioural Sequelae of Post-Traumatic Stress Disorder on the Credibility of Asylum Seekers' (2015) 21(2) *Psychology, Crime & Law* 139; Diana Bögner, Jane Herlihy and Chris R Brewin, 'Impact of Sexual Violence on Disclosure during Home Office Interviews' (2007) 191(1) *The British Journal of Psychiatry* 75; Jane Herlihy and Stuart W Turner, 'Asylum Claims and Memory of Trauma: Sharing Our Knowledge' (2007) 191(1) *The British Journal of Psychiatry* 3; and see generally Judith Lewis Herman, *Trauma and Recovery* (BasicBooks, 2nd ed, 1997).

[58] Marita Eastmond, 'Stories as Lived Experience: Narratives in Forced Migration Research' (2007) 20(2) *Journal of Refugee Studies* 248, 259.

[59] Walter Kälin, 'Troubled Communication: Cross-Cultural Misunderstandings in the Asylum-Hearing' (1986) 20(2) *International Migration Review* 230, 236; Evans Cameron, above n 57.

APPLICANT: One of the things the Delegate [the first instance decision-maker] raised was the dates; Ethiopia has a different calendar. It's very hard for me sometimes to switch to this calendar; honestly, if you call any Ethiopian and ask them what is the day today, people would say "I do not know." It is not only for me, but the Delegate took it as a point of not believing.

MEMBER: Well, that was I think in relation to when you were released from prison, was it? You've told me some other dates today, but the date you said you were released from prison, that was 11 May when you converted, wasn't it?

APPLICANT: Yes.

In the above excerpt, the applicant mentioned to the Member the cultural nature of one's relationship with time and the difficulty of translating dates across different national or religious calendars. To this, the Member responded by asking the applicant for confirmation of a specific date in his evidence.

The *Zeidan* hearing took place before the RRT and involved a female applicant from Lebanon and her daughter, who were making a claim with the mother as the primary applicant. This hearing is particularly relevant due to an exchange that the applicant initiated with the Member concerning the applicant's self-identified difficulty with remembering the dates and timing of events. The exchange took place at the beginning of the hearing, after the Member had explained the hearing process and after the applicant had amended some errors in her written application:

MEMBER: [*Exasperated.*] Is there anything further you want to change or add to your claim?

APPLICANT: No, but there is one thing that we can concentrate on. I have a problem with dates.

MEMBER: Do you want to explain that? What do you mean you have a problem with dates?

APPLICANT: I have a problem with dates because I went through so many things and so many events happened one after the other and . . . I have a problem with dates – I cannot say this happened on that date, I cannot say that.

MEMBER: That's fine – when I am talking to you about the timing and when various things happened, what I'd like you to try and do is think about the order things happened and how long it was between various things happening. If you are able to give me approximate dates, that is also useful.

In the above exchange, even though the Member said that it was 'fine' that the applicant had issues with dates, the Member then went on to confirm the requirement for the applicant to place events in order, and 'if able', to give approximate dates. This placed the applicant in the invidious position of being reassured that her inability to remember dates was 'fine', but still being expected to try to do so and provide temporal details where possible.[60] The applicants had also submitted a psychological report indicating that the applicant mother had diagnoses of post-traumatic stress disorder, major depression and symptoms of 'worsening in memory and concen-

[60] This contradicts a mostly standard element of the opening section of the hearing in both jurisdictions, in which decision-makers emphasise that if an applicant does not know the answer to a question, they should 'not guess', with some decision-makers adding that guessing may affect credibility assessment later on.

tration'.[61] The Member referred to and quoted the report but did not rely upon it in his final credibility assessment. And although not the focus of this chapter, the failure to accommodate an applicant's capacity to give evidence in line with expert medical opinion is reinforced in other research on the tendency for decision-makers to dismiss mental health and psychological reports and expertise.[62]

Throughout the *Zeidan* hearing, the Member did not refrain from asking questions about timing and time, despite the applicant's comments. To the contrary, the Member asked extensive questions about the dates of particular events, the amount of time between events and the order of events. When the applicant was unable to answer these questions, the Member nonetheless pressed her to attempt to do so. The excerpt I draw upon is lengthy. It was difficult to listen to without some level of personal discomfort, due to the applicant's palpable difficulty in providing dates. Despite the applicant's continual expression of distress and her attempts to communicate that she was having difficulty, the Member persisted with questions that required calculations of time or estimations of dates:

MEMBER: When did you open your beauty salon in [XXX]?
APPLICANT (IN PERSON): [*Pause.*] Umm, oh my god . . . I'm sorry. [*Sigh.*]
APPLICANT: The problem is I say a date, that's it, the date goes away from me.
MEMBER: Do you remember how long you had your salon in [XXX]?
APPLICANT (IN PERSON): I have had it for years; I am not sure. [*Sigh.*]
MEMBER: In your statement, you said you opened it around mid-2007. Would that be about right?
APPLICANT (IN PERSON): Yeah, yeah.
MEMBER: And before that, what were you doing?
APPLICANT: I was working at a salon called [XXX], and after that, I opened the salon.
MEMBER: And how long did you work at the other salon, roughly?
APPLICANT: [*Pause.*] About a year. More or less, around that [*sic*].
MEMBER: And what days and hours were you working in your own salon?
APPLICANT: At my salon?
MEMBER: Yes, when you opened your own salon.
APPLICANT: From morning, say nine or ten, till six; it depends on the work.
MEMBER: And what days?
APPLICANT: Ahh . . . sometimes all week, sometimes if I had something to do on Sunday, Sunday as well, sometimes Saturday . . . No, I always worked Saturdays.
MEMBER: Do you remember how long before you left [the country] you stopped working at the salon?
APPLICANT: [*Long pause.*] Few months.. . .
APPLICANT (IN PERSON): Sorry I do not, I do not . . .
MEMBER: So do you remember roughly what month the salon closed?

61 *Zeidan* [2014] (RRT Decision and Reasons) [11].

62 Jill Hunter et al, 'Asylum Adjudication, Mental Health and Credibility Evaluation' (2013) 41(3) *Federal Law Review* 471; on expert evidence generally, see Iris Berger et al (eds), *African Asylum at a Crossroads: Activism, Expert Testimony, and Refugee Rights* (Ohio University Press, 2015).

APPLICANT (IN PERSON): Um, um I think. [*Pause for three or four seconds.*] I think . . . I think three or four, I think March or April.
MEMBER: In 2004?
APPLICANT: Yes.
MEMBER: So how long before the salon closed had you stopped working, or were you working right up until it closed?
APPLICANT: I just stopped working because there was no more work to do, and then after I was attacked I stopped working for about a month.. . .
MEMBER: [*Interrupting.*] Sorry, so you were attacked and you stopped working for about a month?
APPLICANT: About a month and a half.

The following excerpt relates to key events in the applicant's life, including the birth of her child, her marriage and her divorce. It strikes me as the Member's attempt to coax the applicant into creating something of a timeline. Each time the applicant struggled to recall a particular date, the Member sought a further detail.

MEMBER: And when did you get married?
APPLICANT (IN PERSON): Just a year before my daughter was born, in '87. My daughter was born in '89, maybe in '88, no sorry, no '98.
MEMBER: So your daughter was born in '98?
APPLICANT: Yes.
MEMBER: So you got married around 1997, is that right?
APPLICANT: Yes.
MEMBER: And when did you get divorced?
APPLICANT (IN PERSON): Ummm. [*Sigh.*] I remember . . . I had a big celebration in 2011.
MEMBER: And how long before that did you actually separate from your husband?
APPLICANT (IN PERSON): [*Pause. Sigh.*] From when he left . . . umm, 2007. 2007, yes, '07.

Questions about time are, fundamentally, attempts to sequence events and to 'get the story straight'. The Member repeatedly pressed the applicant to put things in order, even when those things were not 'in order' for the applicant. Even where questions on time and timing were not asked in an interrogative manner, or did not ultimately have any bearing on credibility findings, much time was spent on the dates and order of the evidence. Yet the excerpts reveal that neither the order of events nor the exact years or dates of their occurrence were central to Ms Zeidan's understanding of her evidence. Yet, the Member's fixation on timing, combined with the applicant's inability to pinpoint particular years or sequences, made the applicant appear uncertain and unreliable. While the Member did not make a direct finding as to the applicant's overall credibility, she found the majority of her claims to be implausible and therefore not credible. The applicant's daughter also gave testimony. In assessing the daughter's credibility, the Tribunal found that '[w]hile the Tribunal has some concerns in relation to the applicant mother's claims which are discussed above, it found the daughter applicant to be a credible and persuasive witness and is satisfied she holds real fear'.[63]

[63] *Zeidan* [2014] (RRT Decision and Reasons) [44].

Throughout the hearings, questions regarding dates, sequencing and quantities of time persisted as a focal point. Such questions were often posed in order to test the credibility of evidence, with the expectation that credible applicants would be able to accurately answer these questions.[64] These questions of time and decision-makers' demands for specific times, dates and quantities highlight two points that are relevant to this book's overall argument and purpose. The first is the extent to which demands for details about time and sequencing prevented the applicants from putting together coherent narratives by interrupting the evidence being given. The second point is the extent to which the questions exposed a demand for a neatly linear narrative and for a sense of plot, in which the applicant moves towards a decision to seek status and to becoming, above all other narrative resolutions, a refugee.

6.3 Conclusion

In several of the hearings I attended in person, the applicant's advocate took a moment prior to entering the hearing to explain to the applicant how the hearing would run. Sometimes this advice was given on the basis of the advocate's experience of the particular member listed for the hearing; at other times, the explanations were more general. I accompanied the applicant and advocate in attending the *Mbassi* hearing before the RRT. The applicant expressed just before the hearing began that he was nervous about how the hearing would go. In response, his advocate gave him a brief account of RRT procedure, describing the order of questioning and the role of the Tribunal officer who opens and closes the hearing. The advocate further explained that the hearing would not be 'like a court' because it was an informal hearing. Ultimately though, the advocate did not explain the hearing in great detail. This was perhaps because the advocate herself could not know exactly how the hearing would run.

As it turned out, the *Mbassi* hearing was particularly long, and the Member's questioning style was interrogative and hostile. The Member asked a large number of closed questions, and asked questions in a tone that was frequently impatient. Questions about several issues were repeated and even returned to despite the applicant's inability to answer, and the applicant was given no opportunity to outline his claim without his answers being interrupted or fragmented. As soon as we left the hearing, the applicant said repeatedly 'that was not what I was expecting'. The applicant's surprise at how the hearing ran lingered, and he continued to express his shock as we left the RRT building. The capacity to narrate at all depends upon the nature of the narrative occasion; that is, on the conditions for testimony and the 'norms of performance and content'.[65] The response of Mr Mbassi at the close of his hearing, described above, reveals the unpredictability of the hearing as a narrative occasion.

Narrative theory's attention to the spaces (or occasions) of narrative illuminates just how difficult it might be for a refugee applicant in an oral hearing to convey an effective narrative if the terms of that narrative's telling are unknown, or worse still, entirely unpredictable. The outset of this chapter explored what decision-makers told applicants at the start of the

[64] Significantly, often such questioning did not make it into the final written decision and reasons, nor was it referred to in credibility findings – revealing the gap between the hearings as they occurred and what is recorded in the decisions.

[65] Patricia Ewick and Susan S Silbey, 'Subversive Stories and Hegemonic Tales: Toward a Sociology of Narrative' (1995) 29(2) *Law & Society Review* 197, 197.

hearing, about the conduct of the hearing and the applicant's role within it, which did very little to accurately inform applicants about either topic. This fact is particularly troubling in instances where applicants are led to believe they will have the opportunity to present their narratives on their own terms, but are never given this chance. My critique of the contradictory mandates placed upon refugee applicants gathers force in the book's final chapter, which argues that decision-makers evinced an expectation that applicants perform the role of an omniscient narrator, and engage in pure but confident speculation about their own and others in their testimony's motivations and interiority. In making this argument, I return to the 'stock narrative of becoming a refugee' discussed in Chapter 4 to argue that the genre of acceptable refugee testimony aligns with the genres of human rights discourse and the realist novel,[66] which imagine that the seeking of refugee protection enables the resolution of the refugee story, and realisation of a full liberal personhood, marked by self-possession, autonomy and readiness to become a future refugee-citizen.

[66] Joseph R Slaughter, *Human Rights, Inc.: The World Novel, Narrative Form, and International Law* (Fordham University Press, 2007).

7

Beyond the Demand for Narrative: Genres of Refugee Testimony

This final chapter interrogates the impossible narrative position faced by refugee applicants during the oral hearing by examining how specific narrative genres enter the hearing room and further determine the 'authentic' refugee that states are willing to accept. The chapter's focus is on the specific genre or genres of testimony that refugee applicants must present to credibly and successfully move from an outsider-refugee applicant to an acceptable refugee-citizen. Each chapter of the book has incorporated a critique of the claim that law is separate from literature, and of law as a stable system of rules that must seek out narrative forms as sources of insight, virtue or moral good. This chapter's focus on the requirement that refugees provide testimony as particular kinds of narrators and in line with specific genres further builds my argument that a demand for narrative restricts rather than enables access to protection, and that narrative and genre operate as disciplining and exclusionary forms within RSD.

The *Bildungsroman*, or 'formation novel', is a coming-of-age genre historically associated with eighteenth-century Germany and the realist novel more broadly. Slaughter's 'provisional gloss' on the genre explains it as involving an 'outsider' protagonist who moves, through a process of acculturation and education, from a state of conflict with society to one of harmony, assimilation and incorporation.[1] In Slaughter's critique of human rights discourse, he argues that human rights and the *Bildungsroman* are 'mutually enabling fictions' as 'each projects an image of the human personality that ratifies the other's vision of the ideal relationship between individual and society'.[2] Applying Slaughter's work, I argue that just as in the *Bildungsroman* genre, refugees must be able to present their evidence in the form of a linear narrative in which they move from an outsider status and marginalisation towards self-possession, sovereignty and willing incorporation in a new state and status. Crucially, the story must resolve in an unambivalent decision to seek both refugee status and incorporation into the nation-state. Indeed, the 'narrative of becoming a refugee', which I developed in Chapter 4, is marked by the generic conventions of the *Bildungsroman*, with the refugee applicant-as-protagonist who journeys as a social outsider towards a modern, liberal self, who is 'rational, unitary, and assured of [her] free agency'.[3] Reading refugee

[1] Joseph R Slaughter, *Human Rights, Inc.: The World Novel, Narrative Form, and International Law* (Fordham University Press, 2007) 3.

[2] Joseph R Slaughter, 'Enabling Fictions and Novel Subjects: The Bildungsroman and International Human Rights Law' (2006) 121(5) *Publications of the Modern Language Association* 1405, 1407; Slaughter, above n 1.

[3] Sujatha Fernandes, *Curated Stories: The Uses and Misuses of Storytelling* (Oxford University Press, 2017) 11.

testimony through the genre of the *Bildungsroman* reveals the relationship between testimonial forms, the subject of human rights, and the refugee-citizens that Global North states are willing to accept.

Considering the breadth of what we can reasonably define as a narrative, part of my argument in this chapter is that the contention that RSD processes demand that refugees present testimony in a narrative form, if left at that, is almost axiomatic. So, this chapter continues to provide a more precise account of the *kind* of narrative that is required of refugee applicants by employing the concept of genre. Alexandra Georgakopoulou, critiquing the tendency of narrative-based analyses to essentialise and homogenise all narratives as 'one archetypal genre', observes that such analyses rely on a narrowly defined version of narrative as a well-structured story, with a beginning, middle and end, building up to a complicating event that is usually resolved in the end.[4] The narrowly prototypical narrative form that Georgakopoulou critiques has been central to my analysis because I argue it is precisely this conventional narrative form against which refugee testimony is judged. In this chapter, though, I demonstrate that a more precise investigation of narrative *genre* within refugee decision-making raises important questions about the origins of the conventions that govern how refugee applicants give testimony; and about how these conventions relate to existing styles of narration and political conceptions of 'refugeeness' and liberal citizenship.

My exploration of genre within the RSD oral hearing focuses on two aspects of refugee testimony. The first aspect is the narratorial voice with which refugee applicants are expected to speak, which I argue is that of an omniscient narrator. That is, as narrators, refugee applicants are not simply required to recount the events that form the basis of their claim. They are required to provide an all-knowing account of events, outcomes and to explicate their own and others' decision-making and actions, especially those actions which a decision-maker deems 'implausible'. Indeed, alongside the demand for self-possession and interior knowledge, applicants are required to account for the decisions and interior worlds *of others* in their narratives. My contention is that these demands call to mind the generic device commonly associated with certain realist novels, of reliance upon an 'omniscient narrator able to adjudicate the development of the narrative from a beginning to a middle to an end', where subjects are 'knowing, responsible and autonomous', in full possession of themselves and of their language.[5] As with the processes of fragmentation I charted in the previous chapter, the demand to account for oneself and others was constant throughout the hearings, and constituted a further expectation about *how* applicants present and explain their evidence. The second expectation of refugee narrative that I explore is the style of plot that characterised the evidence that decision-makers considered to be credible. By returning to the narrative of becoming a refugee described in Chapter 4, I argue that the genre demanded of refugee testimony aligns with what Slaughter has identified as the related genres of human rights discourse and the *Bildungsroman*.[6]

[4] Alexandra Georgakopoulou, 'Narrative Genre Analysis' in Lisa M Given (ed), *The Sage Encyclopaedia of Qualitative Research Methods* (Sage, 2008) 541; and see further Alexandra Georgakopoulou and Anna De Fina, 'Analysing Narratives as Practices' (2008) 8(3) *Qualitative Analysis* 379.

[5] Maria Aristodemou, *Law and Literature: Journeys from Her to Eternity* (Oxford University Press, 2000) 6.

[6] Slaughter, above n 1; Slaughter, above n 2; and see also Robert Meister, *After Evil: A Politics of Human Rights* (Columbia University Press, 2013); Karin Van Marle and Stewart Motha (eds), *Genres of Critique: Law, Aesthetics and Liminality* (Sun Press, 2014); Mark Antaki, 'Genre, Critique, and Human Rights'

7.1 Genre and the Law

Like narrative, genre is both part of our everyday vocabulary and a term of art used within and across disciplines. Mary Chamberlain and Paul Thompson write, '[g]enre is not an easy matter to discuss; on the one hand the term is relatively new for social scientists, while on the other it has a very long and at times confusing history in literature and the visual arts'.[7] The concept of genre goes back to the basic distinction made in Ancient Greece between the dramatic, epic and lyrical forms of literature – 'a distinction made partly in terms of mood and theme, and partly of mode of presentation and the relationship with the audience'.[8] Chamberlain and Thompson note that genre is most recently understood

> not as a rigid form of classification but more akin to language, with its fundamental flexibility, but at the same time [as creating] common assumptions between writer, speaker and audience of conventions, manner and tone, forms of delivery, timings, settings, shapes, motifs and characters.[9]

Stewart Motha and Karin Van Marle draw on Jacques Derrida to explain the way in which genre is a normative force, creating a commitment to certain forms and conventions even when those rules and conventions are undermined or broken:

> To speak of genre is to draw a line, invoke a limit, mark a boundary. As Derrida pointed out, 'when a limit is established, norms and interdiction are not far behind'. A genre announces a line of demarcation, belonging, purity and also the anomaly that lies beyond that limit.[10]

In Derrida's essay on genre, he writes that there is no such thing as a pure or natural genre; instead, genre arises where 'one has deemed natural structures or typical forms, whose history is hardly natural but, rather, quite to the contrary, complex and heterogeneous'.[11] At the same time, though, Derrida observes that 'a text cannot belong to no genre, it cannot be without or less a genre'; since '[e]very text participates in one or several genres, there is no genreless text; there is always a genre and genres, yet such participation never amounts to belonging'.[12] Wai Chee Dimock agrees with Derrida that the law of genre is an impossible law, since it contains within itself a

(2013) 82(4) *University of Toronto Quarterly* 974. The term 'human rights discourse' is used by Robert Meister in *After Evil: A Politics of Human Rights* (ibid). Much of this work fits into a broader field which critiques human rights discourse more generally. I do not address that literature here, instead focusing on various assessments of the genres of contemporary human rights.

[7] Mary Chamberlain and Paul Thompson, 'Introduction' in Mary Chamberlain and Paul Thompson (eds), *Narrative and Genre* (Routledge, 1998) 1, 1.

[8] Ibid. Though, as they note, genre became a term that could be applied to almost all written forms of literature, even though it originally referred to three spoken or theatrical forms: at 1.

[9] Ibid 4.

[10] Stewart Motha and Karin Van Marle, 'Introduction' in Karin Van Marle and Stewart Motha (eds), *Genres of Critique: Law, Aesthetics and Liminality* (Sun Press, 2014) 17, 19; citing Jacques Derrida, 'The Law of Genre' in Derek Attridge (ed), *Acts of Literature* (Routledge, 1992) 221, 224.

[11] Jacques Derrida, 'The Law of Genre' (1980) 7(1) *Critical Inquiry* 55, 60.

[12] Ibid 65. He goes on to note that this lack of belonging is not 'because of an abundant overflowing or a free, anarchic, and unclassifiable productivity, but because of the trait of participation itself, because of the effect of the code and of the generic mark': at 65.

'principle of contamination'.[13] She suggests that genre is best invoked 'less as a law, a rigid taxonomic landscape, and more as a self-obsoleting system, a provisional set of rules that will always be bent and pulled and stretched by its many subsets'.[14] Dimock also cites Alastair Fowler, who rather charmingly writes, '[g]enre is much less of a pigeonhole than a pigeon', and that genres are best understood not as 'permanent classes' but as 'families subject to change'.[15]

Analyses of law and legal forms have, on occasion, turned to genre to reveal forms of writing (and of reading) that are implicated in or explain practices of interpretation or 'world-building' within the law.[16] In Agnes Woolley's application of Slaughter's work on genre and human rights law, she argues that 'the process of claiming asylum follows its own rigid plotlines, producing an idealized refugee personhood rooted in the 1951 Convention'.[17] Woolley makes this argument primarily by reference to the secondary literature on credibility and refugee law rather than decision-making in practice. However, she also examines how notions of a fixed asylum story and the discoverable truths of authentic refugeehood have shaped fictional, documentary and literary engagements with asylum.[18] Recognising that law draws upon particular practices of representation can make law's genres visible and allow us to challenge refugee law's narrative conventions as constituting a genre that necessarily grants access to the truth.[19] That is, we can challenge the extent to which legal authority governs in a realist register or as form of 'aggressive realism', as van Rijswijk describes it.[20] This attention to literary genres, as implicated in law's claims to authority and its capacity to adjudicate the truth, is quite distinct from turning to pieces of literature, or literary genres, on the rather optimistic basis that they allow us to empathise with particular subjects or to see the 'other', which is at times how genre has been utilised within legal scholarship.[21]

7.2 Omniscience in the Oral Hearings

Paul Dawson notes that, despite orthodox accounts of the omniscient narrator that locate the phenomenon in the eighteenth- and nineteenth-century novel, the term has taken on

[13] Wai Chee Dimock, 'Genre as World System: Epic and Novel on Four Continents' (2006) 14(1) *Narrative* 85, 86.

[14] Ibid.

[15] Alastair Fowler, *Kinds of Literature: An Introduction to the Theory of Genres and Modes* (Clarendon Press, 1985) 37.

[16] See Slaughter, above n 1; Samuel Moyn, *The Last Utopia* (Harvard University Press, 2010); Van Marle and Motha, above n 6; Agnes Woolley, 'Narrating the "Asylum Story": Between Literary and Legal Storytelling' (2017) 19(3) *Interventions* 376; and see also Lynn Hunt, *Inventing Human Rights: A History* (W. W. Norton, 2008); Martha C Nussbaum, *Poetic Justice: The Literary Imagination and Public Life* (Beacon Press, 1995). Mark Antaki writes that 'of course, Lon Fuller's work reminds us that sensitivity to questions of "form," including especially to the form of "rules," is not new to so-called legal theory': Antaki, above n 6.

[17] Woolley, above n 16, 378.

[18] Woolley, above n 16. However, she also promotes the capacity of certain literary narratives to challenge the normative expectations within the legal asylum regime: 379.

[19] Honni van Rijswijk, 'Archiving the Northern Territory Intervention in Law and in the Literary Counter-Imaginary' (2014) 40(1) *Australian Feminist Law Journal* 117, 120.

[20] Ibid 127.

[21] Compare Nussbaum, above n 16.

various meanings and come to describe different features of narrative voice and focalisation depending on the period and context to which it is applied.[22] In tracking contemporary theoretical debates about omniscience and its inexactitudes, Jonathan Culler's list of four textual phenomena that can constitute omniscience in narrative is instructive, and describes omniscience as including: (1) the performative authority of reliable narrative declarations about the fictional world; (2) the reporting of characters' private thoughts 'such as are usually inaccessible to human observers'; (3) overt, self-reflexive and authorial narration 'where the narrator flaunts her godlike ability to determine how things turn out'; and (4) the synoptic overview of events as a means of producing a kind of universal wisdom.[23] While Culler's purpose in describing these multiple elements is to argue that the term omniscience is ultimately unhelpful because it cannot adequately cover each of these elements of narrative style,[24] these multiple meanings of the term 'omniscient narrator' are useful to my argument that a version, or indeed versions of omniscience, are required of refugee applicants.[25]

Two of Culler's elements of omniscience were openly demanded of refugee applicants during the hearings I observed. These were first, the performative authority of reliable narrative declarations about the world, and second, the reporting of each character's private and internal thoughts.[26] This approach to omniscience follows Gérard Genette's formulation of omniscient narration, which defines it as a mode of focalisation where the 'narrator knows more than any character, or more exactly, *says* more than any of the characters know'.[27] Decision-makers conspicuously and repeatedly asked refugee applicants in the observed hearings to narrate their own *and* other characters' (or actors') private thoughts and motivations, as well as to account for why they and others made particular

22 Dawson writes that despite these variations in meaning, literary theorists are nonetheless accustomed to 'an historical trajectory of the novel which holds that modernist and postmodernist fiction throughout the twentieth century can be characterised, in part, as a rejection of the moral and epistemological certainties of omniscient narration': Paul Dawson, 'The Return of Omniscience in Contemporary Fiction' (2009) 17 (2) *Narrative* 143, 143.

23 Jonathan D Culler, 'Omniscience' (2004) 12(1) *Narrative* 22, 26.

24 Culler agrees in part with Nicholas Royle, who first employed the term 'telepathy' instead of the concept of omniscience, and who argues that telepathy 'calls for a quite different kind of critical storytelling than that promoted by the religious, panoptical delusion of omniscience': Nicholas Royle, *The Uncanny* (Manchester University Press, 2003) 261; Culler, above n 23, 29. The concept of telepathy, alongside the more familiar but perhaps less specific 'omniscience', works well to explain the instances that I extract below – and it is a helpful idea to keep in mind when reading exchanges between decision-makers and applicants.

25 Dawson notes that Culler objects to the theism and to the analogy with God that omniscience implies. Dawson does not share Culler's anti-theism, since 'none of the existing alternatives quite manages to encompass the narrative freedom (in terms of panoramic scope and narratorial judgement) which the trope of a "godlike" narrator suggests': Dawson, above n 22, 145.

26 This is also described within narrative theory as 'focalisation'. Internal focalisation is where the story is mediated through the point of view of the focaliser, often with access to the internal world of that narrator. External focalisation occurs when the narrator presents information that is only externally observable. Gérard Genette first used the terminology of homodiegetic and heterodiegetic to distinguish between types of narrators: homodiegetic (a narrator who is also a character) and heterodiegetic (a narrator who is not a character and narrates all-knowingly from 'outside' the story). An autodiegetic narration takes place where the narrator is also the story's main protagonist: Gérard Genette, *Narrative Discourse: An Essay in Method* (Cornell University Press, 1983) 244–48.

27 Ibid 189 (emphasis in original); see also Dawson, above n 22, 148.

decisions. Applicants were asked to explain why and when certain events had occurred, and why other people behaved as they did. The applicants were required to make clear, reliable declarations about the story they presented and exactly why it took a particular course.

The significance of this requirement for omniscience, in the context of RSD, is that the applicant is not a self-conscious author of literary fiction or non-fiction, styling a story to produce a particular literary effect or to convey a lesson. Rather, the applicant is recounting events that they understand to be, or have been told to be, relevant to a claim for refugee status. Inevitably, the applicant narrates the story as a narrator who participates in it. But then, in decision-maker questioning, applicants are frequently asked to meet the expectation that their narratorial role be accompanied by a performance of narratorial omniscience, indicating that they have both 'self-knowledge' and access to the action and interiority of other actors in the story.

The Refugee Convention definition of a refugee requires that the applicant fear persecution '*for reasons of* race, religion, nationality, membership of a particular social group or political opinion' – a definition that creates a causal requirement in relation to *why* persecution takes place.[28] This nexus requirement, that alleged persecution takes place because of one of the Convention grounds, has frequently given rise to the discomfiting demand that applicants be able to account for the actions and motivations of their persecutors.[29] However, there is a substantive difference between presenting available *evidence* of a particular persecutor's motivation, and being required to *know* why particular actors in one's narrative behaved as they did. Notably, in the hearings I observed, applicants frequently met demands for omniscience with a display of agency and a willingness to challenge decision-makers.[30] Indeed, in such challenging moments, applicants often refused to engage in speculation or to answer questions that they identified as being outside of their knowledge. Still, in instances of narrative contest and demands for omniscience, applicants were asked and indeed encouraged by decision-makers to express pure speculation, including in relation to why their persecutors chose to harm them, as testimony.

Before turning to an exploration of how demands for applicant omniscience featured in the *Zahau* hearing, I note that in the observed hearings, modes of questioning that required the applicant to knowingly account for themself and others were so common that it was challenging to choose a single hearing to focus on.[31] I witnessed egregious examples of the demand for omniscience. In certain hearings, when applicants failed to account for their own internal worlds, they were met with hostile and incredulous questioning. Decision-makers often grew impatient when applicants could not present fully realised versions of themselves, free of ambiguity, with full sovereignty over their decisions and their

28 Refugee Convention, as amended by the 1967 Protocol Relating to the Status of Refugees, art 1A(2) (emphasis added).

29 On this point, see Michelle Foster, 'Causation in Context: Interpreting the Nexus Clause in the Refugee Convention' (2001) 23 *Michigan Journal of International Law* 265.

30 See, especially, *Valdez* [2013](IRB); *Rostami* [2013](IRB); *Adere* [2012](RRT); and *Zeidan* [2014](RRT).

31 The applicant was required to account for their own or others' interiority and decision-making making processes in all the Australian hearings. This requirement was less present in the *Jadoon* [2013](RRT) and the *Pillai* [2013](RRT) hearings, where it was only raised briefly in relation to two or three events. In the Canadian hearings, applicants were required to account for their own or others' interior decision-making processes in multiple instances in all of the hearings except the *Flores* [2013](IRB) hearing.

narratives.[32] Often the decision-makers' incredulity led them to question why applicants could not explain their own or others' decisions, rather than focusing on the evidence that applicants provided. Critically, only some applicants were able to describe and explain their own internal motivations or to posit and speculate about the interiority of others. Many applicants could not meet this expectation, and others still openly resisted and contested it.[33]

7.2.1 *The* Zahau *Hearing*

The *Zahau* hearing before the RRT involved a single female applicant from Burma. It was a long hearing, running for more than six hours over two days. For most of this time, Ms Zahau was required to give oral evidence.[34] Her application was on the basis of her persecution on the grounds of her religion, as a Christian in Burma, and on the basis of political opinions. Her claims in relation to her political opinions were based on membership of the Chin ethnic minority, as well as her anti-government views. She detailed her participation in pro-democracy activities in Burma as part of her general opposition to the Burmese government.

The *Zahau* hearing exemplified the 'culture of disbelief' described in the literature on credibility assessment. At certain points, the Member in this hearing could be described as either incredulous or as openly derisive. The excerpts below further illustrate the argument of the preceding chapter, insofar as they demonstrate the overwhelming directive and discretionary power of the decision-maker over how the hearing is structured. The extracts here could equally be described as narrative contests, like those I detail in Chapter 5. Independently of the decision-maker's distrustful manner, the excerpts also exemplify decision-makers' demands for omniscience in the applicant; first in relation to accounting for others, and then in relation to her own decisions and actions.

7.2.2 *Accounting for Others*

In each of the excerpts in this section, Ms Zahau was called upon to explain the motivations, mindsets and inner worlds of the people who played a part in her narrative, including those who were involved in and responsible for her persecution. Ms Zahau, as the narrator, was able in several instances to provide a plausible motivation for the characters in her story; she successfully, albeit hesitantly, took on the role of an all-knowing narrator.

The decision-maker required Ms Zahau to explain the actions of several other actors who were mentioned in her evidence about her political involvement. The following exchange

32 On this point, see Simon Behrman, 'Accidents, Agency and Asylum: Constructing the Refugee Subject' (2014) 25(3) *Law and Critique* 249.

33 Specifically the applicants in the *Adere* [2012](RRT), *Zahau* [2012](RRT) and *Bhatti* [2013](IRB) hearings all displayed a truly exceptional ability to meet decision-makers' expectations that they account for the decision-making processes of both themselves and others in their narratives. These applicants both attempted to explain internal motivations for particular actions or choices and sought to make these motivations or decision-making processes 'comprehensible' for decision-makers by highlighting how and why decision-making processes might differ from those expected or articulated by the Member; or might vary on the basis of differing cultural contexts or experiences.

34 The hearing also included the brief examination of a witness who appeared on Ms Zahau's behalf, as well as her lawyer's closing submissions.

came midway through the hearing, on day two, after the Member has asked Ms Zahau to describe the various political activities she was involved in while in Burma. A key part of Ms Zahau's evidence related to her helping her brother's academic tutor, a political activist, to pass on sensitive or illegal information. Ms Zahau explained that the tutor was wanted for arrest by the authorities. Ms Zahau's involvement included picking up a letter and passing it on to another teacher on behalf of her brother's tutor, whom the decision-maker characterised as a pro-democracy activist.[35] In the exchange below, the Member repeatedly asked, amongst other things, why Ms Zahau's brother's tutor would ask her for this favour; why the tutor could not do it himself; and why the tutor could not have just called his friend by telephone to express the sensitive information. In response to each question, the applicant tried to account for the tutor, who on her own admission she did not know personally. Ms Zahau offered compelling answers to these questions and established possible motivations for the tutor, but ultimately she admitted that she did not know why he made the choices he did:

APPLICANT: Rather than going to protest without no [*sic*] real outcome, I thought I should do something that would lead to a better outcome, so I went to my brother's teacher who teaches English, and he was involved in the '88 revolution. My brother told us that his teacher was involved during the '88 revolution although he did not know all the details and he was wanted for arrest. . .

MEMBER: So you went and met him personally?

APPLICANT: I knew this teacher before the Saffron revolution began because my brother was unwell and his leg was not good, so with his tutorings [*sic*] either me, my sister or I [*sic*] had to take him, so I met this teacher occasionally, but it wasn't personally. So I knew him through that, and maybe because he knew me at that time, he asked me to get this letter to someone.

MEMBER: How did you . . . how did he tell you to get the letter?

APPLICANT: He called me on the phone and said he wanted to write a letter to his friend and he could not give it to him personally and, um, because my brother was quite young he could not do it, so he asked for my help instead. Because I was very interested in those things, I said I would help him, but even after saying that, I could not help him immediately.. . . His friend was a teacher, so I delivered the letter to him. Even when I was delivering the letter, I could not meet that friend personally because he was hiding just like the other teacher, so I asked the secretary of the school to hand it to him.

After asking the above questions, the Member went on to ask Ms Zahau to explain the tutor's behaviour, and then to pose his own version of what could (or to his mind, should) have happened, if the tutor in question wanted to communicate with his friend in relation to politically sensitive topics:

MEMBER: [*Long pause.*] Why could not he just call his friend?

APPLICANT: Burma is very different from here, and making phone calls is very expensive, and all internet access and phone lines are controlled by the Burmese authorities, so they were probably afraid.

MEMBER: [*Sceptical.*] But he called you.

[35] *Zahau* [2012] (RRT Decision and Reasons) [86]. In this hearing, the interpreter made frequent grammatical errors in her translations, which I have noted in the transcript but not amended.

APPLICANT: I was only his student's sister, and I could have been one of his students, so it might not [have] been dangerous for him to contact me, but he might have had other ways of contact with that other friend [*sic*].

Following this exchange, the Member explained at length why he found the applicant's version of the tutor's actions and motivations implausible. The Member's scepticism of the applicant's account primarily concerned her explanation of the tutor's interior decision-making processes. As difficult as the Member's musings are to comprehend when reading the passage below, his musings were even more difficult to follow during the oral hearing:

MEMBER: I am just not sure that it makes that much sense for this person [XXX] to be calling the sister of one his students, who he barely knows; he barely knows you and to ask you to do something very dangerous, pass on a letter to another person and you cannot even get to the other person, so you pass it to a third person. Sorry. [*Gentle laugh.*] I will break this up into separate pieces. So, there could be two ways to communicate about things. One is to pick up [the] phone and to speak to the person. The other way is to write a letter, to pass it on to the other person. And I understand that he may be afraid of using the telephone, but he picked up the telephone and rang you. Then, he does not know you very well, but he decided to trust you; you had to meet two days later, and then you could not even get to his friend, so you had to give the letter to a third person, the secretary. And all of this is for what you say is, you thought is a short letter. If communication technology is not very advanced in Burma, would not it be safer just to ring up on the phone? [*Forcefully.*] Or why could not the secretary go to [the tutor] and get the letter from him. Why did you have to go?

Ms Zahau then tried to account for each aspect of the tutor's behaviour, including details of his reasoning processes:

APPLICANT: The secretary did not know who my brother's teacher was, and it was my brother's teacher wanting to pass the letter, not the friend wanting to pass the letter back to my brother's teacher, so it was the other way around. And, although he barely knew me, he knew me better than most people. And I do not know why he decided to trust me, but he did ask for my help. The reason the secretary did not go to [the tutor] was because it wasn't them who needed to pass a letter to [the tutor].

MEMBER: I understand, but if they meet then [the tutor] can pass the letter to the secretary. In the same way you did not know the secretary but identified him, why could not [the tutor] meet him? They could ring each other up on the phone and [the tutor] would say, 'Let us meet tomorrow at such and such a place, I will be wearing red and something or other, and that's how you will recognise me and I will give you the letter.'

APPLICANT: I do not know why he decided to do that, but what I think is because most teachers are involved in political activities in Burma, it is more dangerous for them to use the school phone to call and talk to each other about political activities and meetings for them.

MEMBER: So that was it, was that what you were involved in prior to arrest, or were there other things as well?

In the above exchange, the member posits a series of alternative decisions – in his view, better-reasoned ones – that the tutor could have made in order to more 'safely' and easily pass on anti-government or politically sensitive information. The Member proposed a completely alternative story, which included the Member making up dialogue and imagining that the applicant's brother's tutor could have worn a red jumper so that he might be recognised upon an imagined secret meeting with a secretary. The applicant was then required to explain her brother's tutor's decisions and to account for why the tutor's approach was different to the imagined scenario proposed by the decision-maker – who seems to have taken the applicant's place as an omniscient narrator. In this instance, the applicant must also, as omniscient narrator, make her own culturally located narratives intelligible to the decision-maker and/or fall into line with the 'stock stories' that constitute the decision-maker's view of what is credible and true.

Questions that demanded the applicant perform the role of an omniscient narrator were especially troubling when they were asked in relation to an applicant's alleged persecution or persecutor. This occurred twice in the *Zahau* hearing. I do not address each occurrence in detail,[36] but briefly summarise one exchange. On day two of the hearing, the applicant provided evidence in relation to her experience as a forced porter, after being stopped by the Burmese army whilst travelling. The applicant described being forced, while she was held captive, to 'massage' and please the soldiers at night and to carry heavy goods during the day. The Member did not question her about the details of this alleged abuse. The applicant then described her attempt to escape, which she did by going to the toilet in the night and then running away with another person who was also being held captive by the army.

After she had described the sexual and physical abuse she had suffered before attempting the escape, the Member wanted the applicant to explain why the soldiers had not followed her to the toilet. The applicant responded, 'I am not sure why, but maybe they could not be bothered or maybe because the toilet was not far away'. The Member then asked the applicant to explain her own decision to escape via the toilet: 'If the soldiers were about to go to bed and they could not be bothered to follow you, could not you just say "go" with the nod of your head or just say "run" [to the other escapee, rather than going to the toilet together].' The Member questioned other details about her escape, including the order in which she and her co-escapee left for the toilet, and then changed the topic, to discuss the fate of the applicant's other political friends. Here, the decision-maker's questioning also reinforces existing literature on the assessment of gender-based harms within RSD, which demonstrates that there is a tendency for decision-makers to minimise or pass over allegations of sexual assault when testing evidence, and an especially strong culture of disbelief towards women making allegations of sexual harm.[37]

7.2.3 *Accounting for Oneself*

As an omniscient narrator, Ms Zahau was also required to explain her own actions and to articulate her decision-making process, as if all her decisions were rational, knowing and

[36] Another relevant example from the *Zahau* hearing occurred when the applicant provided evidence about being abducted and beaten by government authorities and the decision-maker wished to know why, after her abduction, her captors chose to drive her home.

[37] See Helen Baillot, Sharon Cowan and Vanessa E Munro, 'Reason to Disbelieve: Evaluating the Rape Claims of Women Seeking Asylum in the UK' (2014) 10(1) *International Journal of Law in Context* 105; Hana Cheikh Ali, Cristel Querton and Elodie Soulard, 'Gender-Related Asylum Claims in Europe: A Comparative Analysis of Law, Policies and Practice Focusing on Women in Nine EU Member States (GENSEN)' (May 2012) <www.asylumaid.org.uk/data/files/Genderrelated_asylum_claims_in_Europe.pdf>.

self-consciously made. In the following passages from the hearing, the Member asked the applicant to explain the circumstances of her arrest. In response to this, the applicant described the events that led up to her arrest, including her involvement in helping another politically active friend, who is referred to in the excerpt below. In the excerpt, Ms Zahau's friend asked her to collect some things from his house, as he was in hiding from the authorities. The excerpt once again features Ms Zahau's brother: she sent her younger brother to her friend's house instead, as she believed this was the safer option. In response to this, the Member could not fathom how, in the earlier incident (when delivering a letter for her brother's tutor) she went *instead of* her brother because she thought this was the safer option and then, on a later occasion and in a different circumstance, she chose her brother to undertake a risky task. The Member requires the applicant to explain this perceived discrepancy in her reasoning, and to present herself as a self-possessed narrator and as someone who makes decisions confidently, consistently and consciously:

MEMBER: So tell me about the arrest.

APPLICANT: Before the arrest of [the friend], ahh, he was trying to escape, and he asked me to go to his house and pick up some money, clothes, and his passport, identification card from his house, but I was afraid to do that myself, so I asked my brother to do that. My brother decided to take a friend with him, but when they reached the house, the house was guarded and the guards told them that they could not go in and they said they were afraid to go in so they came back and did not get any of his things.

MEMBER: Why did you send your brother?

APPLICANT: Because I was afraid to go there by myself, and my brother was younger and he was like a student and it was normal for him to go there and it wasn't just [the applicant's friend] living at that house, it was like a shared house. So, he could go and ask the other people that lived there for that.

In the above extract, the applicant was required to clearly account for why she made a particular decision. Directly after, the Member doubted the applicant's internal reasoning because it appeared inconsistent with her thinking and decision-making on a previous occasion:

MEMBER: But, hang on a second. [*Long pause.*] But . . . but . . . with, with the letter you said the exact opposite, that your brother was too young at the time so that is why you did not send your brother to pass on [the tutor's] letter to his friend. But then when it comes to doing something more dangerous, to pick up stuff from [your friend's] house, you send your brother. Isn't he too young?

APPLICANT: The difference is that with delivering a letter he was young he might not have had tactics and if he was get caught with his letter [*sic*] then that would have been more dangerous. But as he is young and he is a student, going to his teacher's house is quite common. And, if he goes in there and asks the people that [the friend] lives with for those things, and picks it up then the authorities would not know what he picks up [*sic*].. . .

MEMBER: But you understand what I am trying to say, that . . . that . . . I cannot see why one logic would apply to the letter and another logic would apply for you for going to [the friend's] apartment to pick up his things. If your brother is younger and more vulnerable then he should not do either of these things. If you are more vulnerable because you are involved in political activities, then you should not do either of these things.

In the above line of questioning, the Member not only required the applicant to explain how and why she made a particular decision, but also expected her to use the same 'logic', as he calls it, in making all of her decisions.[38] The Member's questions also imply that the applicant could have modified her political behaviour, if she knew or might have known her actions would create danger for her or others. This recalls the use of now broadly impermissible 'discretion reasoning', which posits that if (primarily) gay and lesbian applicants are discrete or private about their sexual preferences they can avoid persecution, and therefore the need for protection. In the *Zahau* hearing, the applicant provided very compelling reasons as to why she willingly put herself in danger and why she did not apply the same 'logic' in all situations. She told the Member that sometimes our reasoning processes are wrong, and that we often act on impulse or instinct:

APPLICANT: Sometimes our reasons and logics could be wrong [*sic*], but at that time, what I thought was that because my brother was his student and as a student it was common to go to a teacher's house, I just thought that the police would not care if they saw him go in there.

The final excerpt below dovetails with the last section of this chapter, addressing human rights discourse and its relationship to the genre of the stock narrative of becoming a refugee. In the below excerpt, the Member requested that Ms Zahau explain exactly why she chose to leave Burma on the day that she did. He also pressed her to explain why she would *voluntarily* go to the police to be questioned if she feared for her safety vis-à-vis government forces. Exasperated, Ms Zahau explained that presenting herself to the police might not have been the best decision, but that it was the one that she made at the time. In the excerpt, at first Ms Zahau tries to explain her decision-making process in retrospect, but then ultimately presents the decision to leave as something that struck her as the right thing to do in the circumstances – not as reasoned and premeditated as the Member insists:

MEMBER: Now, the last thing is what happened or what you claim happened to you just before you left Burma. You were in [the town of XXX] and you wanted to leave Burma, in December and the beginning of January. Is that right?

APPLICANT: Yes.

MEMBER: And then you go back [to your hometown] on the [XX]th January and your mother says the police want to talk to you. But you had already decided to leave the country, so why do you go to the police to talk to them?

APPLICANT: First of all, now thinking back it may seem stupid, but at that time I did not have any advisers around me, all the decisions I made I had to make by myself no matter what situation I was in. I had already decided I was going to leave the country, but I also wanted to see the police. Although both police and soldiers have authority in the country, umm, the citizens are just scared of the soldiers, but we aren't that afraid of police. Some of them we are afraid of, but it is not like the soldiers. The reason I went was because I wanted to know how much they knew about me and I also had to think about my family, what could happen to them. I just wanted to know how much they knew about me, what exactly did they knew about me and how dangerous it was for me, and I also wanted to know how it could affect my family.

[38] Herlihy et al found that 'an assumption of consistency of behaviour also ran through a number of [UK] determinations. If someone had not acted due to fear in one situation, it was not accepted that they might then act in a similarly fearful situation at another time': Jane Herlihy, Kate Gleeson and Stuart Turner, 'What Assumptions about Human Behaviour Underlie Asylum Judgments?' (2010) 22(3) *International Journal of Refugee Law* 351, 358.

At the close of the hearing, the Member summed up his issues with Ms Zahau's case and gave her a chance to respond. After dealing at length with a number of issues the Member had raised, Ms Zahau closed her testimony by assertively explaining once more that while she was required to narrate her reasoning for various actions, her actions were simply what she had done 'at the time'. She explained that it was not in her power to make these things less 'suspicious' to the Member or to make them better conform to the Member's sense of how the story (and her own internal reasoning) should have run:

APPLICANT: With my case, some of my decisions may not make sense or may be suspicious, but when you are in situations like this, you are in danger. There might be something that I can do better [*sic*], but that is what I did at that time.

This explanation is remarkable for both its clarity and arguably, its calm defiance of what the decision-maker expects of Ms Zahau and her decision-making processes. She refuses to present her decisions as perfect, sensible or correct and instead characterises them as what she did at the time and reminds the decision-maker that it was a time marked by danger and fear.

The fundamental question within refugee law and RSD is whether the applicant has a well-founded fear of being persecuted if returned home.[39] As most refugee law texts emphasise, the test for determining whether the applicant has a well-founded fear of persecution is future-focused, since the question is whether the applicant will face persecution in the future.[40] It is decision-makers who must finally determine this question, via what Guy Goodwin-Gill and Jane McAdam call 'essays in prediction' and hypothesis.[41] At the same time, applicants are routinely given the opportunity to explain 'what would happen' if they returned to their country of origin and why this would place them in danger. Crucially, the applicant is often called upon to state both 'what' would hypothetically happen and then 'why' their persecutors would 'still be interested' in the applicant or why past persecution would continue. Consequently, one of the fundamental demands for the applicant to act as an omniscient narrator comes in relation to questions of what the future holds for the applicant; of how the story might end if the applicant returns home. However, there is once again a substantive difference between asking an applicant what they *believe* might happen if returned to their country of origin, and requiring the applicant, as narrator, to frame such speculation as a self-assured account of how the future will unfold and why, and to execute 'a specific rhetorical performance of narrative authority'.[42]

Ms Zahau's appeal to the RRT was successful. The RRT decision-maker, though, rejected a number of her claims and in doing so meticulously recorded her inability to

39 For discussion of the requirement, see Chapters 4 and 5.

40 See generally James C Hathaway, 'Michigan Guidelines on Well-Founded Fear' (2005) 26 *Michigan Journal of International Law* 492.

41 Guy S Goodwin-Gill and Jane McAdam, *The Refugee in International Law* (Oxford University Press, 4th ed, 2021) 58.

42 Dawson, above n 22, 147.

account for the behaviour of her brother's tutor,[43] and for herself in relation both to her departure from Burma[44] and to her decision to send her brother to her friend in hiding's house (instead of going herself).[45] The Tribunal rejected as implausible Ms Zahau's account of her departure and her experiences of being sexually assaulted as a forced porter but accepted that she had been politically active as a student and in assisting her brother's tutor.[46] The Member found she would be persecuted on the basis of her real or imputed political opinion and that 'just because the applicant may have exaggerated or even fabricated some of her claims', it did not necessarily follow that she had not been truthful in relation to other aspects of her claim.[47]

The literary conceit of omniscience, and the evidentiary expectation of being sovereign over oneself, function here as part of law's generic demands and expectations of refugee applicants. The challenges of fully accounting for one's self, however, are particularly acute for refugee applicants in oral hearings, who must perform this sovereign version of self, whilst narrating a difficult and unsettled autobiography for the purposes of protection. As well, they must do so in a fragmented, often-adversarial and unstructured oral hearing. Applicants are not necessarily equipped to meet the demand for evidence in a particular narrative or generic form. Indeed, Ms Zahau's ability to contend with these questions was exceptional – and parts of her evidence were nonetheless found to be lacking credibility when she could not account for herself or others.

7.3 Human Rights Discourse and the Genre of the Refugee Story

As the preceding chapters have demonstrated, the multiple narratives, events and topics that become the focal points of the RSD oral hearing may be idiosyncratic, unexpected and vary from one hearing to the next depending on the style, impulse and narrative-based expectations of the decision-maker. However, in the fifteen oral hearings that formed the basis for this research, onshore refugee applicants in Australia and Canada were required to contend with a particular stock story, a narrative of becoming a refugee, against which decision-makers assessed testimonial evidence. In this narrative, 'genuine' onshore refugees when faced with persecution or the risk of persecution, take decisive action to flee this persecution and/or their country of origin. They then travel as directly as possible to a place where refugee protection can be sought, and having arrived there, seek the host state's protection at the earliest opportunity. According to this narrative, they take these steps decisively and with certainty. Once having fled, refugee applicants certainly do not contemplate the possibility of returning to their home country and they do not equivocate about the decision to seek protection in a new nation-state, which resolves the narrative and complication of refugee flight.

The genre of the stock narrative of becoming a refugee, with its elements of journey, personal development and resolution, has much in common with Slaughter's critique of the

[43] In the written decision, the Member paraphrases these exchanges at length: *Zahau* [2012] (RRT Decision and Reasons) [87]–[88], [139].
[44] Ibid [111].
[45] Ibid [89].
[46] Ibid [173], [178].
[47] Ibid [175]–[176].

genre of human rights discourse as tied to that of the *Bildungsroman*. Slaughter argues that international human rights law and the nineteenth-century genre of the *Bildungsroman* 'are mutually enabling fictions'.[48] He writes that 'each projects an image of the human personality that ratifies the other's vision of the ideal relations between individual and society'.[49] In so doing, Slaughter points to the complicity of literary and cultural forms in disseminating and naturalising human rights norms and in presenting the imagined liberal subject of human rights. Slaughter builds this critique by revealing how both international human rights law and the early *Bildungsroman* elevated the 'bourgeois, white male citizen to universal subject'.[50] The *Bildungsroman*, writes Slaughter, is a reconciliatory genre[51] that 'conventionalized a narrative pattern for participation in the egalitarian imaginary of the new bourgeois nation-state, a plot for incorporation of previously marginalized people as democratic citizen-subjects'.[52]

Resonating with Slaughter's account of the *Bildungsroman* as involving the outsider protagonist's education and acculturation, Mark Antaki describes the genre as involving a linear narrative, which 'allows the protagonist, often retrospectively, to take responsibility, as author, for his or her own development'.[53] This genre is mirrored within international human rights law, which harbours a 'developmental narrative' and, as Slaughter explains it:

> consists of two actors (the human person and the state), a probable conflict between them, a means of remediation in the human personality, and a temporal trajectory that emplots a transition narrative of the human person's sociopolitical incorporation.[54]

Slaughter emphasises that, 'the development of human rights personality assumes a progressivist telos, a linearity'[55] which Robert Scholes and Robert Kellogg considered the 'central technical innovation enabling the modern novel'.[56] Antaki writes that the novel's teleological, coming-of-age narrative, in which the protagonist becomes what they were always called to be, 'undergirds much human rights discourse both as grand narrative of world history . . . and as the goal of human rights for each individual human being and nation: the opportunity to "develop" his or her or its own distinctive capacities'.[57]

48 Slaughter, above n 2, 1407.
49 Ibid.
50 Ibid.
51 Wilhelm Dilthey, *Poetry and Experience: Volume 5 of Selected Works* (Princeton University Press, 1985) 336; Slaughter, above n 2, 1410.
52 Slaughter, above n 2, 1410.
53 Mark Antaki, 'From the Bridge to the Book: An Examination of South Africa's Transformative Constitutionalism's Neglected Metaphor' in Karin Van Marle and Stewart Motha (eds), *Genres of Critique: Law, Aesthetics and Liminality* (Sun Press, 2014) 49, 68, as part of Antaki's reading of Slaughter; and see Slaughter, above n 1.
54 Slaughter, above n 2, 1409.
55 Ibid.
56 Slaughter, above n 2; Robert Scholes and Robert Kellogg, *The Nature of Narrative* (Oxford University Press, 1966) 236. Slaughter's work on this topic involves a detailed genealogy of international human rights law and its relationship with German idealism, of which his argument about the *Bildungsroman* and its relationship to rights forms one part.
57 Antaki, above n 53, 56. Though cf Mikhail Bakhtin's account of the novel as the most accurate approximation of the complex relationship between representation, time, language and experience, through its heteroglossia (multiple voices), multiple temporalities and 'chronotopes'. The novel, he writes,

The fantasies that Antaki and Slaughter have described as attaching to the genre of human rights and the realist novel are those I have described as characterising the stock narrative of becoming a refugee: a linear, teleological progression towards a new status, closure of the past, access to the interiority of self or self-knowledge, and eventual sovereignty over one's self and the future.[58] However, in charting the journey from non-citizen to citizen, from exclusion to inclusion, the subjectivities or character of the asylum seeker are also multiple and contradictory. In Makau Mutua's influential work on archetypal figures within human rights narratives, he argues that human rights discourse is 'marked by a damning metaphor' of 'savages, saviours and victims'.[59] The narrative of becoming a refugee is a stock story that features the tropes of refugee-as-victim, the benevolent state-as-saviour, and the attaining of refugee status as the ultimate closure. Certainly, the subject represented in the stock narrative of becoming a refugee conforms closely to Mutua's description of narratives of the ideal victim, who is powerless, despairing, and lacks agency. The refugee in this narrative, however, occupies a paradoxical subject position. The refugee must be both vulnerable and dependent in order to be saved, but the genuine refugee must also act with certainty and resolve in response to persecution, exercising immense agency in the decision to seek refugee status.[60] The paradox is irresolvable: the applicant must be the victim of certain out-of-control events, in urgent need of protection, and yet also present themself as an omniscient narrator knowingly journeying towards self-possession and full citizenship. Applicants as narrators must navigate and occupy the contradictory positions of deserving, powerless victim and the educated, self-possessed refugee-citizen. It is precisely this tension that the plot trajectory of the *Bildungsroman* seeks to – but cannot fully – resolve.

The narratorial voice that decision-makers in the dataset required of refugees was also that of the enlightened and autonomous liberal subject, a voice which conveys both self-awareness and self-consciousness and that contradicts conceptions of refugees-as-supplicants or victims. The requirement of refugees as narrators also goes well beyond international refugee law's requirement that they fear persecution on Refugee Convention grounds, are outside their country of origin and are unable to attain the assistance or protection of their home state. Indeed, in Ms Zahau's above exchanges with the decision-maker, she was required to coherently account for how she responded to circumstances of danger and harm, despite the traumatic circumstances she faced; to demonstrate consistent self-knowledge; and to be sure of her decision to seek refugee status. Like the *Bildungsroman*, the resolution of Ms Zahau's narrative, in escaping and seeking refugee protection, was interrogated and tested as a kind of coming-of-age or formation narrative.

David Murray also identifies a hegemonic 'migration to liberation nation' narrative as structuring decision-making in relation to LGBTQI refugee claimants and media depictions

'reflects more deeply, more essentially, more sensitively and rapidly, reality itself in the process of its unfolding': Mikhail Bakhtin, 'Epic and Novel' in Michael Holquist (ed), Caryl Emerson and Michael Holquist (trans), *The Dialogic Imagination* (University of Texas Press, 1981) 3, 7; and following this approach, see Desmond Manderson, *Kangaroo Courts and the Rule of Law: The Legacy of Modernism* (Routledge, 2012); Robert F Barsky, 'Narratology and the Convention Refugee Claim: Re-ontologizing the Subject in Canadian Immigration Hearings Discourse' (1988) 1 *Discours social/ Social Discourse* 265.

[58] Antaki, above n 6, 988.

[59] Makau Mutua, 'Savages, Victims, and Saviors: The Metaphor of Human Rights' (2001) 42 *Harvard International Law Journal* 201, 201; and see Makau Mutua, *Human Rights: A Political and Cultural Critique* (University of Pennsylvania Press, 2013).

[60] See Behrman, above n 32.

of queer refugees in Canada.[61] The 'migration to liberation' narrative tracks closely alongside Slaughter's argument about the idealised subject of human rights discourse. Both narratives imagine social outsiders moving in a progressive manner towards full incorporation as citizen-subjects. As Murray explains, the hegemonic narratives that shape IRB and media conceptions of LGBTQI refugees are:

> literally and figuratively straight in their temporal, spatial and sexual orientation in that they follow an essentialist linear path of sexual identity development . . . [this] coincides with unidirectional spatial migration towards the nation of refuge, culminating in the liberating moment of the refugee hearing where the claimant can officially 'come out' to the state who will protect her . . . and expect passive, docile citizenship in return.[62]

Drawing on Sara Ahmed's theorisation of multiculturalism and its demand for a 'happy migrant',[63] Murray sees a similar imposition of 'a happiness duty' as part of the refugee narrative, which encompasses 'a kind of moral training in which the migrant is supposed to gratefully learn the ways of the civilised empire'.[64] This demand for a happy migrant, and with it a 'happy ending' is implicit within the stock narrative of becoming a refugee that I have traced and analysed within the oral hearings. Murray's description of the 'liberating moment' and culmination of the refugee hearing and determination of status is, in my argument, the narrative resolution that structures the judgment of refugee testimony and credibility.

7.4 Conclusion

In my application of Slaughter's critiques of the *Bildungsroman* to the refugee narrative, the methodological aims and argument of my book come together. Analysing the genres of refugee testimony reveals that literature and literary forms may be complicit in law's authority and power, rather than a means of improving or challenging law's 'truths' and judgments. Patricia Tuitt openly rejects the position that aesthetics and literature are necessarily transformative of the law's determinative and positivist nature, and she argues that we should recognise where aesthetics are part of law's violent, biopolitical projects.[65] She writes that if we wish to recognise the place of aesthetics in law, this necessarily implicates aesthetics in the control of legal subjects.[66] Within RSD, applicants may be judged against stock stories and multiple, intersecting 'standard' narratives, which apply to different cultural, racial and gendered identities that the applicant is perceived to inhabit. Applicants may also, however, be judged by virtue of the forms of the stories that they tell. For the purposes of my argument in

61 David A B Murray, 'The (Not So) Straight Story: Queering Migration Narratives of Sexual Orientation and Gendered Identity Refugee Claimants' (2014) 17(4) *Sexualities* 451, 452.

62 Ibid 453.

63 Sara Ahmed, *The Promise of Happiness* (Duke University Press, 2010) 130.

64 Murray, above n 61, 453 citing Ahmed, above n 63.

65 Patricia Tuitt, 'Literature, Invention and Law in South Africa's Constitutional Transformation' in Karin Van Marle and Stewart Motha (eds), *Genres of Critique: Law, Aesthetics and Liminality* (Sun Press, 2014) 75, 78.

66 Ibid.

this book, the difficulty with generic requirements within RSD – with these literary *forms* – is that they govern access to 'truth' by determining how certain subjects do or should behave, and whose testimony will be judged as credible. Genre and voice, in the refugee context, add a set of expectations not merely about how applicants behave, but how they narrate and interpret their own histories and stories. The demand that applicants act as omniscient narrators was a dominant theme in my analysis of the dataset for both the IRB and the RRT and was exemplified in the *Zahau* hearing before the RRT.

Even as I adopt a critical view of literature and narrative in law, as well as a deep scepticism of the valourisation of narrative, I retain some hope for the potential of certain literary genres to challenge law and to aid legal and interdisciplinary scholars and writers in their critiques of legal forms.[67] Antaki writes that while some literary genres call to be critiqued, others are acts of critique in themselves and can unsettle state law's taken-for-granted assumptions and fantasies of closure and sovereignty.[68] While the *Bildungsroman*, in its fantasies of sovereignty over self, others and the future,[69] is implicated in the law's power to define the terms on which refugee applicants may speak, other critical works 'call these fantasies into question and may therefore invite an experience of affective dissonance'.[70] This point relates to the foundations of outsider storytelling scholarship and arguments that certain narratives disrupt and undermine legal authorities' stock stories about legal subjects.[71] I certainly do not want to abandon or refuse the possibility that certain genres and narratives can expand our understandings of legal questions, rhetoric and speech. Nor the idea that certain legal texts, including judgments and administrative decisions handed down within refugee law, can re-write or revise law's stock narratives. These counter-narratives can offer ways of reading, interpreting and being a refugee that do not conclude, solve or impart direct moral meaning, that permit or dwell in ambivalence, uncertainty or even a lack of self-knowledge and self-realisation. Turning to genre, and to narrative style, reveals yet one more term upon which refugee testimony is assessed – but equally pries open a space within and beyond legal adjudication for new narratives, which contest generic, familiar and rigid accounts of the (refugee) self.

67 In Slaughter's reading of the relationship between the realist novel and the human rights project, he is critical of human rights discourse. And yet, in his critique, he retains hope for the normative project, and indeed the genres, of human rights. Slaughter argues that instead of treating rights discourse's 'imaginary egalitarianism' and its paradoxes as a shameful limitation, we should attend to the productive possibilities of human rights discourse, whereby 'such a project must consider not only the content of human rights discourse but also its logical and rhetorical forms, from which its content is in fact inseparable': Slaughter, above n 2, 1413.

68 Antaki, above n 6, 975–77; Manderson, above n 57, 17.

69 Antaki, above n 6, 977.

70 Ibid. See also Robin West, 'Communities, Texts, and Law: Reflections on the Law and Literature Movement' (1988) 1 *Yale Journal of Law & the Humanities* 129.

71 As I highlight in Chapter 8 such a claim has been central to the literary style and genres that Behrouz Boochani and Omid Tofighian have used to theorise the violence of Australian refugee policy, and in particular refugee expulsion to and imprisonment on Manus Island: Omid Tofighian and Behrouz Boochani, 'Narrative, Resistance and Manus Prison Theory' (2020) 54(2) *Review of Middle East Studies* 174; Omid Tofighian, 'Introducing Manus Prison Theory: Knowing Border Violence' (2020) 17(7) *Globalizations* 1138.

8

Conclusion

In the absence of other means or written forms of evidence to prove their claims, the refugee applicants who participated in this research needed to be able to present and explain their oral evidence in a way that met the core elements of a compelling narrative form. This fundamental aspect of the interrogation and judgment of refugee oral testimony encompassed an expectation for oral evidence marked by linearity, direct and explicable causal connections between events and outcomes, and some sense of both plot and closure. The hearings before the IRB and former RRT demonstrated how such demands structured the reception, testing and, ultimately, the judgment of refugee oral testimony. The book has also addressed how applicants contended with the challenge of providing a coherent narrative account of themselves, and the at-times-impossible task of trying to convey a 'good' story that moves from beginning to middle to end, during the fragmented and unpredictable conduct of the RSD oral hearing. Indeed, applicants who possessed the 'narrative resources' to do so,[1] questioned or resisted decision-maker expectations that their testimony fit into a neat narrative form. Such contestations took place during hearings in which applicants were expected to present evidence in narrative form, yet by virtue of the oral hearing's conduct and structure, were actively impeded from doing so. Further, decision-makers' demands for testimony that met the core elements of a conventional narrative form both reshaped and redirected an applicant's account of evidence and the testimony that formed the basis of the claim.

Judging Refugees' focus on the assessment of refugee applicants' oral testimony places it squarely within an interdisciplinary body of scholarship that has critiqued the tenuous straws at which RSD processes have grasped – principally, coherence, consistency and plausibility – to appraise and determine credibility. The criteria governing RSD credibility assessment are inaccurate measures of the credibility of *any* form of autobiographical testimony, and wholly inappropriate when applied to the trauma-inflected, cross-cultural, multilingual and adjudicative environment of the RSD hearing. The book has argued in favour of placing the (often inaccessible and closed) conduct of the oral hearing at the centre of studies of the politics and practice of individualised RSD and credibility assessment. The empirical aspect of the book examined the precise nature and conduct of each hearing, to ask how the hearing itself governs refugee applicants' ability to present their testimony as credible – that is, to meet the narrative mandate that the book describes and critiques. I explored these issues using the framework of narrative theory to analyse fifteen RSD oral

[1] Jan Blommaert, 'Investigating Narrative Inequality: African Asylum Seekers' Stories in Belgium' (2001) 12 (4) *Discourse & Society* 413; Katrijn Maryns and Jan Blommaert, 'Stylistic and Thematic Shifting as a Narrative Resource: Assessing Asylum Seekers' Repertoires' (2001) 20(1) *Multilingua* 61.

hearings before the IRB and former RRT. Alongside my argument about the place of the narrative form in the presentation and testing of refugee testimony, I have argued that (refugee) law's turn to literature and narrative must be attentive to the function of narrative as a means of disciplining certain subjects and of refusing access to rights, justice or recognition before the law.

Each of the arguments that I develop in *Judging Refugees* was framed by Chapter 3's account of the history of the oral hearing. In that chapter, I demonstrated that the introduction of a statutory and semi-independent hearing in Australia and Canada took place as means to both enhance the procedural fairness and independence of RSD processes, as well as to ensure that only 'genuine' refugees were granted asylum. In Australia, this occurred as the government was attempting to limit the arrival of onshore refugees and judicial oversight of migration decisions, and alongside the introduction of the notorious and enduring policy of mandatory immigration detention. In Canada, the right to a hearing was introduced in a less cynical mode and as the result of litigation testing refugee applicants' right to be heard under the *Canadian Charter of Rights and Freedoms*. Nonetheless, this similarly took place in the context of renewed government rhetoric and policy aiming to prevent unauthorised arrivals from reaching Canadian territory.

Chapters 4 and 5 addressed how narratives and the narrative form fundamentally structure the conduct of the RSD oral hearing and the interrogation of refugee testimony. Chapter 4 revealed that a fixed, narrow and unimaginative stock narrative of becoming a refugee formed the basis for judging the form and content of refugee applicants' testimony. Chapter 5 exposed how decision-makers tested evidence during hearings. Specifically, that decision-makers engaged in a form of narrative contest with applicants, presenting counter-narratives to applicants as to how their histories *might* have taken place if they were true or credible, and expecting applicants to contend with these alternative narratives. The counter-narratives frequently related to small details in an applicant's evidence, such as an injured arm, a phone number or the items that an applicant had decided to pack prior to leaving. These normative expectations held by decision-makers were often implicit, deeply subjective and difficult to connect to the core elements of the Refugee Convention's definition of a refugee and its domestic enactments.

In Chapter 6 I considered the conduct of the RSD oral hearing as a narrative occasion. I examined the form of the hearing; the types of questions that decision-makers posed; and how, when and in what order topics were raised by decision-makers. Did the questions and topics follow any kind of pattern? To what extent were applicants allowed to answer questions, and on what terms? What happened when applicants provided an answer that the decision-maker judged unsatisfactory? I concluded that the hearing and applicants' testimony with it were frequently and severely fragmented due to the plenary control exercised by decision-makers over refugee testimony, and the manner, sequencing and style of questioning in the hearings. The process of narrative fragmentation led to the troubling finding that, in the majority of hearings observed, the applicant was both expected to present evidence in narrative form and actively impeded from doing so. Further, if applicants displayed confidence and an ability to present evidence in a narrative form, and to 'argue and justify'[2] their own story, this was done in spite of, rather than because of, the structure and conduct of the oral hearing.

2 Robert F Barsky, *Constructing a Productive Other: Discourse Theory and the Convention Refugee Hearing* (John Benjamins, 1994).

Chapter 7 analysed the demands placed on refugee testimony as they related to specific narrative genres. This last chapter showed that the requirement for 'credible' oral refugee testimony called for a particular kind of narrator and refugee subject: one who has knowledge over self and others, who displays omniscience in relation to their story and its complications, and who acts out and narrates a linear path from an 'outsider' and asylum seeker to successful incorporation into a new liberal state and status. In identifying the place of the realist novel in casting the refugee story as a narrowly reconciliatory genre, I suggested that this is but one of the genres that shape the judgment of refugees. Multiple genres structure RSD and the judgment of different classes of refugee claims. There is much ground for further engagement as to how specific generic expectations and standard scripts function across different types of claim, sites of decision-making and jurisdictions.

8.1 Repairing the Oral Hearing?

Narrative expectations and resources, then, are 'at the heart of the power asymmetry that characterises encounters between asylum seekers and the state'.[3] This fundamental inequality within asylum procedure shapes 'who can talk when, in what ways and with what effects'.[4] Crucially, it is an inequality that cannot and will not be corrected with the implementation of more guidelines or minor variations to the norms or procedures that govern RSD.[5] This is absolutely not to dismiss or undermine work that has studied, critiqued and sought to address the worst excesses of fact-finding and credibility judgments within RSD. The repeated, thoughtful and sometimes exasperated interventions by cross-disciplinary scholars, advocates and international bodies to improve fact-finding and credibility assessment within RSD are necessary and urgent.

There is little hope, however, for repairing the oral hearing or the judgment of refugee testimony within individualised RSD processes while the current credibility criteria remain in place. This is because the prevailing criteria of coherence, consistency and plausibility (and to a lesser extent, demeanour) are an absurd and unworkable means by which to test the truth of a refugee applicant's oral testimony. The criteria are even less workable in Australia and Canada in the context of the oral hearing in its current form. Gregor Noll, who also uses the strong but appropriate language of absurdity to describe evidentiary assessment in asylum procedures, surveys existing proposals and solutions put forward in response to the dysfunction of current practice and standards.[6] After careful consideration of the myriad options that experts, advocates and states have contemplated, including *prima facie* or 'group-based status determination' rather than individualised RSD,[7] he comes to the somewhat plaintive conclusion that there is no 'clear cut resolution to the problems of

[3] Blommaert, above n 1, 444.

[4] Ibid citing; Charles L Briggs, *Disorderly Discourse: Narrative, Conflict, & Inequality* (Oxford University Press, 1996) 13.

[5] Blommaert, above n 1, 444.

[6] Gregor Noll, 'Credibility, Reliability, and Evidential Assessment' in Cathryn Costello, Michelle Foster and Jane McAdam (eds), *The Oxford Handbook of International Refugee Law* (Oxford University Press, 2021) 607, 617–20.

[7] Ibid 622. Noll argues that group-based determination simply displaces the problem of evidentiary and credibility assessment onto a new question, of whether the applicant is a member of the group that is eligible for *prima facie* recognition. But, see also the following project in train at the time of writing and its much needed investigation into the possibilities of group status determination: Cathryn Costello, Caroline

evidential assessment in the asylum procedure'.[8] Moreover, he states that this is the case even though 'we have enough information to reject the way evidence and credibility is currently assessed in asylum cases'.[9]

I agree. As I have argued, the absence of a simple solution to credibility assessment and RSD's demand for narrativity is, in part, due to the connection between credibility assessment and Global North asylum regimes' near-singular objectives of stopping, discrediting or removing people who dare to seek protection within their territories. The refugee applicant whose credibility is tested during the oral hearing is also the asylum seeker who eluded a state's multiple sites and means of border policing to access the Refugee Convention's protections. However, while the credibility criteria provide a clear means for states to identify 'genuine' refugees and exclude 'bogus' claimants, they do not fully account for the multiple, contradictory narratives demanded of asylum seekers within RSD processes as a basis for access to safety and protection. These narratives define the acceptable and 'good' refugee-citizen for Global North states. They are implicated in (and constructed in contradistinction to) discourses of 'deceitful', 'opportunistic' and 'fake' refugees. Indeed, the narrative of becoming a (good) refugee, authored, repeated and reinforced by states, entrenches the exceptionalism of the 'genuine' refugee, so as to legitimately reject those outside of this narrative frame.[10] For a refugee applicant to present a different script risks the denial of protection and safety altogether.

Even though the objectives of the book were not to investigate or advance precise reforms to RSD, in reflecting on what suggestions for reform arise, it is tempting to suggest that if the oral hearing must be a narrative occasion, it should be a less surprising and more predictable one. To put this another way, where applicants' evidence is tested against standards of plausibility, coherence and consistency, and expected to fit within cognisable narrative forms, the hearing should provide the opportunity to meet these standards. Further, the opportunity to convey one's evidence, in a consistently structured hearing, should be afforded to refugee applicants even where the decision-maker has already read a written version of the evidence, or an existing decision about refugee status is being administratively reviewed.

The problem though, that arises as soon as the suggestion is made, is that such a reform would do nothing to address the narrative mandate that I have traced throughout the book.[11] To improve the terms on which refugees may present their evidence during the hearing may just as soon entrench the demand for a 'good' refugee story and narrativity rather than undermine it. And, as Bohmer and Shuman have shown, even if refugee applicants are given an opportunity to present their claims fully and frankly – or to successfully modify the messy evidence of life and experience into a neat narrative form – telling a story that happens to be too neat, too familiar or too 'textbook' can be detrimental

Nalule and Derya Ozkul, 'Recognising Refugees: Understanding the Real Routes to Recognition' (2020) 65 *Forced Migration Review* 4.

[8] Noll, above n 6, 622.

[9] Ibid.

[10] Sara Ahmed, *The Cultural Politics of Emotion* (Edinburgh University Press, 2nd ed, 2014) 46–49.

[11] Though, structuring the hearing in some kind of consistent manner and limiting decision-makers' subjective and unpredictable interventions into applicant evidence *may* improve efficiency and prevent credibility assessment from 'blowing out' during the hearing, as observed by Kneebone in relation to the RRT's early operation: Susan Kneebone, 'The Refugee Review Tribunal and the Assessment of Credibility: An Inquisitorial Role' (1998) 5 *Australian Journal of Administrative Law* 78, 84.

to the success of the claim.[12] Indeed, refugees are required to meet a demand for narrative, but the precise terms of this demand, as with the assessment of refugee credibility, is shifting, unpredictable and subject to narrative sensibilities (amongst other things) of the individual decision-maker.

At this point, I want to emphasise that in my critique of the burdens on refugee testimony during the oral hearing in Australia and Canada, I am not advocating for the removal of hearing or oral interview within individualised RSD processes. I have not addressed this suggestion in the book and nor have the book's questions or methods provided a sufficient basis to mount a specific reform agenda. This is worth stating clearly since, as I have addressed throughout *Judging Refugees*, contemporary reforms of RSD continue to be motivated by crude discourses of 'efficiency', speed and gate-keeping. This in turn has resulted in limiting refugee applicants' access to status determination procedures, oral interviews or hearings, and in diminishing the quality of RSD procedures. As long as predominantly closed, individualised and discretion-driven executive and administrative RSD procedures persist, any move to constrain or abolish the oral hearing would provide refugees with even less of an opportunity to present their claims. Further, this would reduce access to much-needed advocacy and legal advice and diminish an applicant's capacity to understand or respond to even the most explicit legal and procedural bases on which their claims are determined. Moreover, diminishing the quality of first instance decision-making will not make RSD more efficient or effective, being two of the ostensible concerns articulated by refugee-receiving states.[13] However, I am cognisant that the faster and more limited that 'fast-track' processes become, there is a growing tendency among states to legitimise RSD procedures by providing access to *any* kind of hearing or indeed perfunctory 'screening process' as a means of fulfilling Refugee Convention obligations. This is a dangerous trend. Access to an accelerated oral interview alongside only minimal (if any) oversight of short shrift, first-instance decision-making widens 'the margins of subjectivity and irrationality' and creates yet another barrier to access to protection.[14] This reinforces my argument that attention to the conduct and quality of the hearing is crucial to the evaluation of RSD, and that despite near-constant reforms to refugee law and procedure, the centrality of the oral hearing for onshore refugee applicants in both Australia and Canada remains remarkably constant.

8.2 Resisting Narrative Closure

This book has critiqued the demand for narrative within RSD processes. It has argued that the narrative form is implicated in how law exercises power and authority, rather than being outside of law or better than 'legal' forms of language and rhetoric. However, it has also argued that certain genres of narrative do not demand chronology, linear causation, closure, a rational interior self or a rejection of uncertainty. As LaCapra puts it, 'there are forms of narrative which do not unproblematically instantiate the conventional beginning-middle-

[12] Carol Bohmer and Amy Shuman, *Political Asylum Deceptions: The Culture of Suspicion* (Palgrave Macmillan, 2018).

[13] Gregor Noll, 'Introduction: Re-mapping Evidentiary Assessment in Asylum Procedures' in Gregor Noll (ed), *Proof, Evidentiary Assessment and Credibility in Asylum Procedures* (Martin Nijhoff, 2005) 1.

[14] Indeed, the acceleration of asylum procedures and removal of avenues of review for asylum decisions means that 'the opportunities to explore the evidentiary dimensions of a claim are severely reduced': ibid 6.

end plot . . . [or seek] resonant closure and uplift'.[15] Certain texts and genres present us with a way of imagining narrative outside of the strictures currently placed on refugee applicants seeking protection. Others still pose discomfiting questions in relation to state processes for judging refugees and their testimony. Indeed, writing at the intersection of literature and the politics of asylum has held open the possibilities of literature, narrative and art as a means of recasting the epistemologies and standard stories of the refugee experience found within law and beyond it. This is not just a kind of counter-storytelling but also about the potential of counter-genres. Omid Tofighian, for example, has put forward the idea of an 'anti-genre' for refugee writing and knowledge, as well as 'horrific surrealism', to best interpret Behrouz Boochani's book *No Friend but the Mountains*, which is (amongst other things) an extended and polyphonic critique of the stifling range of refugee stories that can be told by or about people seeking safety and protection.[16] Tofighian applies the horrific surrealism genre to Boochani's narration and analysis of imprisonment and torture in Australia's offshore detention regime on Manus Island in Papua New Guinea. Again, this is one part of an asylum seeker's experience of arrival in Australia, as a Refugee Convention-signatory state, but certainly not a part of the refugee story addressed within RSD and its reconciliatory narrative frame.

***

Dauvergne observes that refugee applicants who cannot establish their identity or claims credibly must contend with the fact that '[o]ne's account of self is not sufficient – a truth that most of us are spared from confronting'.[17] In the oral hearings I observed, refugee applicants had to deal with this fact – that their accounts of self were insufficient – directly and in person, whilst also contending with demand for evidence in a particular form in a necessarily stressful adjudicative setting. This experience – of one's credibility and plausibility being judged in real time during the oral hearing, and then later in a final decision – is a core part of RSD procedure and what Cathryn Costello et al identify as refugee status recognition's 'degradations'. As they put it:

> [I]t is not only the outcome of refugee recognition that is important. The processes themselves shape lives profoundly . . . many asylum seekers recount the indignities of waiting, prolonged uncertainty, and indeed the degradations of asylum interviews. The recognition processes, while they ought to be a gateway to protection, often entail obstacles for applicants, with a profound and long-lasting negative impact on well-being and rights.[18]

[15] Dominick LaCapra, *Writing History, Writing Trauma* (Johns Hopkins University Press, 2nd ed, 2014) 54.

[16] Omid Tofighian, 'Translator's Tale: A Window to the Mountains' in Behrouz Boochani (ed), *No Friend but the Mountains: Writing from Manus Prison* (Picador, 2018) xxix; see also Omid Tofighian and Behrouz Boochani, 'Narrative, Resistance and Manus Prison Theory' (2020) 54(2) *Review of Middle East Studies* 174. Anna Poletti argues the book represents a 'new form of transnational life writing', which is both a work of theory and life writing that 'responds to and seeks to understand the logics of the nation state' based on an account in real time of the lived experience of refugees incarcerated on Manus Island: Anna Poletti, 'Introduction: A Forum on Behrouz Boochani's No Friend but the Mountains: Writing from Manus Prison' (2020) 43(4) *Biography* 685.

[17] Catherine Dauvergne, *Humanitarianism, Identity, and Nation: Migration Laws of Australia and Canada* (UBC Press, 2005) 104.

[18] Costello, Nalule and Ozkul, above n 7, 4.

The final decision and determination of each refugee claim might mark a beginning or an end, a transformative event, a life-threatening complication, or none of these things. For refugee applicants in Australia who were granted only temporary forms of protection, and whose refugee claims were therefore required to be redetermined every three or five years, a positive outcome may have marked very little outside of the start of new period of waiting for a further determination of their claims.[19] The refugee story presented for judgment, however, is endlessly more compelling if the making and determination of the claim marks a final resolution, an ending, whereby the 'other' is received into the state and incorporated into a citizen or refused entry and expelled. However, the lives, histories and experiences of refugee applicants presented in the adjudicative settings I observed did not order themselves into neat narratives. Of the fifteen refugee applications included in this research, none of the stories presented to refugee decision-makers were marked by a clear and obvious beginning nor did any of the narratives end with the seeking of refugee status. And yet, the ability to shape testimony into a narrative form, and then to articulate and rearticulate this narrative, to explain and account for it in person during the oral hearing, fundamentally shaped the terms on which a refugee's credibility and access to protection was determined.

[19] A regime of temporary protection for certain refugees who arrived without a valid visa in Australia was repealed in 2023: Andrew Giles Minister for Immigration, Citizenship and Multicultural Affairs, 'Delivering a Permanent Pathway for Temporary Protection Visa Holders' (Media Release, 13 February 2023).

Appendix

Applicant Name	Place of Hearing	Date	Country of Origin	Gender	Basis of claim	Details of claim	Credibility	Outcome	Type of Data
Canada									
1. *Bhatti*	Canada (Montréal)	2013	Pakistan	M	Religion, particular social group (PSG)	- Religious persecution due to conversion from Islam to Christianity - Persecution on basis of imputed homosexuality - Persecution by religious and government authorities	- Positive credibility assessment	Positive	In person hearing observation
2. *Flores*	Canada (Montréal)	2013	Cuba	F	Political opinion	- Persecution due to expression of anti-government sentiment through art and poetry - Persecution by government authorities	- Positive credibility assessment	Negative	In person hearing observation
3. *Jabbar*	Canada (Montréal)	2013	Afghanistan	M	PSG, political opinion	- Persecution due to membership of PSG: people working for foreign NGOs - Persecution due to perceived anti-Taliban political opinion - Persecution by Taliban forces	- Positive credibility assessment	Positive	In person hearing observation
4. *Perera*	Canada (Vancouver)	2013	Sri Lanka	M	Political opinion	- Persecution due to imputed political opinion as a perceived member of the Liberation Tigers of Tamil Eelam - Persecution by Sri Lankan authorities	- Negative credibility assessment	Negative	In person hearing observation

5. *Rostami*	Canada (Montréal)	2013	Iran	F	PSG, political opinion, religion	- Persecution due to membership of PSG: women subject to spousal violence - Persecution due to participation in anti-government protests, perceived anti-regime opinion and alleged immorality - Religious persecution due to conversion from Islam to Christianity - Persecution by government and former spouse	- Positive credibility assessment	Positive	In person hearing observation
6. *Valdez*	Canada (Vancouver)	2013	Mexico	M	PSG	- Persecution due to gang-related politics and violence - Persecution by local gangs	- Negative credibility assessment	Negative – applicant excluded under section 1F (b) of the Refugee Convention	In person hearing observation
7. *Solemani*	Canada (Vancouver)	2015	Iran	M	Political opinion, PSG	- Persecution due to perceived anti-government activity, membership of an anti-government and pro-democracy organisation - Persecution by government authorities	- Negative credibility assessment	Negative	Audio recording of the hearing

(*cont.*)

Applicant Name	Place of Hearing	Date	Country of Origin	Gender	Basis of claim	Details of claim	Credibility	Outcome	Type of Data
Australia									
8. *Adere*	Australia (Melbourne)	2012	Ethiopia	M & F (husband & wife)	Political opinion, PSG	- Persecution due to perceived anti-government and pro-democracy opinions, and work with 'Western' NGOs - Persecution by government authorities	- Negative credibility assessment	Negative	In person hearing observation
9. *Jadoon*	Australia (Melbourne)	2014	Pakistan	M	Political opinion, PSG	- Persecution due to membership of a local Peace Committee and anti-Taliban political opinions - Persecution by Taliban forces and members of the army loyal to the Taliban	- Positive credibility assessment	Positive	Audio recording of the hearing in full and transcript
10. *Malik*	Australia (Melbourne)	2013	Pakistan	M	Political opinion, PSG	- Persecution due to imputed anti-Taliban political opinion; membership of a village defence committee; and refusal to give land to the Taliban - Persecution by Taliban forces		Positive	Audio recording of the hearing in full and transcript

11. *Mbassi*	Australia (Melbourne)	2012	African state (details omitted for anonymity)	M	Political opinion	- Persecution on basis of opposition to government corruption; whistle-blower status; and anti-government political opinion - Persecution by government and government-sponsored secret police	- Negative credibility assessment	Negative	In person hearing observation
12. *Mena*	Australia (Melbourne)	2014	Egypt	F	PSG, religion	- Persecution due to status as a Christian woman, and as an unmarried Christian woman - Persecution by Islamicist forces, in particular Muslim Brotherhood members	- Negative credibility assessment	Negative	Audio recording of the hearing in full and transcript
13. *Pillai*	Australia (Melbourne)	2013	Sri Lanka	M	Race, political opinion	- Persecution due to imputed anti-Tamil political opinion, and refusal to support Tamil organisations - Persecution by Tamil paramilitary groups	- Positive credibility assessment	Positive	Audio recording of the hearing in full and transcript
14. *Zahau*	Australia (Melbourne)	2012	Burma	F	Political opinion, race, religion	- Persecution on basis of Chin ethnicity and political activities in support of Chin people; Christian religion; and pro-democracy political activism - Persecution by government authorities, army forces and pro-government groups	- Negative credibility assessment of certain claims; acceptance of some key claims	Positive	Audio recording of the hearing in full and transcript

(cont.)

Applicant Name	Place of Hearing	Date	Country of Origin	Gender	Basis of claim	Details of claim	Credibility	Outcome	Type of Data
15. *Zeidan*	Australia (Sydney)	2014	Syria & Lebanon	F & F (mother & daughter)	PSG	- Mother: persecution on basis of owning a beauty salon and perceived 'anti-Islamic' behaviour - Daughter: persecution on basis of being a young, unmarried, female child - Persecution by family members (threat of forced marriage), and by Islamic militias	- Negative credibility assessment of the mother's claims - Positive credibility assessment of the daughter	Positive	Audio recording of the hearing in full and transcript

INDEX

For EU product safety concerns, contact us at Calle de José Abascal, 56–1°,
28003 Madrid, Spain or eugpsr@cambridge.org.

www.ingramcontent.com/pod-product-compliance
Lightning Source LLC
LaVergne TN
LVHW081933200926
848484LV00009B/2422